Advance Praise for *Getting to "Yes And"*

"You don't have to spend years on stage to be good at the art of improvisation. In his new book, *Getting to 'Yes And,'* improv veteran Bob Kulhan shows you how improvisation techniques can positively impact almost any business situation. Read this intriguing book and get ready to take communication at work to a whole new level."

—Ken Blanchard, coauthor of *The New One Minute Manager®* and *Collaboration Begins with You*

"Prescriptive, educational, and funny, this book is filled with disarmingly easy improv techniques to up our game at work. *Getting to 'Yes And'* has earned its place on the bookshelves, desks, and nightstands of savvy business readers. It's Dale Carnegie Training for the 21st Century."

—Jack Canfield, CEO, The Canfield Training Group, and bestselling author of *The Success Principles*™

"For years, the business world has echoed 'yes and,' but we were light on details—until now. In a fun romp from Chicago's Second City to Duke University's Fuqua School of Business and beyond, this book threads together improv and business essentials such as negotiation, sales, goal setting, and conflict resolution. Read it, follow it, and you'll get better results, maybe even a few laughs along the way."

—Dave Logan, USC Marshall School of Business and bestselling coauthor, *Tribal Leadership*

"Improvisation is the key to collaboration and innovation, and Bob Kulhan is an improv star! This book shows you how to use improvisation for business success. It's filled with specific, practical, actionable advice, and it's lots of fun to read."

—Keith Sawyer, author of *Group Genius* and *Zig Zag*

"Kulhan is an experienced improviser with a deep understanding of the art form. And, he is a talented teacher with years of experience translating the essence of improv into valuable business lessons. His no nonsense (yet entertaining) style is perfect for anyone in either business or improv who wants to bring the two worlds together."

—Daniel Klein, Stanford Graduate School of Business, Department of Theater, and d.school

"Kulhan came early to the realization that we are constantly innovating in business and in life, and that there is a method to doing it better. He brings very sharp tools to promote collective success, through motivating, making decisions, energizing, building ideas, and managing status differences. Although a key insight in the book is that improvisation isn't synonymous with comedy, nobody will mind that Bob presents these important ideas in a lively and fun way."

—Paul Ingram, Columbia Business School

"*Getting to 'Yes And'* is a transformative book. With focus, care, professionalism, and good humor, Kulhan delivers a how-to guide for implementing improvisation in business. At the Center, we will definitely be incorporating his techniques into our future programs."

—Rick Barrera, COO, The Center for Heart Led Leadership, and author of *Overpromise and Overdeliver*

"I don't know anyone who likes this more or commits harder than Bob. Bob is an improviser's improviser. Buy this book!"

—TJ Jagodowski, improviser and author of *Improvisation at the Speed of Life*

"When it comes to the application of improv tenets in the business world, there is no one better than Bob Kulhan. Any university, business, and (now) reader is fortunate to have him as their lead facilitator. If I ran the business world, I would insist this book be a part of every curriculum, in every company."

—Susan Messing, instructor and performer, iO, The Annoyance, and The Second City, and Adjunct Professor, DePaul University, The University of Chicago, The School at Steppenwolf, and The World

"I have known Bob Kulhan for a damn 20 years. He's a great improviser, a great teacher, and an o.k. guy. His commitment to improvisation is spring loaded and fuel injected. He's super positive (too positive) and rather smart! Read this book because why not?"

—Mick Napier, founder, The Annoyance Theatre, and author of *Behind the Scenes* and *Improvise*

"Bob Kulhan's skills as an improvisational teacher and player offer an insightful and energetic point of view to any group. I have thoroughly enjoyed playing with this dummy for almost twenty years now. And, I look forward to many more."

—Jack McBrayer, actor, *30 Rock, The Middle, Wreck It Ralph*

"Bob is a thoughtful and caring teacher of improvisation. He's a tireless champion of the art form and he'd stop me from singing his praises if that didn't directly contradict improv's first rule: acceptance. Deal with it, Bob."

—Jordan Klepper, correspondent on *The Daily Show with Trevor Noah*

GETTING TO "YES AND"

The Art of Business Improv

Bob Kulhan
with Chuck Crisafulli

STANFORD BUSINESS BOOKS

An Imprint of Stanford University Press • Stanford, California

Stanford University Press
Stanford, California

© 2017 by the Board of Trustees of the
Leland Stanford Junior University.
All rights reserved.

Special discounts for bulk quantities of Stanford Business Books are available to corporations, professional associations, and other organizations. For details and discount information, contact the special sales department of Stanford University Press. Tel: (650) 725-0820, Fax: (650) 725-3457

Printed in the United States of America on acid-free, archival-quality paper

Library of Congress Cataloging-in-Publication Data
Names: Kulhan, Bob, author. | Crisafulli, Chuck, author.
Title: Getting to "yes and" : the art of business improv / Bob Kulhan with
    Chuck Crisafulli.
Description: Stanford, California : Stanford Business Books, an imprint of
    Stanford University Press, 2017. | Includes bibliographical references and
    index.
Identifiers: LCCN 2016030504 | ISBN 9780804795807 (cloth : alk. paper)
Subjects: LCSH: Creative ability in business. | Improvisation (Acting) |
    Communication in management. | Psychology, Industrial.
Classification: LCC HD53 .K85 2016 | DDC 650.1—dc23
LC record available at https://lccn.loc.gov/2016030504
ISBN 9781503600959 (electronic)

Typeset by Classic Typography in 11.25/15 Baskerville

To businesspeople: I believe in you.

To Martin de Maat: I honor you.

To Denise, Casey, and Baby no. 2: I love you so much.

Grassroots efforts are real.

Grass cannot grow if someone is standing on it.

Where are you standing?

CONTENTS

GETTING TO "YES AND"

Introduction

MORE THAN ONE WAY
TO HIT A PIÑATA

IN A CONSTANTLY SHIFTING BUSINESS ENVIRONMENT in which every player seeks a competitive edge, there is little to be gained from platitudinous morale boosting. Yet over the last ten years a flourishing cottage industry has arisen, providing companies with exactly that. Almost every brand-name sketch comedy group has developed some kind of corporate outreach program, in which teams of comedians lead businesspeople through improvisational games and exercises, ostensibly to hone business skills. Quite often these games are exactly what a college student would participate in during an introductory level improv class.

Corporate America pays handsomely for the chance to play these games. In 2013 U.S. firms spent over $70 billion on corporate training and approximately $15 billion on leadership development, with much of that money spent on "intangibles training"—programs focused on such unquantifiable skills as leadership and creativity.[1] Companies often pay at least $5,000 a week to send a VP-level employee to a top business school, and it has become common for comedy-oriented improv groups to run these programs or be a significant part of them.

For a young drama student improv games may provide a wonderful first step into the world of improvisational comedy. For businesspeople such games may provide a bit of fun, a pleasant day out of the office, or a chance for the VP of sales to finally learn the names of those IT folks (it's Pat and Deanna, by the way). So, does the simple act of bringing traditional improv games to a corporate setting provide businesspeople with anything of substance? Anything practical? Anything that might be useful in the real business world? In a word, Nope.

And yet a true understanding of the art of improvisation can offer businesspeople the most impactful, culture-changing, success-enabling tool imaginable. There's much, much more to improvisation than games and giggles, and for the past 16 years my company, Business Improv, has specialized in teaching improv techniques to corporate executives with the express intent of developing skills that allow these serious people to accomplish serious business in the most effective way.

Though the techniques of improv can be used to entertain, in the following pages I will show you how these techniques can be used just as easily to run a meeting, handle negotiations, spark a brainstorming session, and positively influence those around you. The tenets of improvisation can help you help yourself, your team, your department, and your entire company to succeed beyond what you think you're capable of. Yes, a great improviser can be a very funny person. And great improvisers don't just play games.

Consequently the work that goes into becoming a great improviser is a little more involved than simply binging on episodes of *Whose Line Is It, Anyway?* To make the best use of this art, we have to draw on the range of communications-related sciences: behavioral decision theory, cognitive psychology, social psychology, and behavioral economics. Together these foundations point us toward a smarter way of reacting, a more effective way of adapting, and a deeper way of engaging—the things true improvisation provides.

It is a driving passion of mine to get people to understand that improv skills can be effectively translated into the business world with powerful results. I thirst to make this connection for people. For those who might react to the idea of "business improv" with apprehension and skepticism, I have a confession: I empathize with you. Yes, improv techniques are often taught without a detailed exploration of substance. If your negative assessment of the value of improv was crystalized when you invested good money to spend a day playing Zip, Zap, Zop—a basic improv game with no practical business value—I feel your pain. There is no Zip, Zap, Zop in this book. "Return on investment" means something to me. And that is what you will get if you suspend your disbelief and follow me through these pages. I enjoy the challenge of winning over the skeptics, and the first step in notching up those wins is to emphatically and decidedly debunk the two biggest myths around improvisation.

Myth One: Improvisation Is Comedy

Improvisation is in fact not comedy. Nor is it simply an approach to acting. Those are two specific types of improvisation, unique to the context in which the improvisation is taking place. There are many more contexts for improvisation, though. Improvisation is a key element of busy emergency rooms; it takes place on NBA basketball courts; it's a part of the skill set for every policeman cruising the streets—all contexts in which comedy is certainly not intended to be part of the picture. The context dictates the style of improvisation required. The improvisation an emergency room doctor uses in performing a lifesaving operation is unique to that situation, and the kind of improvisation a starting point guard employs in facing an unexpected defensive strategy only makes sense on the basketball court.

A fantastic example of high-level improvisation took place in 2011 when a team of highly trained U.S. Navy SEALs undertook Operation Neptune Spear—the deadly raid on Osama bin Laden's compound in Pakistan. This mission had been meticulously planned; the SEALs trained for it over months and several contingency plans were developed and put into place. Still, when one of the navy's Black Hawk helicopters crashed within the compound, a very specific kind of improvisation was required if the mission was to succeed under shifting circumstances.[2] In this case improvisation had everything to do with adapting to changes within a strategy to achieve real, tangible outcomes.

I certainly concede that the most common understanding of improvisation is as a form of comedy. *Curb Your Enthusiasm*, the aforementioned *Whose Line Is It Anyway?* and the films by Christopher Guest all showcase amazing comedic work that is based on improv. On a personal level I've been incredibly fortunate to spend an enormous part of my professional life on the great Chicago stages of The Second City, the Annoyance Theatre, and iO (where I was coached by Tina Fey and Amy Poehler and performed alongside such notable folks as Jack McBrayer, Ike Barinholtz, Thomas Middleditch, Jordan Klepper, Jason Sudeikis, and Seth Meyers along with many other famous and less famous, equally brilliant comedic improvisers). In that context we were performing with the focused purpose of delivering comedy. The payoff we were after was audience laughter and a great show.

Laughter is not the payoff a surgeon, a jazz musician, or a SEAL team is after, though, and it's certainly not the payoff a businessperson is looking for either. If you're in front of the board of directors after a dip in fourth-quarter sales and you get thrown a hardball question, the challenge is not to quickly come up with a way you can use your necktie as a comedic prop to make the board laugh (lest that necktie become a noose with which you strangle your career). Instead you must react and adapt to the circumstances and communicate in an engaging and inspiring way.

The takeaway here: improvisation as it applies to the business world is a specific type that works in the business context. The heart of this book is to explicitly demonstrate how the art of improvisation can be used as a serious means of getting serious results.

Myth Two: Improvisation Is Making Stuff Up as a Last Resort

What we've got here is both a misconception and a matter of semantics. If you grab five random items out of your refrigerator, throw them in a pot of water, and bring it up to boil, technically you might say you were "cooking," a word that could describe the simple application of heat to foodstuffs. But we all know that the simple act of cooking can be raised to an elite art form, one that depends on skill, training, technique, thoughtfulness, and imagination. A hot pot of gross mush and an elite chef's tasting menu may both be cooked, but there's quite a tastable difference in the quality of the cooking there.

Similarly we sometimes call it improvising when someone is driven to make things up on the spot after discovering that plans A, B, and C have all fallen apart. This kind of improvisation is a sort of survival skill and coping mechanism, and can certainly be relied on when all hell breaks loose and the scramble-sweat is flowing. However, this is a terribly limiting definition—improvisation as an emergency measure or last-ditch effort. This conception of improvisation does not factor in technique, training, practice, and thoughtfulness and seems to imply that the need for improvisation is only dictated by the level of chaos one finds oneself in.

In fact improvisation at its most effective is a deliberate strategy that draws on intelligence in concert with instinct. Improvisation isn't simply panicky reaction; it's a way in which people can actively explore possibilities, synthesize available information, and innovate in response to a challenge in real time. Improvisation thrives where planning meets execution, and the art of improvisation is really about making fast decisions and adapting when faced with unanticipated situations. The quality of those decisions—of the improvisation—is in direct proportion to an improviser's abilities and the degree to which those abilities have been developed through training and preparation. Improvisers don't really make stuff up in the moment; they have been trained to draw on everything around them and on everything they've learned right up until the moment they have to improvise.

Preparation and awareness are hugely important parts of improvisation. Those Navy SEALs carried out their mission effectively even when their planning did not specifically cover the circumstances they encountered. The SEALs trained extensively for the raid on the bin Laden compound, created scale models of it, and drew up several contingency plans to cover what-if scenarios such as a Black Hawk helicopter going down—a previously experienced contingency that unfortunately had very real mortal consequences in Mogadishu,

Somalia.[3] When the raid finally took place, the SEALs discovered that the intelligence they'd based their plans on was not entirely accurate. There were a number of unknown variables (how many people they would encounter, the types of people, the weapons, the doors and hallways, etc.).[4] So they had to improvise—not by making things up but by drawing on every bit of skill, training, and knowledge their preparation had equipped them with.

I recently spoke with Navy SEAL captain Jamie Sands, who at the time was working at the Joint Special Operations Command at Ft. Bragg, and was preparing to take command of SEAL Group 2. Our conversation focused on how planning, preparation, and training affect the way people react and adapt when a plan cannot be executed flawlessly. Not so surprisingly the improvisational thinking required of SEALs is not a matter of "making things up" but instead one of drawing on a previously developed skill set.

"Training to a very high standard is an imperative," said Captain Sands. "It provides the foundation for everything else and creates muscle memory. The fact is, repetition matters, as it affects all aspects of performance: mental, physical, situational preparation, communication. Shooting, for example, is a perishable skill. You need repetitions to be at the highest level of proficiency. Training prevents brain freeze."

Whether you're on the battlefield or in the boardroom, practice and repetition of the specific skill set required for the task at hand puts you in a position to succeed when that task must be carried out in times of uncertainty or even chaos. Regarding the specific skills required for throwing oneself out of a plane, Sands had this to say: "When you first start free-falling, your awareness of space is very small and you can only focus on what's right in front of you—gauges, timing, ripcord. Around your tenth or twentieth jump, you begin to feel comfortable. However, it is only after your fiftieth jump that you're seeing the whole sky and even thinking about what your next moves are once you land."

The point here is that no matter what you do—cooking, accounting, playing sports, jumping out of airplanes, or embracing business improv—your skill level is achieved and maintained through practice. Especially in times of crisis, you want to be able to rely on well-developed muscle memory, not on making stuff up.

In theatrical improvisation one of the common phrases is "performing at the top of your intelligence," a concept that is about 180 degrees away from simply working off the top of your head. If you think about some of the other great improvisers I mentioned earlier—the soldier, the athlete, the chef—they don't respond to unpredictable events by doing just anything, willy-nilly. They work at the top of their intelligence, drawing on all their skills, training, and experience to make fast choices about the actions they will take. When musicians improvise, they "make up" the music in the sense that they are playing notes of their extemporaneous choosing. However, the success (and listenability) of that improvisation depends on the players' musical knowledge and skills and their ability to communicate with fellow musicians and an audience. If you don't actually know how to play a trumpet, improvising on one isn't going to help you sound any better.

Even when improvisation is actually about comedy, it's not just about making stuff up. Somewhere around 1996, very early in my improv career, I was serving as the host of the iO's evening shows and I described to first-timers in the audience that the improvisers onstage would be "making things up off the top of our heads." Offstage I was promptly and vehemently reamed by improv legend Noah Gregoropoulos, who impressed upon me how insulting that phrase was in relation to the level of work done by improvisers. Lesson learned. This resonates strongly with me to this day. Performing at the top of your intelligence is a lot different from flying by the seat of your pants.

The myth that improv is a means of last resort dismisses the knowledge and training, coordination, focus, and intellect needed to perform in the moment. If you are drawing upon everything you know and working at the highest level your abilities allow, you are improvising at the top of your intelligence—a stunning feat when seen.

•

With that debunking out of the way, you've got a better sense of what improvisation isn't. So what the heck is it then?

Improvisation, when stripped down to its basic building blocks, is about *reacting*, *adapting*, and *communicating*. You see what's happening around you. You quickly consider how to respond. You communicate to others. And then you do what needs to be done to succeed. Repeat as necessary.

The first step in any improvisation is indeed reaction. This is not reacting blindly or out of panic, however. With effective improvisation, reaction involves being focused and present, being in the moment, and being completely open to the idea of responding honestly to whatever it is that requires a response. There's a parallel force existing alongside reaction, and that's adaptation—the skill of being ever aware of the shifting parameters one is working within while keeping in mind the specific objective that needs to be achieved. Reacting and adapting are channeled together to create the true resultant force of improvisation: communication. Communication in this context refers to productive engagement in any form—between individuals, within or between groups, as part of a process, or the final stage of decision making.

Why would this definition of improvisation make sense in a business setting? Because improvisation is a method of dealing with situations in which we need to send and receive messages accurately, effectively, efficiently, and quickly.[5] Of course as a businessperson and an improv veteran I'd say it's always important to set proper expectations, so one of the things that has bothered me incessantly over the last decade is the overpromising that takes place in corporate training sessions—promising often done by smiling (though great) improv coaches who honestly want to spread the message that if you simply relax, adopt a positive attitude, and trust your instincts, your business will thrive, your job title will turn to gold, and you'll receive the keys to glorious executive washrooms that can only be discussed in whispers.

I love these people. I am friends with hundreds of improvisers who teach this way. They are awesome performers, coaches, and teachers, and without question their approach to business improvisation is ineffective, because it does not dive more than an inch below the surface of a sea that is thousands of feet deep.

Improvisation is not a panacea or a silver bullet. It is an art and a discipline—a set of techniques that have to be used at the right time and in the right place. Improv can improve the way ideas are generated. It can open a free flow of communication. It can boost the sense of organization within a workplace. It can help you manage the unexpected. And it is not the ultimate or only way to run a business. Potential improvisers, whether actors, athletes, or business leaders, all have to decide when and how improv techniques will be valuable. There's more than one way to hit a piñata and improv is only one possible stick to swing—though I've found it to be a very effective stick when it comes to opening that sucker up and getting the sweet stuff inside.

Improvisation is not so much a creation of something out of nothing as much as it is the creation of something out of everything—everything one has been taught, everything one has experienced, everything one knows. Improvisers observe all and try to take advantage of everything around them: every word, every movement, every sound; every facial expression, body gesture, moment, data point. Improvisers will pull from all information at their disposal and will not dismiss anything that might possibly be useful. A great improviser can look at the tiny details and the big picture simultaneously. Improvisers observe everything for its worth and assess every situation as accurately and honestly as humanly possible. Great improvisers aim for the best possible overall solution in the moment, as opposed to "This is the best I could do given a set of circumstances." And seasoned improvisers acknowledge that the unknown will happen no matter how well they attempt to plan things out. Murphy's Law states, "Anything that can go wrong will go wrong." For improvisers these aren't words of caution but a rallying cry: when you are performing at the top of your intelligence, you not only expect the unexpected; you embrace it.

In the following chapters, then, let me guide you toward becoming a great improviser in your career. Here's the path we'll take: from personal development to interpersonal application, to team application, to creating culture. We'll begin with a practical overview of how improvisation can be used as a tool to break through the barriers to creativity and collaboration that are common in workplace environments. Then we'll get into the nuts and bolts of improvising by way of improvisation's core principle: "Yes, and . . . " We'll look at the ways improv can be used for personal growth and empowerment—a method of strengthening your personal brand. We'll also explore improv's role in manipulating energy and attitude. Moving beyond personal growth, we will chart a path to implementing these techniques outwardly in dyadic and small group conversations. Then we will examine how improvisation can impact team dynamics by looking at its practical applications in fostering better group ideation and the breakdown of silos—a persistent workplace problem. We'll then take these foundational blocks to show how improv techniques can improve leadership skills and how improvisation can be used as a catalyst for positive change in a corporate culture. In the final pages of this book we'll focus on transferability and sustainability—how to utilize improvisation in your workplace immediately.

I do not teach with talks or seminars alone. Instead I favor intensives based on experiential learning. In that spirit I've packed this book with step-by-step instructions for some of my most effective and practicable exercises. I hope you'll give them a try.

It is my explicit intention in these pages to get you to think differently about yourself, your work, your company, and of course your use of improvisation. No matter what your particular business is, the goal here is success. I promise I won't ask you to take a trust fall or participate in a group hug. All I ask is that you commit to helping yourself. Done? Alright then, let's go!

Chapter 1

THINKING OUTSIDE OF THINKING OUTSIDE OF THE BOX

WHAT EXACTLY DOES IMPROVISATION have to do with business? Think about the major trends in the business world. Emerging technology continues to increase the speed of business. Moreover technology itself continues to change at an accelerated pace (Moore's Law purports a doubling of processing speeds every two years).[1] Business now relies on instantaneous, 24-hour communication as well as remote access to vital information, and any business that has trouble communicating that way is considered to be at a severe disadvantage.

The global community—corporate, consumer, and geographic—is upon us, and adopting new methodologies for effective communication and collaboration must take place between and across cultures.[2] Even within individual workplaces the potential for diversity in perspectives—the probability that those around us see things differently than we see things—is greater than ever before and must now be factored in to how business gets done. Put it this way: reacting, adapting, and communicating are not a matter of choice for businesspeople; they're a matter of basic survival. This has always been so, but in today's environment the stakes are higher.

The skills of focused thinking and rapid decision making that improvisation strengthens can easily be put to use in many of the day-to-day challenges in your competitive landscape: dealing with personnel demands, overcoming analysis paralysis, developing creative solutions, increasing general efficiency, handling conflict, managing crisis, encouraging adaptive problem solving, and fostering intrinsic motivation in others. The same skills that make for exceptional comedic improvisation—intense listening, focus, energy, engagement, teamwork, authenticity, adaptability—are skills that any businessperson can use to make positive changes in the workplace.[3]

Beyond the scope of our rapidly changing workplace lies the simple truth that we are still human—creatures of immense gifts, and limitations—and we will always have to interact with each other on a basic, personal level. This need for human connection is very powerful and is the stem for the socially conscious Millennial. Improvisation is a powerful tool for fostering interpersonal communication, making connections and building strong relationships.

Corporate culture has become an ever more important focus in the business community. A slew of common buzzwords and phrases get thrown around whenever companies discuss the kind of corporate culture they're after: creativity, risk taking, innovation, flexibility, strong and supportive teamwork, empathetic connection, authentic leadership, and of course thinking outside the box. Everyone seems to agree these end goals are positive. However, using a tired phrase like "thinking outside the box" to pay lip service to the idea that creativity should be encouraged is not going to get the job done. If you want change and fresh ideas, then don't think about that same old box at all. The challenge for us businesspeople is not in coming up with catchier ways to describe our end goals. The challenge is in whether we actually know how to get to these end goals within today's corporate climate.

Do you know concrete steps to create a culture in which people are not afraid to fail and are not afraid to openly share ideas? Do you know how to instill trust and mutual support in your team? Do you know how to inspire an attitude of openness and acceptance in others? Do you know how to connect and engage with people quickly to build strong relationships? If you want to say yes, then improvisation can give you the tools to make it so. In the following pages we'll lay a foundation for the entire book by demonstrating how improv is used in business, describing the skill set necessary for improvising well, defining the barriers to successful improvisation, and examining the core concepts of divergent and convergent thinking.

Training Smart

To understand the way that improv will work for you, let's take a look outside the business world for a moment. In the world of professional athletics, competition has never been fiercer; long-standing records of achievement are constantly being broken. Athletes have responded to increased competition—and increased rewards for their success—by training harder, smarter, and ever more scientifically. The way athletes compete has changed and the great competitors accept the fact that there's now a premium on well-muscled bodies that operate at peak physical fitness. There are not a lot of pro athletes who look like Babe Ruth anymore.

Businesspeople, like athletes, must respond to the competition and challenges in their fields by training harder and smarter. Improvisation techniques work on the brain the same way physical exercises work on muscle groups. The brain that's been tuned and toned by improvisation may be capable of much quicker decision making; however, the speed of decisions is a side effect of the process. The primary, desired result of improvisation is not that decisions get made quickly; the objective is to increase the probability that a great decision gets made. At its heart improvisation is about better decision making, and in your case better decisions make for better business.[4]

Let me contextualize this with a brief quiz: take five minutes to jot down your own barriers to creativity, collaboration, improvisation, and change. In other words what keeps you from being creative? What blocks collaboration from taking place? What impedes successful improvisation? What stops you from embracing change? If it helps to separate these four items and just focus on one of them, that's fine too! You will find that the barriers to creativity are likely the same as the blocks to collaboration, which are identical to that which keeps people from improving successfully and driving change.[5]

So, what are the barriers? For most, the answers commonly start with

- Fear (of losing control, of uncertainty, of being wrong, of looking like a fool, of the repercussions of being wrong or right, of not being aligned with the boss)
- Organizational structure (bureaucracy, rules, rituals, space, silos, hierarchy)
- Status (the boss speaks first, so you follow what the boss says; one or two vocal people dominate the meeting with their version of the right answers)
- Time
- Money
- Insufficient motivation ("It's not my job")
- Personal biases (previous success, complacency, status quo bias, "If it's not broke, why break it?")[6]

As you will learn, the tenets of improvisation can be used to remove these barriers. Individually, improvisation is going to allow you to defend against all distractions and bring a laser-like focus to the task you want accomplished. Within a group, improvisation opens up communication and ensures that there is a meritocracy of ideas. The businessperson who embraces improvisation is taking a qualitative, proactive step to keep his or her brain—and thus business skills—in top shape.

Improvisation, again, is a tool and as with all tools you have to know what it does and how and when to use it. The hammer is a great tool, though it does nothing for you just hanging on the pegboard over the workbench. If you want it to help you get the job done, you've got to grab it, hang on to it, and put some effort into swinging it at its target. Improvisation is that kind of tool—if you want it to work, you've got to commit to it. On stages where improvisers are trying to entertain, the moment one of them starts thinking about the audience, or about how they're going to get the next laugh, or about anything outside the process of improvising, the improviser disengages and the show suffers. Everybody onstage has to commit fully and consistently to the same goal at the same time. The business applications of improvisation are going to require that kind of commitment as well.

Wait! Why Should I Listen to You?

Hold on though. Before I begin to tell you specifically how improvisation can serve business needs, let me answer a question that may have occurred to you a few pages back: "Who the heck is this Kulhan guy and why should I listen to what he has to say about improv or business or business improv?"

To put it quite plainly, I am a businessman and a professional improv comedian, and I absolutely love the art form of improvisation with all my heart. I learned about comedic improvisation the first week of college at Illinois State University when I read a "Local Girl Does Good" newspaper write-up about Megan Moore Burns performing with The Second City in Chicago. Reading about what The Second City actually did—improvisational comedy—was a revelation. I promptly tracked down Megan (which in 1990 took a fair amount of sleuthing). Megan's advice to me was to begin learning the art of improv at the Players Workshop of The Second City. The next summer I moved roughly four hours north from my hometown of Effingham, Illinois, to Chicago to take classes at the Players Workshop. For two punishingly hot, humid months I slept on an ever-deflating air mattress on my cousin John's living room floor and ate past-expiration pies and cupcakes I'd bought for 35 cents from the Hostess Thrift Shop across the street. I walked about a mile to and from improv class. That summer I studied solely under Martin de Maat, the man who would eventually become my mentor and who is credited for cocreating The Second City Training Center with Sheldon Patinkin (also a brilliant and kind man who I'd have the good fortune of working under at Columbia College roughly ten years later). I could not have been happier.

I became so impassioned and committed to this art form that when an opportunity arose for me to accept my very first term of employment with The Second City I jumped at the job—as a walking trash can. Technically the job was to be a "mascot" for The Second City, a costumed character who would walk around the grounds of the famously rambunctious Taste of Chicago festival handing out fly-ers that announced the theater's new show. And it just so happens that the show The Second City was doing that summer was called "Winner Takes Oil," playing on the Persian Gulf War. The mascot was to be a cross between an oil barrel and the old Depression-era cartoon caricature of a guy who had lost everything. I was directed to wear nothing but shorts and shoes, and hoist a giant plastic keg over myself, which would be held up by two lengths of tug-of-war rope over my bare shoulders. If I kept that barrel on and spent a day handing out Second City flyers, I'd make $5.50 an hour. This sounded like an unbelievably sweet deal at the time.

It was a fairly clever costume and I wore it in service of a really great show—the cast that summer included such incredible talents as Steve Carrell, Michael McCarthy, and Jill Talley with more than oc-casional doses of Stephen Colbert. I'll be the first to say that Chicago is an amazing city that really knows how to get exceptionally festive at the Taste of Chicago. What I had not counted on was that to a crowd of several hundred thousand Chicagoans who had spent the day downing 16-ounce plastic cups of Old Style beer in the summer heat, a young, scrawny man-boy in a giant plastic barrel looked exactly like a walking trash receptacle. I spent a good deal of time fighting off the crumpled beer cups and half-eaten bratwursts that were slam-dunked in my costume.

If my budding love for improvisation had wavered, I might have just left that barrel next to a real trash can and shrugged the whole thing off as a stupid summer job that wasn't worth the mustard stains and rope burn. However, I stayed committed, and through a bit of reacting, adapting, and communicating I worked my way to a payoff that literally changed my life: I got my employment deal sweetened to include a pass to the show on nights it wasn't sold out. So all summer, once my barrel work was done, I watched that Second City show over and over and over, studying every little nuance of the performance and performers and falling more and more in love with the art of improvisation and sketch comedy. I returned to Illinois State University for my sophomore year and then transferred up to the University of Illinois at Chicago (UIC) for my junior and senior years of college, so that I could continue to take classes at the Players Workshop.

Well before I graduated from UIC I also began indulging my budding entrepreneurial spirit. I served as a one-man marketing department for Michael Jackson Software, Inc. (no, not that Michael Jackson)—one of the first companies to put multimedia elements into computer-based training systems. Through that job I got my first taste of mixing improv and business through guerrilla marketing: posing as a delivery person, I got MJSI media packages onto the desk of every prominent business reporter in Chicago. Positive press coverage of the company ensued as did a Bank of America Small Business Award for Creative Marketing.

In the early 1990s, before American eyes had ever seen *Whose Line Is It Anyway?* the term "professional improviser" was an oxymoron. It did not matter—I was thoroughly hooked. I went on to coach and perform improv at iO (Improv Olympic) and the Annoyance Theatre. At iO, I got to study with another improv guru, Del Close, and cofounded the improv troupe Baby Wants Candy ("America's seminal completely improvised musical group"), which toured internationally and won the 2005 Ensemble of the Year award at the esteemed Chicago Improv festival.[7] Baby Wants Candy offered me a chance to fulfill my double passion for entertainment and business; while our focus onstage was improvisation, offstage the troupe had to be run just like any other small business.

I was also frequently part of other improv groups that were called in to do corporate training. After many of those workshops I began to hear the same sort of comment: "That was a lot of fun, but I can't use any of it. In fact, now I have to go back to the office and work harder to catch up on the work I missed while we did this."

It was after one of those corporate gigs that I had my Eureka! moment: Why not create a program that would be enjoyable for businesspeople and would also give them something they could use in the real world? In the fall of 1999 a serendipitous encounter with a professor of management at the prestigious Duke University Fuqua School of Business led to the discovery that one of the deans at Duke Fuqua was soliciting ideas for a one-week intensive MBA course with an experiential learning component. I jumped at the chance to develop a course that showed the true potential of improv in business, and collaborated with academic experts to create the world's first improvisation program in a top-tier business school. In December 1999 "Business Improvisation" (the course) was born.

Since that time Business Improv (the company) has created programs for top business schools in America and has served a large roster of blue-chip clients such as PepsiCo, Capital One, Bristol-Myers Squibb, Ford Motor Company, the U.S. Naval Academy, the United Nations, Hilton Hotels Worldwide, and Starwood Hotels and Resorts Worldwide. I've got a team of a dozen trainers, working with over 3,500 C-level executives and another 2,000 businessmen and businesswomen annually. And though I never fancied myself the academic sort, I have served as an adjunct professor of business administration at the Duke University Fuqua School of Business since 2002. I have also held guest professor spots at the Columbia Business School at Columbia University, and I teach regularly as part of the executive education programs at the UCLA Anderson School of Management. I stay busy in classrooms and conference rooms; however, whenever I get the chance I'm back up on an improv stage, performing in New York City at the PIT, the UCB Theaters, and the Brooklyn branch of the Annoyance Theatre. Baby Wants Candy also lives on!

So those are my bona fides. I'm a professional improviser (now a better-understood vocation), a person who has worked in businesses and is now at the helm of one, and a "pracademic" who works with brilliant business professors to bring the art I love to the business class-room. Looking back over the last 17 years, I can say that I'm proud as hell that the "crazy" notion of teaching businesspeople to do better business by way of improv techniques has led to an extremely high percentage of success stories.

True Story

In order to give you a feel for how exactly those successes can hap-pen—how business and improvisation can interact in the most posi-tive way—let me present you with a case history. A couple of years ago I created an intensive three-day seminar called "Story of a Life-time" conducted at the UCLA Anderson School of Management and sponsored by UCLA Anderson's Executive Education Department. The course details had been clearly laid out in session descriptions and everyone in the room had made the explicit choice to be there. In fact this particular program had been created to reward VP-level financial advisors employed by one of the world's top financial man-agement firms. It was a thank-you from the company to its elite earn-ers. Other rewards had been available; all the enrollees in my program could have opted for spa vacations, trips to Hawaii or Europe, or open enrollment programs at prestigious universities such as Harvard, Wharton, and MIT. They had ended up with no view of a Hawaiian sunset and no chance at a hot stone chakra massage. Instead, they were under florescent lights in a room with me.

The focus of the "Story of a Lifetime" program was to craft stories and to develop the skills to pitch those stories, all to emphasize the importance of storytelling as a form of communication.[8] It seemed to be a perfect program for a Hollywood setting, a town basically built on the art of storytelling. While pitching stories is particularly relevant to the entertainment industry, it's also central to one's success in or-ganizations. Certainly that's the case in regard to the ability to align individuals around a vision; to influence teams for results; to explain key decisions in real time; and to put impactful meaning behind otherwise raw data—abilities that any high-performing corporate executive should want to master.

The core exercise of the program was a storytelling and pitching challenge, in which teams of the participants developed movie ideas and then pitched their best concept to a panel of judges made up of creative types with some real Hollywood credits (a screenwriter, a producer of the TV show *Drunk History*, a former *Saturday Night Live* cast member). The program was designed not so that these top-level financial planners could have the thrill of pretending to be Oscar contenders; rather, so that they could develop skills immediately transferable to their work: engagement, commitment, influence, persuasion, adaptability, passion, and most of all, of course, storytelling.

Every client coming to a financial planner is in essence telling a story—a life's story. A planner has to hear that story, understand its underlying meaning, recognize the client's needs, and be able to answer with a story of his or her own that addresses those needs and connects with the client. The planner's story has to explain how the financial planner is working in the client's best interests. You can't shape a story like that unless you get used to thinking creatively, and you can't tell a story like that unless you've got some specific communication skills in great shape. Adaptability plus communication equals improvisation. The goal of the program was for these execs to head back to the office and use their newly learned improvisation techniques while analyzing a client's portfolio, putting together a quarterly report, facing a board meeting, connecting with an investor, or in any number of other real-world business challenges.

Here is what we did.

The first step in the challenge was to break the class of 25 into smaller teams. Each team was tasked with coming up with a master list of movie ideas they might want to develop further. I stressed to the teams that at this stage in the process, they were to be focused on generating a quantity of ideas without judgment of their quality, so some improv-related rules would be in effect:

1. All ideas are to be encouraged, and no ideas should be quashed—at all.

2. There are no creative boundaries, and no idea can be judged unusable on the basis of any aesthetic, technical, or budgetary concerns. Dream big!

3. If an idea can be expressed and understood, it's on the list.

4. Everyone must participate.

The rules were met with considerable eye rolling and some exasperated grunting. But the teams did get working. After only 30 minutes it was apparent that some groups had taken the task seriously and had created a list of 25 or so movie ideas. Others—the grunters—barely had half a dozen. What had at first been presented as a brainstorming challenge now went a little deeper, as I began to familiarize the teams with the concepts of *divergent* and *convergent thinking.*[9]

In divergent thinking, ideas radiate from a single point of origin. The ideas are free to head in any direction and are not to be hampered by self-judgment or by a fear of judgment from other participants. Divergent thinking in a corporate setting might be the ideal opening strategy for an exceptional brainstorming session, or it might be the way in which creative solutions to a conflict begin to take shape. However, divergent thinking is only half of the process. To be effective, divergent thinking must be followed by focused, convergent thinking, in which members of a group or team now apply critical judgment to determine the most workable ideas and bring that wide range of initial thoughts back to a single, productive conclusion. In a corporate setting convergent thinking would close the brainstorming session or lead toward an innovative resolution.

In the next phases of the challenge, then, the teams were asked to take their divergent lists and apply convergent thinking in order to narrow the lists down to their top three story ideas. Then the process was repeated using the same mix of divergent and convergent thinking to turn the three basic ideas into three fully fleshed-out, who-what-why-when-where-how storylines. The more skeptical members

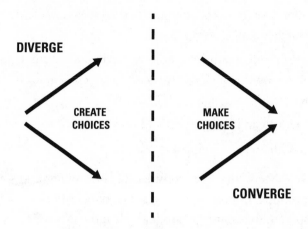

DIVERGE

CREATE CHOICES

MAKE CHOICES

CONVERGE

Divergent and Convergent Thinking

of the group thought this process sounded ridiculous. "Why not just vote right away on a best idea and then get to work coming up with a pitch?" The answer was that the exercise was not about time saving and efficiency; it was about how to pull a great idea out of a team through a process of creativity and collaboration. The process of fleshing out the three ideas might lead to the realization that elements of the "weaker" storyline actually work better than what was originally deemed the "best" idea. Then, in piecing together the best elements of disparate ideas, the groups might find they've arrived at an even better "best" idea than they would have gotten to otherwise. I implored the groups to follow the process, though I didn't yet emphasize the point that in doing so, they'd be putting improvisation techniques to use.

A few aha! moments began to happen. The teams most open to the process were discovering that what they thought was their best idea didn't hold up when stretched out into a movie-length narrative. Some teams were finding that parts of their three good ideas fit together to make an entirely new premise. Others were finding unexplored depth and breadth in the story and character development. The techniques of divergent and convergent thinking weren't quite so abstract now; they were getting results.

The teams applied convergent thinking once more to pick a single, best movie idea. Then it was back to the divergent cycle for them to fully develop that idea. Each team's best idea had to be completely thought through and shaped into a real, deliverable movie pitch. It had to have a concise logline—a one-sentence summary of the story capturing the basic concept and unique hook of the movie idea. Teams also had to consider a narrative arc, a sense of character development, and a way to convey the impact the movie would have on its audience. After some prep time each group was only going to have five minutes to pitch their movie to our expert panel. They had to be succinct, on point, and impactful.[10]

I was thrilled when the team that had been most resistant to the process conceded that they would not be showcasing the idea they had quickly and stubbornly trumpeted as their best—a "Tommy Boy"-goes-to-Washington story based on the wild exploits of former Toronto mayor Rob Ford (Ford had recently been in the news, and the tales of his public drunkenness, his admissions to smoking crack, and his general boorishness were on everybody's mind—four of the eight teams started with Mayor Ford movies on their lists). The team of skeptics would now be pitching a movie about a U.S. GI working as one of the unheralded "tunnel rats" during the Vietnam War, who gets trapped behind enemy lines. In working through the repeated divergent/convergent process (about which they had such strong doubts), this team had discovered that this highly emotional war story was actually much stronger than the raucous Rob Ford comedy.

The war story was up against some tough competition. Among the other teams' pitches were

- A high school football drama about a star player who dies after suffering multiple concussions, and whose mother then takes up the cause of making football safer (*Erin Brockovich* meets *The Blind Side*)

- Another football film, in which the NFL is run by corrupt prison wardens and football stadiums have become gladiatorial coliseums in which the games are battles to the death among the prisoner-athletes (*Mad Max* meets *The Longest Yard*)

- A film that follows a serial killer working the speed-dating scene (*Valentine's Day* meets *Silence of the Lambs*)

- A film about a team of robots that plans a bank heist (*Robocop* meets *Ocean's Eleven*)

- A feature documentary that centers on the "nature vs. nurture" debate and examines how an inherently good person can go bad in the wrong environment while an intrinsically bad person can become virtuous in a positive environment (*Freaky Friday* meets *Freakonomics*)

- A film about a wine connoisseur who finds love on a dairy farm (*Sideways* meets Whole Foods)

- A film about a female spy who kicks ass and saves the world (the *Bourne* films meet *The Hunger Games*)

The teams pitched their big ideas, then the judges conferred to pick the four strongest ideas on the basis of clarity, content, the passion of the presentation, and the effectiveness of the storytelling. They went with the two football ideas, the nature vs. nurture documentary, and the skeptics' tunnel rat. The lower groups were folded into the top groups, creating four final groups with new personal dynamics as well as new assets. Each top group was given thoughts and direction about their movie pitches from our judges and then the new, larger team began the divergent/convergent process once more to implement the changes and perfectly hone their pitches. The stakes were high: members of the winning team were going to receive a UCLA hat *and* coffee mug.

At the start of this particular program the energy in the room had been decidedly negative. By the time the four teams of elite financial planners were putting together their final 15-minute pitches for the judges' panel, there had been an observable shift. Nobody seemed interested in questioning or undermining the process—they were all fully committed to go for the win. Every voice felt supported, every idea was properly aired and considered, and every group member had a clear understanding of the group goal and each individual's responsibility. The final pitches were a blast, every group putting so much passion into their presentations that you would have thought there was a real $100 million studio check at stake. The skeptics' team was the most animated, actually crawling around on the floor to bring the tunnel rat story to life, and almost tearing up in the climactic moments when the GI finally makes it back to the States with a newly adopted Vietnamese son.

The judges had a tough decision to make, and the win went to the "NFL as deadly penal colony" movie. The skeptics placed second—a finish they seemed very happy to achieve.

On the last morning of the program there was a final debriefing session with the participants. I asked the group, "What if the challenge now was to come up with a quarterly report, or draft a best practices memo for your department?" Everyone in the room—skeptics included—had a similar reaction: they realized that whatever work they might be faced with, if approached with the same energy, focus, and sense of purpose they had been using on their movie pitches, it would get done better, faster, smarter, more productively, and more enjoyably. Moreover what seems like a basic task—best practices for a new employee engagement, let's say—can in fact be a much more invigorating and insightful exercise in divergent and convergent thinking if structured as such. That's what I call thinking outside of thinking outside of the box.

I am continually amazed at how powerful a change agent improvisation can be when serious people commit and get serious about the process. From boardrooms to classrooms to breakout rooms—no fancy environs are necessary to set a foundation of growth in place. With that in mind let's settle in (wherever you are) and move on from the big picture to the building blocks. We'll start with the principle that is at the heart of all improvisation: "Yes, and . . . "

Chapter 2

JUST SAY "YES, AND . . . "

IF A PERSON KNOWS just one thing about the techniques of improv, it's probably two words: "Yes, and . . . " This phrase describes the cornerstone philosophy of theatrical improvisation around the world. No matter the country or continent, no matter whether what's being taught is short-form games, long-form theater, or classroom exercises, if people are improvising they're using the concept of "Yes, and" (or *si y, oui et, ja und, ye gwa* in Spanish, French, German, and Korean).

In this chapter we'll take a look at what the "Yes, and . . . " philosophy entails and how it can be applied practically and effectively to business. We'll also look at a couple of key outgrowths of "Yes, and": the importance of separating individual perspective from individual agenda, and the ways in which improvisational communication can boost the emotional intelligence of a workplace.

In the realm of comedic improvisation the phrase might actually be spoken aloud in the course of a scene. More importantly, though, each word in the phrase—whether actually spoken or silently implied—represents a key part of the team dynamic and mind-set that must be established between performers. "Yes" represents the unconditional acceptance of an idea that has been presented and established by another performer or a group of performers. "And" means that you take that expressed idea and build directly on it. What this means onstage is that if one performer says, "Wow, it's hot in this kitchen," the second performer does not say, "No, it isn't—I'm freezing," or "We're not in the kitchen. We're in a cruise ship bathroom." Both of these statements deny, negate, and otherwise undermine the offer the first performer brought to the table. A "Yes, and . . . " response might instead be, "Yes, it is hot. And the fact that I set the house on fire probably isn't helping any."

Onstage it's crucial that everyone embrace "Yes, and . . . " In fully improvised musicals for example performers are in a situation where an entire show is inspired by a single suggestion from the audience, and the comedy is going to grow from the series of split-second decisions the performers make about how to create a scene and how to move it forward, in real time. In order for the process of improvisation to work, there has to be mutual trust and understanding that everyone onstage has the same agenda in mind: to work together at peak intelligence as a team and create a process or product that entertains an audience. A violation of "Yes, and" means the scene crumbles, because a performer's pursuit of a personal agenda ("Look at me—funny, funny me!") negates what's been built and doesn't give the other performers in the scene anything to build on. The pure musical equivalent of a "Yes, and" violation would be something like a drummer in a jazz ensemble suddenly taking a wild, extended hard-rock drum solo in the middle of "My Funny Valentine" simply because he wanted to seize the chance to show off his chops in front of a paying crowd.

I like to refer to "Yes, and . . . " as the "scarlet thread" of improvisation—the one element of the improvisational fabric that is always present and ties all other improv techniques together. As simple sounding as the phrase "Yes, and" may be, its practical applications can be varied and nuanced. On a comedy stage a troupe of eight improvisers is usually made up of eight individuals with very different comedic styles, educations, and backgrounds. The fact that they all work together by way of "Yes, and" does not mean they give up their distinctive approaches or all react and engage with each other in the same exact way. "Yes, and . . . " really becomes more a philosophy than a prime directive, encouraging each performer to work toward

a common goal while maintaining an individual intellectual and comedic perspective. In fact the common agenda is achieved on the
strength of each individual perspective that supports it. Consequently
there is a clear recognition that individual perspective is different from
individual agenda.

Watching improvisers onstage, an audience doesn't have to be
aware that any particular philosophy is being embraced by the performers—the audience simply reacts to what's funny, interesting, or
impactful. "Yes, and . . . " should be similarly invisible in a business
setting; what is supposed to shine through is actual communication,
not the usage of a communication technique. The real engine of "Yes,
and" is simply respect. Whether onstage or in a boardroom, those who
use a "Yes, and" approach are demonstrating respect for colleagues,
respect for the idea that a group's common goal takes precedence over
any personal agenda, and respect for the process of communication
and idea sharing. The yes of "Yes, and" is not supposed to be empty
agreement. It's not enough simply to say the word for the sake of
saying it. On its own, "Yes" is an affirmation and acts as a conversa-
tion-stopper when no new information is brought into the mix. The
authentic "Yes" in conjunction with the word "and" is a show of respect because it implies focus and concentration. A "Yes" that comes
out of your mouth when your head has been speeding through an unrelated to-do list while a colleague is talking—that yes is meaningless.
The point is to be present and in the moment. Your "Yes," spoken or
not, must carry the power of thoughtfulness and understanding.

Adaptation

When it comes to the specialized realm of improvisation in business,
an unavoidable and even understandable negative connotation at-
taches to the notion of being "forced" to build directly on somebody
else's idea. "Yes, and-ing" someone else works perfectly well on an
improv stage; however, it occasionally causes mental hiccups in the
business mind. Sometimes the connotation of "building on somebody
else's idea" is misunderstood to mean abandoning one's own critical

thinking to unconditionally support and further what somebody else is saying or doing. But postponing judgment and surrendering one's unique voice are two very different things. Here again we run into the difference between individual perspective and individual agenda: individual agendas are a barrier to open communication and collaboration, while an individual perspective is the unique lens through which each person sees a situation. Both on the stage and in the workplace individual perspectives are to be celebrated and individual agendas are to be realigned to serve the larger process.

Of course the stage and the office are very different spaces and the team dynamic of the theater is not the same as that of the workplace. For the "Yes, and . . . " philosophy to have real value in the business world at large, the definition of "Yes, and" must be tweaked a bit. Not a problem, as the "Yes, and" philosophy is inherently flexible and adaptable. Let's deconstruct what "Yes, and" really means in business.

Recall that improvisation is all about reacting and adapting and communicating. As such the "Yes" in "Yes, and" still represents unconditional acceptance without judging or prejudging the idea or the person talking. "And," however, rather than representing only the act of building on someone else's idea, now represents the building of a bridge to your own authentic perspective—to your unique voice and your honest reaction to whatever is being presented. Once again, "Yes" is (implied) thoughtfulness in regard to what someone else is saying; "and" is the connector that allows for the expression of your own thoughts, which may or may not build directly on the idea you're responding to. That little adjustment makes a big difference. It effectively extends the reach of "Yes, and" from a tool to facilitate a common, specific goal (great brainstorming, creativity, collaboration) to a more broadly applicable philosophy and an easy-to-access communications technique.

It's particularly important in the business setting to remember that unconditional acceptance is not the same as unequivocal agreement. (There is a huge difference between saying "Yes, and" and being a "yes-man"!) In business "Yes" is unconditional acceptance as a show of respect, focus, and thoughtfulness. "Yes" indicates that you have listened fully to what someone has just said, that you've made the effort to understand it, and that you are willing to consider it—at least at face value. "And" then allows you to step across the verbal bridge from someone else's thought to your own response. It is the bridge to the particular way in which you understand what's been said—or how you don't understand. Critically, "and" respectfully opens the door to the introduction of your own perspective rather than your own agenda. Yet while "and" may provide the bridge to how you agree with someone, it may just as easily provide the bridge to how you disagree with someone.

As a means of business communication "Yes, and . . . " can actually have great value as a conflict management tool, wherein you can strongly disagree with somebody and still communicate openly and respectfully. It is incredibly difficult to remain in an emotion-based disagreement with someone when your counterpart is "Yes, and-ing" everything you are saying. In a debate "Yes, and" slows the brain down and requires each individual to listen and understand; however, it does not limit responses. In a business setting if someone says, "We should meet Tuesday to go over the quarterly reports," the accept-and-bridge "Yes, and . . . " response might be, "Yes, and my morning is packed. Let's meet over lunch, on Tuesday." Perhaps, though, you know from experience that one meeting is never enough for those quarterly points. Your instinct might be to turn negative and say, "No, that's not going to work." The more business-oriented accept-and-bridge "Yes, and . . . " response would be, "Yes, and if we have trouble getting it all done Tuesday we'll chisel out some time Wednesday to pick up where we left off."

Why would it be worth the time and effort to make this seemingly small change in tone and language? Well, unless you've managed to find gainful employment as a cave-dwelling hermit in the Appalachian Mountains, you're in the relationship business and the people business no matter what your actual business is. At some point in your business day you need to communicate with others—clients (internal, external), prospective clients, partners, sales reps, employees, the IT guys,

even the UPS guy—and better communication techniques mean better business (and better service). "Yes, and . . . " is a powerful means
to strengthen relationships and help people communicate better with
each other. Making "Yes, and" an element of corporate culture is a
means of emphasizing and celebrating individual perspective. It allows voices to be heard and in doing so it creates a culture that cel-
ebrates diverse opinions and ideas. When more ideas are heard, the
probability of hearing more *great* ideas increases.

Wait. What about all the lousy ideas one might hear?

The glib response would be that bad ideas are the price you pay
for building great relationships in which people are not afraid to come
to you with any idea. However, in a properly run "Yes, and . . . " environment lousy ideas can be openly identified as non-starters. In such
an environment there is plenty of room for dissent and disagreement;
it will just be respectful dissent and disagreement. Again the power
behind "Yes, and" is respect: if employees feel their ideas are worth
respect, they will feel they've got a stake in the way the business is run,
and if they feel they've got a stake in how the business is run, then
they've got a stake in that business's success.

Here's a point of bombshell importance: learning to make use of
business improvisation is not the same as attending etiquette class.

"Yes, and . . . " is not about valuing workplace courtesy over corporate success. The aim is not to create a corporate culture in which
everyone gets along wonderfully while the business itself fails. The
idea is not to create something illusory, a happy atmosphere of Kum-
baya moments and hand-holding sing-alongs around the copy machine. The point—always—is to make a business run better.

In fact a "Yes, and" discussion can sound like a fairly heated argument. A great example of that can be found in any high school or
college debate club. In the debate model you've got teams that are in
direct opposition to each other—the whole point of the endeavor is
to "defeat" the other side. Yet the win is not possible without sharp,
focused, in-the-moment listening. Debaters on one side make points
and their opponents have to listen intently because it's their job to use

those words against the speakers who just made them. A point can't be negated or rebutted without first being accepted and fully understood ("Yes"). A debater has to be present, in the moment, and fully focused on what's being said because the rival's words become the weapons to attack the opposing points and reinforce one's own points. (Political debates, wherein candidates ignore questions and proper rebuttals in favor of redundantly regurgitating prepracticed talking points, are perfect demonstrations of *not* performing in the moment.) The spirit of "Yes, and . . . " isn't mindless cooperation; it is mindful communication. "Yes, and" is a means of being focused and present at the highest possible level, and being aware of what's said and done around you in order to react to it most effectively. "Yes, and" is a means to mindfulness.[1]

The point again of fostering respect and open communication in the workplace isn't so that the business functions like one endless employee appreciation day. The point is to build relationships that create intrinsic motivation in others, that is, the desire to do a great job because you want to do a great job—not because it gets you that much closer to a bonus or a bigger office.[2] A business leader has to patiently and thoughtfully contemplate how to create relationships in which other people will desire to work for him or her. "Yes, and" isn't about avoiding hurt feelings at work because the leader wants to be seen as a nice boss. It's a means of influence, creating a culture of intrinsic motivation in which people work through the weekend or put in extra time because that's what they want to do for you. "Yes, and" becomes a mutually beneficial proposition when people want to do great work for the sake of doing great work and want to do it for people who value their input and allow them to have some ownership of the work.

Postponement

Suspending judgment and surrendering one's own critical thinking to further the ideas of another person or a group is the key to what happens on the comedic improv stage. You do not attempt to forcefully assert leadership in the middle of a scene and you're always in a position to follow someone else's initiations. Forcing leadership or dominance creates something onstage that is jarring, unprofessional, and usually awkwardly unfunny. "Suspension of judgment" is an important concept in almost all improv. When it comes to making "Yes, and . . . " work in a business setting, though, I reframe the concept of "suspending judgment" to "postponing judgment." In business a suspension seems to have a negative connotation ("My son was suspended from school for toilet-papering the gym"), whereas a postponement implies that the inevitable will eventually come.

Importantly the postponement of judgment is not the abandonment of judgment. Postponing judgment holds back our critical thinking skills for a time and allows for the freest flow of ideas and communication. This is crucial because in the business world "judgment" is often actually prejudgment—ideas are dismissed before they are fully presented or even fully understood. Great ideas will never be available if a culture has been created in which people have resigned themselves to having their ideas dismissed.

When used properly, postponing judgment is not simply a way of letting employees feel they're being heard; it's a period that allows for those great ideas and forward-thinking solutions to be freely communicated. To be clear, there are of course moments in any business when a postponement of judgment is not possible; there are times when decisions need to be made by somebody in charge. However, when open communication is the goal, it really is necessary for all of us to take off our critical thinking caps for a predetermined amount of time. Lord knows, there is plenty of time and opportunity for judgment in the workweek. If we can learn how to postpone judgment, we can make sure that the best ideas get heard and the best decisions get made.

Adjusting EQ

A lot of companies have begun to put stock in the concept of emotional intelligence (EQ).[3] That manner of thinking is relatively new in the business world and is probably not something that robber barons of eras past worried much about. Over the last decade though EQ has become a hot topic because the dynamic of the workplace has continued to change. Employees increasingly put a great deal of value in finding a workplace where they feel their talents are recognized and appreciated, and where they feel a sense of belonging.[4] This has become especially true for Millennials in the workforce, who often rank personal satisfaction and individual sense of purpose even higher than paycheck when it comes to the appeal of a workplace.[5]

If we're looking at how workers "feel" about work, we are in the realm of examining emotions, and emotional intelligence is simply the ability to recognize those emotions and make thoughtful decisions based on them. The robber baron may have been able to harrumph away any consideration of employees' emotional states, but these days it makes excellent business sense that if the mind-set of the employee is changing then the role of the employer must change.

According to Daniel Goleman, one of the pioneers in this field and author of "What Makes a Leader: Why Emotional Intelligence Matters," there are five components of emotional intelligence at work: *self-awareness, self-regulation, internal motivation, empathy,* and *social skills.*[6] With improvisation in mind, I would expand on those components this way:

> *Self-awareness.* This is the ability to recognize what you are doing (emotion, actions, and language) in real time so that you can make the intelligent decision to continue that behavior or change it to affect the people in the way you desire to influence them. Take time to postpone judgment to assess your situation, circumstances, and actions as accurately as possible. As important as it is to be self-confident, it may be equally important to be humble. When success arises, credit the people around you who deserve it, and when struggle or failure pokes its head up, be sure to understand what role you played in this situation and where perhaps you—as a leader—missed areas for greater success. Look to define areas for improvement. Once you have an understanding

of your behavior and the role you played in any given situation, create a road map to your growth by objectively evaluating your strengths and weaknesses. Then define simple action steps that you can practice in casual, no-stakes situations so that you can employ your learnings in specific, higher-stakes situations.

Self-regulation. As we've already stressed, postponement of judgment does not mean abandonment of judgment. With a bit of forethought, take deliberate time to use the knowledge you've gained from your work on self-awareness to make subtle tweaks or large changes in yourself, with thoughtful goals of affecting others. Unless your style of leadership is that of a ruthless tyrant, focus on "Yes, and" for adaptability, finding comfort in loosening the reins and becoming open to the unique perspectives of those around you.

Internal motivation. If we are motivated by the head, the wallet, the heart, and the gut, intrinsic motivation comes from the last two—it is the drive that makes your soul sing. While Chapter 4 will show you techniques for manipulating energy to feed intrinsic motivation, you can extend the literal use of the two-word phrase "Yes, and" to create a 'Yes, and' philosophy. This philosophy, which taps into our intrinsic motivation, accepts what is given to us in any given situation at face value (the good, the bad, or the ugly) *and* looks to create paths to success every time (anywhere, with anyone). The "Yes, and" philosophy is a commitment to operating at the top of our intelligence, at all levels, from EQ to IQ.

Empathy. The ability to feel the emotions of others is a powerful leadership trait, engendering trust and building supportive relationships quickly. Use "Yes, and" to slow your brain down to engage and connect fully. "Yes, and" in relation to empathy creates an outward focus, a concentration that is directed to the person or people with whom you are engaged. This level of awareness allows you to react, adapt, and communicate on a personal and impactful level:

- "Yes" = I hear what you are saying. You have my undivided attention. I am fully committed to listening to you and understanding you to the best of my ability.
- "And" = This is how I can relate to you. This is how I can support you. This is how I can be of service to you. This is how I am grateful to you for sharing this with me.

Social skills. The equation to create good social skills contains a constantly shifting set of variables. As you have read, improvisation is an inherently communicative art form; as such it directly lends itself to developing social skills. Cling to "Yes, and" as a technique for finding common ground, for active listening, and for quickly building rapport on both a personal and a team level.

In an era of social media and information sharing, a company's culture is almost as transparent as the lens of a microscope. Recruitment and retention of great, talented employees is increasing, and the perceived EQ level of a company has a huge impact on current and prospective personnel. Just like a person trying a new restaurant on the basis of online reviews, potential hot recruits are more prone to believe in an organization by what the company's employees have said online than by what a recruiter promoted to them. The meat of this meal: talent enticement is impacted substantially through employee engagement.[7] One of the truest and most powerful statements in all of human resources is that employees don't quit companies; they quit people. Given the current interest in EQ, "Yes, and" should be seen as an effective power booster for upping the emotional intelligence of the workplace, because—no surprise—the skill set that improvisation inherently strengthens is the same skill set used to reach emotional intelligence: awareness, focus and concentration in the moment, empathetic listening and communication, unconditional support, postponement of judgment, collaboration, celebration of diverse perspectives, adaptability.

If we are all in the people business and we understand that the extreme majority of people like to feel valued, then "Yes, and . . . " is a priceless EQ addition to the corporate culture because it requires a culture in which you make it clear that you value the person talking to you enough to isolate your thoughts and give that individual your undivided, focused attention and then respond openly and honestly without an agenda. A "Yes, and" culture is a system in which—because everyone is attentive to what each person in the team is saying—the decision-making process can improve, and perhaps even accelerate (if you know your words really count, you won't waste them).

"Yes, and . . . " is adaptable enough to be the underlying foundation for a corporate culture, and it can also be used as a specific tool during any particular interaction. Even so, that does not mean the philosophy will govern every decision. Remember, "Yes, and" is not a panacea or magic elixir to cure all business woes. Sometimes "No" is the right answer. Enlightened leaders must make that decision for themselves, often in real time. "Yes, and" must be applied thoughtfully and strategically, again in real time.

Big Picture

What does a "Yes, and . . . " corporate culture look like? Twitter, IDEO, and many other tech and design companies openly embrace a "Yes, and . . . " philosophy.[8] As CEO of Business Improv—a company that's in the business of promoting a redefined understanding of improvisation—I've found it important to have a workplace where the members of my staff can frame their thoughts to look for opportunities and possibilities for success, regardless of their titular status. I want everyone who works for me to feel encouraged to take on challenges that others might be daunted by. Instead of focusing on the negative—what can't be done—employees should feel free to do something original, fearless, and awe inspiring. (Save the "What went wrong? Who was wrong?" for the after-action review, and then be sure to ask the additional questions, What did we learn? What could we have done differently? How do we keep this from happening again in the future?) The challenge at hand might be in the development of our curriculum; it might be in our travel schedule; it might be in the way we lead a complex program. Whatever the challenge, all employees regardless of company hierarchy or length of time in my organization know they are in a workplace where all perspectives are supported, respected, and valued. Everyone understands communication is an imperative, and decisions are made on the basis of a meritocracy of ideas rather than the status of the person saying them.

Someone involved in a more number-crunching type of business—a banker, actuary, or accountant—may recognize quickly that "Yes, and" cannot be a part of every business decision. True. The numbers themselves are going to dictate some of those decisions. However, even in the bank or the accounting firm you can have a "Yes, and" conversation with somebody else in the office. You can still put a premium on communicating effectively. And you can still be open and present when hearing what somebody else has to say before you judge what he or she is saying. Giving everyone respect doesn't mean that all that is said gets acted on. A financial planner shouldn't rush into an unwise investment simply because a divergent "Yes, and" conversation explored the idea. Leaders still need to lead thoughtfully and hard decisions have to be made. In any type of collaborative environment, though—any place where there is a need for communication—"Yes, and" can improve the quality of that communication.

How does it work? Let's step into the realm of cognitive psychology for a moment. By forcing one to listen and react in the moment, "Yes, and" helps develop mindfulness and makes one aware not only of one's own behavior but also how that behavior influences others.[9] Very often Business Improv gets brought into companies to help instill a culture of more open communication, a culture of acceptance, a "Yes, and . . . " culture. What we most often find we are dealing with is a "Yes, but . . . " culture. Perhaps it doesn't seem like that little shift in a three-letter conjunction could add up to much. The psychological ramifications run deep, though.[10] "Yes, but" is often thought of as a nicer way of saying "No." This is 100 percent, completely and unequivocally incorrect. "Yes, but" is not a politer way of saying no.

In fact it is a condescending way of saying no. People engaged in "Yes, but" communication are denying, negating, restricting, or otherwise redirecting—or at least it feels that way to the person on the receiving end of that interaction, especially when it is delivered consistently over time. Further, "Yes, but" creates a point/counterpoint mentality wherein people tend to spend time figuring out what they're going to say next to defend their perspective rather than listening to what's being said to them. That kind of inferred negation and denial leads to a workplace in which people either feel stuck in the mud because they're not heard, or harbor resentments because what they say gets shot down. Morale and motivation (intrinsic motivation) suffer. Moreover when a workplace gets bogged down in "Yes, but" eventually personal agenda (often in the form of self-preservation) is placed above common goals. Effective communication is quashed and a company has a hard time moving forward.

To turn those cultures of negation into cultures of acceptance, step in and begin modeling the benefits of respect and support over denial, negation, and argument. Again, instilling a culture of acceptance does not mean that every idea brought to the conference table is acted upon unconditionally. It means that the people at the table are now unconditionally open to sharing ideas and opinions and the possibility of new solutions (divergent thinking) and will consider them before judging them (convergent thinking) or ignoring them altogether (no thinking at all). Each person in the workplace must accept responsibility for listening to others and postpone judgment until feeling certain about what has been brought to the table.

New Frames

At the nuts and bolts level, "Yes, and . . . " is made up of three pieces: language, thought process, and desired outcome. When we talk about corporate culture—behaviors, beliefs, values, and language—we are talking about the way people think and communicate within their workplace. In "Yes, and" we are very aware of the looping nature in which thought and language interact. The way we think impacts the language we use, and the way we use language often impacts the way we think.[11] If we want to change the way we think, we must be aware that our choices of language frame the way we think and, over time, train the brain to react a certain way. In that sense "Yes, and" is a framing device—a choice of framing language that can have a tremendous effect on other people, especially when delivered by the same individual over time. Such framing may not be something that people on the receiving end are even consciously aware of; they just get it in their gut and their heart. If you're provoking a negative gut reaction in a colleague, chances are that at some point that negativity will show up in the work or the workplace. If you're speaking to someone's heart, that's when a fiery, intrinsic motivation catches hold.

In short, the small shift from "but" to "and" can tremendously impact the way the message is perceived. "But" eliminates everything preceding it and shuts things down. "And" is an extender and moves things forward. "But" is exclusive; "and" is inclusive.

One small point of resistance I have occasionally heard is that the "Yes" in "Yes, but . . . " might be more important than the "but"; that is, if I'm agreeing with somebody, how can saying "but" be a bad thing? The answer is that whether intended or not, "but" eliminates everything said before it. So even when "Yes, but" does not mean to negate what's been said, it feels that way to the person hearing it because "but" is an emotional trigger for most people and sets off a negative reaction.[12]

This is where "Yes, but" gets dangerous and corrosive in the workplace: the moment you refuse to accept that the language you use is in fact a choice. When you're meaning to say "Yes, and" to engender a supportive relationship and build positively on an idea, and you're actually using "Yes, but," you're using words that train people to react negatively. People walk away from a "Yes, but" encounter feeling like they've been shut down and dismissed because their idea didn't have value. They've been denied the opportunity to be heard. On the receiving end, "Yes, but" makes people feel like they've stepped into a

competitive boxing match to be hit, rather than stepping onto a coop-
erative field to join the rest of the team. Those negative feelings are
eventually going to limit what an employee contributes or attempts to
contribute to the success of a project or a business. How many times
can you feel like you've been shot down by one person just for speaking up before it becomes easier not to bring any ideas to the person
who makes you feel lousy? For most, the better option starts looking
to be the path of least resistance: keep your head down and do the
minimum required to be considered a "good" employee.

For example, if a leader is actively trying to inspire people and
keep energy pumped up and then responds to her team's motivation
with a passionate "Yes, but . . . !" that passion meant to inspire instead
feels like a verbal slap-down: the "Yes" becomes dismissive because
the "but" is a negation. The energy meant to motivate becomes an
emphatic demotivator. Similarly if a team member enthusiastically
presents an idea with pop and excitement and the leader responds to
that idea with a quiet, passionless "Yes, but . . . " it sucks the energy
right out of the process, and out of the person presenting the idea. In
either situation the framing language is a choice that affects outcome:
if the response feels dismissive or impersonal, the person receiving the
response feels disengaged, demotivated, and devalued. With a "Yes,
and" style of response the person receiving it feels empowered, encouraged, and valued. As such you can use framing language to shape
the emotions of others, and to up your own EQ.

What Gets Heard

The old adage "It's not what you say; it's how you say it" has evolved
to "It's not just what you say and how you say it; it's also what the
listener walks away understanding." The key here—and one of the
most powerful components of "Yes, and"—is to be aware not just of
what you mean to communicate and *how* you mean to communicate
it, but also of the effect that specific communication has on other people. In the next chapters we will more fully explore the concept of

mindfulness and of "self-audit"—the ability to recognize what you are doing in real time so that you can make the choice to continue that behavior or change it to get the desired effect on the people you are influencing. For now understand that over time, through our style of interpersonal communication, we train each other on what to expect and how to react to us. We hear something a certain way, and we react a certain way. While no one wants to be thought of as a drooling dog, Dr. Pavlov did have a point.[13] (Now pardon me, I just heard a bell and I have to get something to eat.)

The underlying message of any communication is processed and reacted to even before a spoken reaction is prompted. This is a matter of brain science,[14] and it's also quite evident in our day-to-day lives. At my desk I have a picture of my young son up on the wall, and next to it is a Post-it note that reads "Stay focused." I also have a decorative magnet that displays a favorite phrase of my improv mentor Martin de Maat: "You are pure potential." Some days I'm aware of actually reading these words. Many days they are simply part of the visual backdrop of my workspace—things that dance in my peripheral vision. However, whether I consciously or unconsciously process such words, they have an impact on me and the people who step into my office. When I see these kinds of messages on a regular basis, they affect the way I think and the way I treat other people. Words do indeed train the brain.[15]

If as a leader you are acutely aware of the effect you have on other people and the way your communication style impacts them, and you can see in measurable ways that your impact is positive—fantastic. If however you are simply assuming that you're communicating effectively and having a positive impact just because it feels that way on your side of the desk, I'd ask you to put your communication style under review. Too many people in the business world do not consider whether their style of communication and their language choice have a positive or negative impact. It doesn't even occur to some that impact matters. The impatient, Kumbaya-resistant executive might recoil from considering "Yes, and" on the grounds that it's not his job to care about how other people feel. However, I'd argue that if you want those people to do a better job and you want the business to run better, the language of the workplace is well worth examining. Instead of spending millions on EQ development seminars, why not explore the noncostly alternative of examining how you are personally affecting people, and try embracing "Yes, and . . . " Take this "Yes" test if you don't think language matters:

Have a 3–5-minute conversation with a colleague (or a stranger at a pub), starting every sentence with "Yes, but . . . " Focus internally by objectively looking at the language you use after "but," and focus externally at how the person across from you reacts throughout the course of the entire conversation.

What did you notice?

Now have a 3–5-minute conversation with someone, starting every sentence with "Yes, and . . . " Keep focused internally on your language after "and" and externally on how the person across from you reacts throughout the entire conversation.

What did you notice?

What was the difference between the "Yes, but" conversation versus the "Yes, and" conversation?

A final guiding "Yes, and . . . " principle is this gift from my good friend and improv legend Susan Messing: "Words are gold." If you have a supply of gold, you probably don't want to hand it out randomly to anyone. You bestow your gold to specific people for specific reasons, and you definitely want them to appreciate the fact that they are receiving gold. Similarly if someone gives you gold, you aren't likely to come up with reasons you can't use gold and then simply toss the gift into a desk drawer alongside the paper clips, random batteries, and six-year-old receipts. You cherish the fact that you have received gold. If everyone involved in a business were to adopt a mind-set that puts a premium on communication—on treating everyone's right to speak as something precious, like gold—then there would be a lot less wasted words in the workplace. Less waste is always better business.

Massage the Message

Words are only part of how and what we communicate, of course. Attitude, energy, and mind-set all come through to others and have an impact. And as we've mentioned, our words and our behavior feed off each other. If you make a conscious effort to change the way you think about something, your speech will reflect it. If you put an effort into speaking a certain way, eventually your thoughts will reflect that. Aside from actually saying the words "Yes, and," thinking in the "Yes, and . . . " philosophy will change the intonation of your speech: your tone, your cadence, your inflections. And speaking that way reinforces the mind-set. When we have a positive mind-set we speak a certain way with a lighter cadence, a more energetic rhythm, and a more positive word choice. If we have a negative mind-set our cadence again reflects it. The words themselves sound negative and weighted, like they're slogging through the mud on the way to a shift in the salt mines. Being aware of the impact you have on others means being aware of what your brain and your mouth are doing.

We have said that in "Yes, and" communication the "Yes" represents unconditional acceptance of an offer, not thoughtless acceptance of an action. It means accepting what is happening in the moment. In practical terms this means that you should not mentally jump ahead to judge something that's being expressed in that moment. Deal with this offer in the present and allow actions and reactions to spring directly from that. That kind of attentive mind-set communicates a respect that translates into positive energy. In turn, that positive energy has an impact on how business gets done.

We all know people who can walk into a situation that seems dire and their very presence makes the situation seem lighter, the problems-at-hand solvable. With that kind of presence in the room hard work becomes exciting and every challenge becomes a means to an achievable goal. Positive energy increases the possibilities for success. On the other hand, I'm sure we also know people who can walk into a light, positive, happy environment and immediately suck the energy out of it. That kind of person makes what might have been exciting challenges now seem like dead-end problems. String enough of these positive or negative moments with positive or negative people together, and you've got your positive or negative corporate culture. Any business increases its chances for success when it is full of great people passionately performing at the top of their intelligence and bringing the best they can, authentically and honestly, to any situation. In that positive environment employees feel they are enthusiastically on the same team and working toward a mutual objective. "Yes, and" is a tool that can help you make a positive environment.

If "positive energy" sounds like we've gotten touchy-feely, think about the concepts of "inspiration" and "motivation" and tack them to any number of real-world encounters. When you deal with somebody who's great at what they do—a teacher, doctor, flight attendant, waiter—and they communicate that competence in words, attitude, and energy, they influence you in a positive direction and your load is lifted. You feel that whatever problem being approached can be dealt with effectively. This person inspires you and the interaction is enjoyable, creating an intrinsic motivation in you to work with that person again. If you're treated rudely by waitstaff and negatively influenced, you'll probably not be spending money at that restaurant again, no matter how tasty the roasted chicken is. In business all that positive or negative energy ends up having a real dollar value.

Can You Listen to Me Now?

While "Yes, and . . . " can effect huge changes in corporate culture and in interpersonal dynamics, one doesn't have to focus solely on huge changes to get started down the "Yes, and" path. As Mahatma Gandhi said, "Be the change that you wish to see in the world." So let's start with small things you can do for yourself to help you in your personal development.

If you start using some of the "Yes, and" language of acceptance and support, it will trickle back to the way you think. It's not such a daunting change when it begins with small, practical steps like making the attempt to swap out one three-letter word, "but," for another, "and." No brains have to be rewired in order to do this properly. However, it does take desire and action, focus and concentration; the truth is, when those first small steps are attempted on a regular basis and you begin to create good speaking habits, the rewiring of your brain begins automatically.

A small part of an incredibly effective exercise I execute in most sessions focuses on participants simply closing their eyes and listening. The listening lasts for only 30–45 seconds. When I ask people what they heard during that short span, there are always some obvious responses—the hiss of a radiator, people talking next door, the floor creaking, the clock ticking. When I press a little harder for what else they heard, somebody invariably says, "I heard my own thoughts." When I ask who else heard their own thoughts, on average 85 percent of hands in the room go up. The point of the exercise is to demonstrate how so many of us actually have trouble focusing on what our ears are registering. Even when asked to simply listen for less than a minute, the vast majority of people can't do it and end up getting caught in their heads, thinking about something other than what their ears are picking up: *Why are we doing this? I have to remember to call home. Did I send out that follow-up e-mail? What will I get at the lunch buffet? Whose pants am I wearing?* Our mind needs to be challenged and we unconsciously allow it to drift away from the task at hand—in this case the task of listening. This simple exercise underscores how we communicate in real life as we busily attempt to multitask our way through real deadlines and time crunches and ambient chaos. So how does one learn to listen better amid real-world business stress?

To fully embrace "Yes, and" and make fast, effective decisions in the real-world environment, we have to do something counterintuitive: slow our brain down. Slowing down our thoughts doesn't mean we're looking to diminish the quality of our thoughts. I would argue instead that by slowing down the brain and focusing on the nuances of our communications, we're actually increasing the quality of thought. Let's hit this piñata from another angle. The human brain can process somewhere between 350 and 550 words a minute, while most people usually only speak around 120 words a minute.[16] This means that in virtually every exchange of communication each participating brain has room for 230–375 extra words' worth of thought to float around. Like a captainless ship, that gives our minds plenty of chance to drift and wander, whether we're the one speaking or listening. We easily slip into the basic communication pitfall of drifting away from the person speaking, often thinking about what we're going to say next rather than being focused on what we're communicating or what's being said to us. Rather than wandering off, our focus should be to slow the brain down, put extra emphasis on the words spoken (as if they were gold), engage our partner, and be fully present in the moment.

Throw down the gauntlet and challenge your brain to stay in the moment, in real time. It's all about refocusing the brain to engage in a heightened state of concentration. This is precisely what "Yes, and" accomplishes. At its simplest level "Yes, and" requires you to really listen and understand, in the moment, before you react. The broader concept is that "Yes, and" asks both speaker and listener to be account-able for what is being communicated and what is being received—that is, to be accountable for all parties involved in the communication.

In my programs I move on from our intensive listening exercise to some exercises in interpersonal collaboration. We begin with a dem-onstration of what's really happening when we say we're listening but are instead allowing those approximately 200 extra words per minute to ricochet wildly in our brains. Participants pair off and attempt to have a "conversation" in which each person must talk over the per-son who's trying to talk to him or her. We only need 30 seconds or so of this to get the point across. Nobody is clear on what was said because speakers were either talking mindlessly while focusing on drowning out the other person, or they were only hearing themselves speak regardless of what was being said to them. So in a conversation in which no actual listening is occurring, there is no reacting, adapt-ing, or engaging taking place—only noise. Even on a comedy improv stage, if two performers are talking over each other it feels rude and confusing to the audience. There's a slim chance that the performers are in mutual agreement to find comedy in the pointless noise of talking over each other, though most of the time that's not what's happening. Instead when two improv performers are talking over each other it means each is trying too hard to pull a high-status move, get a laugh, or upstage the other performer. They are more focused on a personal agenda than on sharing and accepting personal perspective.

The seminar exercise continues on to the most practical of small "Yes, and" steps: a pair of people have a conversation in which every sentence must begin with the actual words "Yes, and." Whether or not I've prefaced the exercise with the underlying philosophy of these words, people quickly discover that in order to make such a conversation work, they have to listen intensively and make connections to their partner's comments before building a cognitive bridge to their own perspective. The emphasis is on one voice at a time, giving and taking the right to speak in a mutually agreed process. This is the gist of "active listening."[17]

With an eye on transferring this exercise to the real world, in the next round we show how our "Yes, and" conversations can connect in a slightly different way to relationship building and influence. In this round each speaker has the right to speak one sentence at a time, and each partner's response must include specific, significant words used by the last speaker. The idea is to maintain a natural flow of conversation in which each speaker recognizes which of their own words are being used by the other person. (This should be a natural, authentic conversation, of course; simply repeating something common like the word "the" would defeat the purpose.) The goal is that speakers focus their mental energy enough to repeat what's been said to them, and listeners are focused enough to hear what's being repeated back.

When I ask group members how it felt to have a conversation in which they heard their own key words being used by the person they were talking to, the responses are often revelatory: "I felt like I was being listened to." "I felt like the other person cared about what I was saying." "I felt like we were on the same page." "I felt like we were building a connection." "I felt validated."

I ask the participants whether it would be worth employing this simple technique if it could have the same effect on people they speak with in their workplace, and the answer of course is yes. They answer yes not because any of these businesspeople feel the urge to grab a ukulele and get a version of "We Are the World" started. It is yes because they've just gotten a clean taste of how effective communication can create a positive emotional effect in someone else. They got a taste of how to quickly create a strong connection with another person. They got a taste of "Yes, and . . . "

In a final round of the exercise we highlight how language influences real-world workplace relationships. In that real world, conversations don't happen just for the sake of showing off speakers' communication skills. They happen because points of view need to be expressed, explored, and perhaps even debated. With that in mind participants continue to have these "Yes, and" conversations in which every sentence must start with "Yes, and" for about a minute. They then continue their conversation, this time with the direction of starting every sentence with "Yes, but . . . " Participants quickly discover that it's much harder to maintain a flow of acceptance and support in a conversation when starting every sentence with "Yes, but"; and when they don't remain mindful about the process, the "Yes, but" passion quickly turns things into an argument, a one-upmanship grapple for high status, an impassioned defense of one's own opinion by undermining one's partner's opinion, or even a point/counterpoint debate in which the conversation simply moves back and forth like a game of table tennis.

In other words a "Yes, but" conversation is hard work. Conversely a "Yes, and" conversation is smooth, free flowing, inclusive, and easily productive, and the feeling of collaboration is underscored by the depth and breadth of the conversation. In a nutshell, a "Yes, and" conversation is easy and enjoyable. By extension a "Yes, and" culture accommodates passion without shutting other people down. It may take a little effort to establish this culture, and the payoff is tremendous. Let's see if energy in relation to language matters by revisiting our "Yes" test:

Have a 3–5-minute, very excited, very energetic, very passionate conversation with a colleague (or a stranger at a pub), starting every sentence with "Yes, but . . . " Your goal now is to influence the other person with your level of energy and excitement in this passionate "Yes, but" conversation. Take note of how your partner reacts to you and the language they use toward you.

What did you notice?

Now have a 3–5-minute, very excited, very energetic, very passionate conversation, starting every sentence with "Yes, and . . . " Your goal is still to influence the other person with your level of energy and excitement in this passionate "Yes, and" conversation. Audit what happens in this conversation, how your partner reacts to you and the language they use toward you.

What did you notice?

What was the difference between the passionate "Yes, but" conversation versus the passionate "Yes, and" conversation?

The beauty of the "Yes, and" approach is that practicing it doesn't actually require a break from the workday, an empty conference room, or the pairing up of staff. Anyone at almost any time can decide to work the techniques of the exercises through his or her side of an interaction. The persons you communicate with will likely not know that an exercise is being followed, but they will feel the effect. No explanation of the exercise will be necessary—the resulting experience, positive or negative, will speak for itself. Try it!

- Try talking over someone and see what happens.
- Try taking specific words used by the person whom you are conversing with and incorporating them in your follow-up sentences. See what kind of response you get.
- Have a conversation in which you only ask questions. Interrogate your partner and see how that person reacts to you.
- Have a conversation starting every sentence with "Yes, but . . . " and see how the person across from you reacts.

- Similarly have a conversation starting every sentence with "Yes, and . . . " and see how the person across from you reacts.

"Yes, and" techniques can be employed with a boss, a colleague, a spouse, a child—even a flight attendant who looks like he's having a hard day. In fact on several long international flights, motion sickness bags full of mini booze bottles have been surreptitiously handed to me by stressed-out attendants who greatly appreciated a smile, positive attitude, and a little attentive listening. Just a few moments of awareness and "Yes, and" word choice on my part were enough for these attendants to feel they were being heard and understood. If you still doubt that the positivity and clear communication of "Yes, and" gets noticed and has an impact, those tiny bottles of Bombay Sapphire don't lie.

Now that we've learned the importance of "Yes, and . . . " as a foundation of personal development, let's take a look at how it can be used to develop one's own voice and presence in the workplace.

Chapter 3

I'M WITH THE BRAND

OVER THE LAST 15 YEARS, discussions of "personal branding" have become ubiquitous in the business world, to the extent that the concept has now been stretched to encompass everything from self-improvement strategies to social media profiles. However, unless I've seriously misjudged the target audience for this book, you are not a tube of toothpaste, a cola, or a box of cereal. So when I speak of branding, you should not be thinking of yourself strictly as a commodity—a widget for sale whose chances for success in the marketplace can simply be manipulated through a new and improved formula or a flashy redesign of packaging. For our purposes "branding" really stems from one key attribute: awareness. Your brand is fashioned directly from a clear, honest awareness of your inner strengths (and weaknesses) as well as a focused awareness of your outward presence—the effect and impact you have on those around you in the workplace.

You are a uniquely talented, driven individual with an authentic voice and with thoughts and opinions that have been cultivated from your background, your family and relationships, your education (formal or informal), and your personal experiences. This combination of variables has created the person you are today, and the sum of these variables is your personal brand. Your brand is represented in the workplace in the way you consistently react, adapt, and communicate. In this chapter we will look at how to develop your brand through the practices of mindfulness and self-auditing, and how to maintain your brand and "promote" it in the workplace.

I've described the "and" of "Yes, and . . . " as the bridge to your authentic perspective. Your brand is to a great extent the delivery system for your perspective. Your brand pulls together the unique way you have of looking at problems and opportunities, and the particular skill sets you have available to you in addressing those problems and opportunities. Your brand is drawn from your knowledge of what you bring with you to any team or any challenge, and it is equally defined by how you put that knowledge into action—how you conduct yourself in various situations, with ease or difficulty, energetically or lethargically, stress free or DEFCON 1.

Effective branding is not the result of a more expensive haircut and a better outfit. It really does have to connect with your authentic self. Of course "authenticity" is another one of those currently fashionable buzzwords—one of those slippery leadership training terms that can be defined a number of ways. What I mean by authenticity is pretty straightforward: your brand is authentic if it connects honestly and directly with who you actually are, at your core. You may act differently—and think differently—when you're hanging out around a tub of beer with college friends at a barbecue as opposed to when you're working with colleagues over a cup of coffee around the conference table. That doesn't necessarily mean though that in one of those situations you're expressing the "real" you and in the other you're living a lie. Given the situation, you may put forward a different version of your brand and each version can still have authenticity because it is an honest expression of who you are in that situation. There is an unchanging, authentic you that can be branded in different ways depending on your circumstances, your "audience," and your goals. To pull a metaphor from the wardrobe department, a person can be capable of wearing many hats without putting on any masks.

To get a little more theatrical, the comedic improv groups I've been part of have always had their own authentic perspective. Take Baby Wants Candy for example. BWC completely improvises hour-long musicals with a full band (the "Yes Band!"). Since 1997 this is the only form of improv we have performed and the only form audiences want to see us perform. This is the Baby Wants Candy brand. However, the specific way Baby presents that sensibility in performance depends entirely on context and circumstance. A completely improvised musical we perform for a church group differs immensely from the improv musical we'd perform in a frat house. At a bare minimum we'd refrain from using profanity or entering into adult humor in front of the family-oriented churchgoers, whereas those comedy blue bombs are not only appropriate with the drunk fraternity kids, they are expected! In a nutshell churches expect a G-rated show and fraternities expect an R to NC-17 rating. However different the show might be, the goal—an amazing, completely improvised musical that results in audience laughter—doesn't change. The performance though has to be adapted—rebranded—to the particular time and place in which it's being presented to meet the expectations of that specific audience.

Sorting out your authentic self, best-possible business brand, and appropriate adaptations of your brand requires a high level of candor and self-awareness. One of the most effective ways to achieve that level of awareness is by turning the philosophy of "Yes, and" inward, through a process of self-discovery. So far I've spoken of improv as an outwardly directed technique that applies to how you react, adapt, and communicate in small-group, interpersonal contexts. The technique can just as easily, and equally rewardingly, be applied inward to one's own thinking. In short, one of the greatest obstacles to clear communication may not come from others undermining our authentic perspective; it may come from ourselves undermining our authentic perspective. Sad and true, we are often our own worst nay-saying "Yes-butters." So one of the keys to successfully developing your personal brand is in getting comfortable with "Yes, and-ing" yourself.

If the idea of "Yes, and-ing" yourself sounds complicated or confusing, it doesn't have to be. The process can begin with a few simple, practical steps:

1. Take pride in yourself! If you don't, no one else will.

2. List five things you'd like to change about yourself at work.

3. Prioritize your list.

4. Baby steps! Take on each action item one at a time. Focus on conquering the first one before moving on to the next one.

5. Be diligent! Hold yourself accountable to make the change happen.

6. Ask a peer to hold you accountable as well.

7. Spend five minutes before you get to work to refocus on your goals.

8. Take five minutes in the evening to evaluate your progress.

9. Celebrate your successes with the person who is holding you accountable.

Day of Postponement

We like to assume that we are always putting our best self forward at work, that we naturally do a good job of brand development and promotion. Actually, though, in the business setting we are very good at being our own worst enemies. This is because in so many workplaces it's considered the smarter move to play defense. So we edit ourselves extensively, shooting down, fine-tuning, or otherwise judging our own ideas before they have a chance to become fully expressed. (Think back to the blocks to creativity, collaboration, and change that you defined in Chapter 1.) Mentally we focus on why things aren't going to work as opposed to looking for ways in which they can work. We are also very good at limiting our thinking and our exposure to perceived threats. This self-limiting has an impact not just on creative processes but on more straightforward thinking as well. Whether we're developing a marketing campaign or writing a proposal, too often the governing principle in our work-related tasks is CYA (covering your aft-quarters). The problem is, if all you're focusing on is CYA then all you're doing is CYA. And there is so much more to life than just aft-covering.

At the beginning of all my programs I stress three principles emphatically—all based on postponement of judgment. First, I ask that participants postpone judgment of the exercises I am going to ask them to do, and trust that the value of those exercises will become clear as the program moves forward. Second, I ask participants to postpone judgment of each other; we're in this together and everyone present should feel comfortable enough to say what's on their mind. The third request is the toughest: I ask that participants postpone judgment of themselves. Each participant must make the effort to allow him- or herself to speak up honestly in the moment.

It is this third request—postponement of self-judgment—that will help us get out of our own heads and stop the self-censoring process as it relates to the creation of material, and it is each individual's job to take this challenge head-on. Stop worrying about what others might think, and stop trying to be perfect the first time, every time. In personal creation (a project, proposal, or pitch) "Yes, and" yourself to remove the barriers to creativity within yourself. Allow your first draft to be messy and take this time just to release all of your thoughts onto your paper. Your second and third drafts will be for fine-tuning, editing, and otherwise making sense of the first, rough draft of thoughts.

How do you know when you're in your own way? Well, we can begin by going back to the neuroscience introduced in Chapter 2 that tells us our brains can process 350–550 words a minute while most of us only speak around 120 words a minute. That extra processing power can allow the mind to wander during interpersonal communication, and it's just as able to wander away from our own central thoughts. In essence we're quite capable of not listening to ourselves and can almost instantaneously spend our brain power on unnecessarily shooting ourselves down, creating counterarguments, deflections, and distractions every time we try to think something through or simply create material. Just as the human pitfall of "thinking what to say next" can interfere with interpersonal communication, a related pitfall of "thinking that what we are thinking is not right or won't work" can pull us away from the mindfulness necessary for being in the moment.

Think Slow to Move Fast

There is an old improv phrase which may be good to remember in times of stress, risk, and uncertainty: "Think slow to move fast." This may seem counterintuitive; however, by thinking quickly you may actually be missing the solutions right in front of you and getting farther away from something that would be a perfect outcome to the challenge you're taking on. When you slow down and focus on being present in the moment, you may discover "offers" and opportunities right in front of you—gifts that might be unnoticed or ignored when you're moving (or thinking) too quickly. Slowing the brain down can actually get you to your destination faster. As a result others will see your brand as a voice of clarity in times of stress, risk, and uncertainty.

Anyone who works in the higher levels of the modern business world would no doubt recognize that speed and complexity are hallmarks of that world. Speed and complexity don't help us to become better thinkers though. Speed alone simply turns everything into a race in which we are eager to push forward and get somewhere first, whether that "somewhere" is a new product or a perfect pitch for a Hollywood blockbuster. Speed gets confused with progress: "If I'm moving quickly, I must be getting somewhere." Nope, not necessarily. In fact poor decisions can come from uncontrolled or rushed decision making.

As for the matter of complexity there's a tendency to believe that if you're doing a lot of things and juggling a bunch of responsibilities, then things are being accomplished. The problem is that while most people think they are good at multitasking, the literature consistently demonstrates that we're pretty terrible at it.[1] Instead of doing one job effectively for an hour, we get in the habit of doing ten jobs ineffectively for 20 hours. We feel like a lot has been done because we've been so busy, when in fact time has been wasted and results are not optimal. Singular focus on what needs to be done at one particular time ends up being much more effective and efficient.

In turning "Yes, and" inward then, we aim to slow down our brain in order to recognize and understand what is happening in real time and to simplify, to find the root of the matter. To get that job done, one of the most powerful concepts in business improv is the self-audit. And any good self-audit begins with mindfulness.

Mind the Gap

"Mindfulness" is a popular term in American business these days. However, I've found that there is a gap in defining this key business word. So just to make sure we are all on the same page, the definition we are going by is this:

> Mindfulness is a state of active, open attention on the present. When you're mindful, you observe your thoughts and feelings from a distance, without judging them good or bad. Instead of letting your life pass you by, mindfulness means living in the moment and awakening to experience.[2]

The improvisational self-audit is the ability to recognize what you are doing in real time. This means mindfulness plus awareness of language and action. With a self-audit you can make an intelligent decision to continue your behavior or change it to get the desired effect on the people you are hoping to influence. This involves making subtle changes in real time based on how you perceive your message is being received and interpreted. A self-audit is mindfulness on steroids.

If you're thinking through a problem on your own, the self-audit helps you consider whether you are properly focused and whether you are truly making progress rather than just letting yourself appear busy. If you're addressing a coworker or a team, the self-audit gives you a chance to consider whether you are having the impact you want to have and what adjustment might be necessary. In interpersonal and group settings the self-audit is the moment in which you decide whether you are doing a good job of representing your brand by affecting your audience the way you desire.

The purpose of the self-audit is to strengthen the "muscles" needed to be aware of yourself, to be aware of how you are fitting into a situation, and to be aware of a team and how you are impacting that team. It's about being mindful of how you lead and how you follow—how you affect people on a one-to-one basis and on a group basis. In that sense other people will always be the barometer in gauging the accuracy of your self-audit and how well you are projecting your brand.

In practice the first step in a self-audit—the first step to better branding adjustments in real time—is commitment. This implies commitment to being present in the moment, to putting yourself under a high-powered microscope for a brief time. If you are really aiming for authenticity, then honesty has to go hand in hand with this commitment. If a self-audit is going to work, it must be an honest attempt to see yourself in real time, and it must be an honest assessment of what you see.

After mental awareness the next step is physical awareness. At a basic physical level a self-audit asks these questions:

Is my posture erect or slumped?

Do I look wide awake or about to pass out?

Am I making eye contact?

What is my facial expression? (Am I smiling?)

What's my tone of voice like?

At what level is my personal energy?

Am I engaged by the person or people with whom I'm communicating?

It is said that of the messages we receive we understand 55 percent of a message from body language, 38 percent from tone of voice, and 7 percent from the actual content of words.[3] What nonverbal messages are you embodying yourself and communicating to others? Every little element of our physical presence is an expression of something: our head gestures, body gestures, degree of eye contact, eye rolling, or eyebrow raising. Our breathing can be deep and relaxed or shallow and quick. Are you sighing or exhaling in a way that signifies exhaustion or frustration? Maybe the frustration is warranted. Maybe you are not just frustrated; you are also extremely tired. Neither of these states of mind has to be denied. The point of the self-audit is to be aware of what you're doing, not necessarily to judge it. When you are aware of your actions, you can see how they affect others. This is where the power lies. To be aware of how your physical state impacts both your thinking and the messages received by those around you puts you in the position to make subtle changes along the way.

At a higher level of self-auditing there are additional questions to consider:

What is my word choice like?

What is my intonation (how am I delivering my message)?

Am I being clear and concise or overexplaining?

And the most important question of all: Am I affecting the audience the way I want to affect them?

And if not: What subtle adjustments can I make in real time to adapt and get the results I desire?

The purpose of the self-audit is to understand what you are doing and to recognize whether what you're doing is increasing or decreasing the probability that you are affecting people around you the way you want. In short, it's a moment of mindfulness centered on whether or not you are properly managing your brand.[4] The self-awareness one achieves through a self-audit doesn't necessarily lead to a list of dos and don'ts. Improv is about performing at the top of your intelligence in the moment, and whether onstage or in a business setting that moment must always be assessed and adjusted to.

Generally if you have your arms crossed and are not participating in a meeting, that gives the signal that you're closed off or in disagreement—judging. And if you're looking out the window rather than at the person you are speaking to, that's generally a signal that you are distracted by something. If you are texting while in the middle of a conversation, that gives the signal that whatever is being discussed or whomever you are talking with is not important enough to give your undivided attention to. However, these physical clues don't always mean the same thing. Perhaps the folded arms are a sign of relaxation that means you are open to the person you are speaking with. Maybe that window stare connotes reflection rather than distraction. Maybe the texting during a conversation is relevant to the conversation itself. Again, check your audience in real time; this is part of the self-audit. If your goal is to build rapport and connect with another person, then in your moment of self-audit it will be pretty clear whether that engagement is being accomplished. As soon as you become aware that all of your nonverbal communication is part of your brand and has an effect on people, it's easy to see whether that effect is positive or whether it needs to be adjusted. Try it:

> Have a brief interaction with one person in which you are self-auditing your behavior, language, and nonverbal communication with an outward eye on how the person is reacting to you. Take a deliberate moment to honestly assess how you are acting, reacting, and communicating, verbally and nonverbally, in real time, with the person across from you. Make subtle changes and observe how these actions affect the person.

When the Going Gets Tough

It's often quite a revelation to my program participants that just a bit of heightened self-awareness can lead to a great improvement in communication skills. However, there are unavoidable moments in the workplace when things are not working out so well and, for any number of reasons, communication is not smooth and clear. It's easy to promote your personal brand and perform necessary self-audits when everything is going right—you're well rested, deadlines have been met, and the people you are talking to are smiling back at you. It's a much harder task to maintain your brand (and your composure) when someone is delivering a difficult message to you or perhaps even attacking your abilities or your integrity.

Let's look at the concepts of personal brand and self-auditing within real-world stresses and pressures. Think about being in a tough interview or in a meeting where superiors are giving you critical feedback. Those kinds of situations happen every day in business and your brand has to be able to maintain its integrity even when the workday gets tough.

If you are curious how the mettle of your integrity holds under attack, please feel free to test it out in "Can You Take It," an extension of the exercise above:

> Find one or two trusted colleagues or friends. Begin a short presentation to them and have the other person(s) interrupt you with challenging questions (distractions), give you hard feedback (pushback), and pick apart everything you say (criticism). Self-audit how you handle these challenges in real time, and then debrief with your team. Get their honest feedback and coaching notes on how well you did under stress. And as always, take notes and be thoughtful about your experience to further deepen your "after-action review" and transfer your learnings to your decision-making abilities in real-life situations.

I've run this exercise hundreds of times, and as a side note it's interesting to me that very few people see much of a challenge in being the person who is criticizing and doing the picking apart. We all seem to feel that we're pretty good at dishing out difficult messages. In truth most people are really bad at this, because they are not self-auditing and gauging the impact they are having. To be blunt it is simply not enough to get a tough message out of your mouth. If you are an

EQ-minded leader—someone who chooses to lead with caring and empathy for others—it is always important to understand the impact you're having on the person receiving the message and equally important that the difficult words are understood properly. In this case, however, "Can You Take It?" is more about being on the receiving end and learning how to hear and process something negative (tough questions, criticism, active pushback) without immediately assuming it is a personal attack. There is no real trick to the exercise—the value is just in running the simulation and getting the opportunity to really feel what it's like to summon self-auditing skills under a very stressful situation.

When you feel your brand is under attack, here are the skills you need to draw on:

1. *Don't let it get personal.* Be consistent with the brand you want to project. Know your hot-button issues and words. Stand up for the points you need to defend without being defensive. Develop your own ways to maintain brand integrity in stressful situations without counter-provoking.

2. *Love thy brand.* Be confident in your brand and who you are as an individual. Your brand has to be sturdy enough to withstand attacks. If it has been developed carefully and with authenticity, it deserves to be protected.

3. *Be open to being incorrect.* You should be open to the fact that there might be some truth in a harsh critique. Remember, if you are going to take strategic risks, mistakes and wrong answers will invariably be made. Your job is not to be right 100 percent of the time (a baseball hitter who succeeds three out of ten times is a superstar); your job is to find the right answers and implement the right solutions and lead teams to success. Base your judgments on professional rather than personal criteria and be open to learning.

4. *Stay physical.* Maintain eye contact. Maintain posture. Control body gestures—don't allow yourself to get to fidgety. Breathe. Breathe. Breathe and smile.

5. *Keep the heat down.* Don't react too quickly or too emotionally to anything. Control the cadence of your reaction time and speech. Empathize: try to look at what someone is saying from their perspective. Stay focused on engagement.

6. *Avoid the riptides.* Don't surrender what you can control—your tone, your presence, the cadence of your thoughts, your non-verbal communication. If you do get caught up responding too quickly in the moment, reestablish the pace. Ask for some time to process and remove yourself from the strong current. Get a breath of fresh air and recompose yourself before reengaging in the conversation.

7. *Be present.* Don't shut down as soon as you hear something negative. Don't get caught in your own head, thinking of counter-arguments while the person addressing you is still speaking. Stay in the moment and process carefully all that is being said. Think slow. Breathe.

Audit vs. Edit: Blurred Lines

The process of self-auditing is a process of taking stock of yourself to make adjustments in accordance with your goals. Way too easily, though, the adjustment that gets made can lead to one of the main obstacles we're trying to avoid: self-editing. Going back to a point made earlier in this chapter, we are all very good at "Yes, but-ing" ourselves. Defensive posturing and fear of failure make it easy for us to embrace self-judgment and self-censorship. We seem to take comfort in the notion that if our self-censor is harsh enough and hardly lets any of our ideas slip past our lips, then we won't ever say anything stupid. True enough. And it's also highly likely that we won't ever say anything brilliant either, because to get to brilliance we have to be willing to take some risks.

Auditing is a means of becoming aware of yourself. Editing is a way of judging yourself—picking and choosing, eliminating, censoring. In self-auditing you are aware of the impact your communication is having on others, and your cue for adjustment comes from outside of you. When you self-edit you are framing and reframing your own thoughts before they even have a chance to reach an audience outside of you. Instead of adjusting to a response, are you adjusting to the fear of what a response may be? If you're in any situation where you need to honestly and directly express yourself (an idea-sharing session for example), it's crucial that you refrain from self-editing.

Ultimately, though, the line between auditing and editing should blur. Every day we are in situations in which our editing functions are engaged, not out of fear but out of knowledge. As such my admonitions against self-editing only go so far. For example, no, it's not okay to wear a supertight, sleeveless, sweat-stained shirt, cut-off jeans, and no shoes to a board meeting just because you feel that's the unedited, authentic you. Edit yourself, damn it, and put the dress clothes back on. The projection of your brand should be a combination of informed auditing and editing. Auditing helps you to be aware of what you wish to communicate, while editing guides how you communicate with a particular audience at a particular time. The best way to protect and promote your brand may in fact be to apply self-auditing to your self-editing. Ask yourself, Am I making a decision to limit my contribution strictly out of fear, or am I using every bit of knowledge I have to tailor my brand to my audience? The self-audit is always useful. The self-edit has to be regulated, and when needed it can be just as useful.

Tight Brands

The advice to express yourself as freely as possible while shaping your message for an audience can seem a bit contradictory. However, that contradiction can be accepted, celebrated, and used as an improv tool all its own. In a theatrical improv scene an audience may have a sense that anything can happen because they know the performers are not working from a script. In truth offers and opportunities for how an improvised scene will transpire are taken as that scene is developed in real time. Rules of time and place are established and respected, as are dynamics between characters, relationships, and situations. If anybody onstage said just anything that came to his or her head, it wouldn't make much sense and probably wouldn't be very funny. The best improvisers instantly accept constantly shifting dynamics, perform within the context of the situation, and build a world of rich realities within those limits.

Zeljko Djukic, a great Chicago theater director I've had the wonderful opportunity to work with on four separate TUTA Theatre productions, once told me to "learn how to operate within a straw." What he meant was that in learning how to operate within what looks like a tight, suffocating, confining space, you find that you start to get comfortable enough that the space isn't so confining anymore. If you can make that shift in your perspective, the tight space opens up and becomes an enormous world. This directly relates to our philosophy of mental framing: if you focus on where you cannot use the tenets of improvisation, you will succeed because that is where you are choosing to focus your mental energy. And if you choose to focus on where you can use them, with whom you can use them, why you should use them, and how you should use them to achieve real-world results, you will succeed here as well because, again, that is where you are choosing to focus your mental energy. So instead of fighting against things you cannot control, you acknowledge and accept the confines and structures and parameters you are working within, and you discover that you've got all the space you need.

This isn't as ethereal as it might sound. Think about learning something that at first seems complicated and overwhelming—a second language, chess, French cooking, riding a bike, improv. The challenge at hand becomes easier once you are comfortable with the required techniques (limits), understand them, and practice them. The possibility for success increases as you accept and learn to thrive in the parameters you are working within.

Mistakes Get Made

In theatrical improv there's an old saying, "There is no such thing as a mistake." The idea is that whatever happens on the stage, we go with it and make it work. Anything that might otherwise be viewed as a mistake becomes an opportunity to successfully put our improv skills to use. If you're aware that a mistake was just made onstage, you put yourself in a position to capitalize on that mistake. However, capitalizing rarely involves simply calling out the mistake—that just makes you look like a jerk for focusing on a partner's shortcomings. For the most part the best course of action is to honestly address the mistake. For example if in an improv scene somebody walks through a part of the stage where earlier in the scene an "invisible" table was established by a fellow performer, shouting "Hey, you just walked through a table there!" at a fellow cast member isn't going to further the scene. (It will likely alienate your fellow cast member though.) If, however, you make a show of continuing the dialogue with the fellow performer, unceremoniously picking the table up and putting stuff back on it as if it were a natural occurrence, the laugh is there. The audience knows what's going on—you're not ignoring something they witnessed and you're not undermining a member of your group. You've found an opportunity to connect with both your colleagues and your audience. Consequently some of the biggest laughs at an improv show come out of what the performers do with their mistakes.

In real life and especially in business life the saying, "There is no such thing as a mistake," doesn't hold up so well. There really are mistakes, and real mistakes can have real consequences that are usually not going to be alleviated by turning them into laughs. There are plenty of ways in which communication mistakes can be made in the workplace—proverbial toes get stepped on; intentions get misunderstood; messages get mangled. However, just as onstage, honest acknowledgment will go a long way toward dealing with a mistake before it becomes any bigger.

Once you develop the workplace habit of maintaining an effective personal brand through self-auditing, a side benefit of slowing the brain down and being in the moment is that you increase the speed of recognition and more quickly become aware of any mistakes you make in real time. That is to say, if you create the work habit of gauging how your communication is being received, you will know right away if you ever unintentionally confuse or even insult somebody. You sense this in real time, so you are instantly able to back up, restate, or apologize if and when necessary. You can even check in, clarify, or qualify what you mean if you sense it has been misunderstood. If in real time you are consistently aware of the impact you are having on others, then you can do whatever's necessary to acknowledge a communication problem so that everyone can move on in a way that is respectful to each other.

This type of mindfulness greatly reduces the probability of misunderstandings and increases the likelihood that you will be able to adjust to any difficult moment. If you know the impact you're having and immediately acknowledge any miscommunication, then a misunderstanding doesn't have the chance to fester into some weird subtext that becomes a bigger problem in and of itself. Self-auditing doesn't guarantee that every communication will end pleasantly; however, it does guarantee a heightened level of awareness of exactly what just got said, what happened, and what your role in it was. That clarity and understanding helps you put your brand across even more powerfully. So relax a bit and strategically give yourself time and room to make a few mistakes. Your brand will survive and perhaps even thrive when you adapt.

Go Team

Let's expand on the idea of personal branding and start laying foundational blocks to team development (coming soon in Chapter 5). Your brand is defined by the consistency of your actions. Moreover we lead by example, not by empty declarations. This means that through the consistency of our actions the people we lead will ultimately mirror our behavior. So model the behavior you want to see in others. Focus daily on connecting, engaging, postponing judgment, and listening to others around you as you react, adapt, and communicate throughout your workdays and within meetings. If you are consistent in your brand, the people around you will understand what to expect and many will follow your behavior and language. Once one or two people around you follow suit, you are well on your way to creating "team branding."

Moreover be thoughtful and deliberate about leading and designing environments in which workers feel valued and appreciated. Take time before an upcoming meeting to make sure you are in the right mental and physical space to create and uphold an environment that is respectful and productive and energetic.

By keeping it simple and laying a foundation of individual brand development based in personal growth, you put yourself in the position to represent your brand the way you want to in a collaborative setting. In a team for example there's nothing to be gained from holding in a thought out of pure fear, worrying whether the thought is correct, acceptable, or even appropriate. Create a space and block of time to "Yes, and" yourself in a team setting and become stronger by being more vulnerable in idea sharing. For many people—especially analytical, left-brain thinkers—this is an incredibly difficult task: to postpone judgment of themselves and let their brand, their authentic perspective, shine in the group. Part of what makes that postponement of judgment so difficult is that many critical thinkers have probably never considered the fact that obstacles to creativity, collaboration, and communication can be self-made. Try applying the steps to personal brand development to how you comport yourself in a team:

1. *Be thoughtful and self-audit.* Before you enter a meeting, take one or two minutes to honestly and objectively think about how you have handled challenges that you've faced in a collaborative team environment in the past. Focus on getting out of your own way, getting out of your head, getting caught in analysis paralysis, and getting held up by self-judgment and editing in an attempt to produce perfection in your first attempt at a project.

2. *Be deliberate.* Lay some ground rules for yourself. "For the first half of the meeting I am going to focus on letting my presence

be known by vocally 'Yes, and-ing' the ideas of others. For the second half of the meeting I am going to focus on bringing (only) one or two of my own ideas forward. I will be vocal and participate in both the divergent and convergent parts of this meeting."

3. *Be forgiving*. Give yourself permission to fail, struggle, and otherwise make mistakes in a controlled environment, for a predetermined time, in a team setting.

4. *Be understanding when reflecting*. After a meeting or a collaborative session take five minutes to accurately and objectively assess your performance. "Yes, and" yourself and note where you continued to struggle, where you need improvement, and where you succeeded.

Keep this simple. You do not have to go into a meeting and do every step all in one sitting. Most businesspeople have many meetings over the course of a month. Start small: "In this one meeting I will do my best to do this one thing." Stay focused on long-term development over short success. Remember, your brand derives from the consistency in your behavior. Honestly chart your progress (mentally or otherwise) as you continue to expand your comfort zone one meeting at a time.

Brand Management

If you've applied due diligence to self-auditing and self-editing and have come to the conclusion that you are always operating at the top of your intelligence and always having precisely the impact you desire on the people you communicate with—then may the sweet Mother Earth bless you with all her glorious bounty. You've got a hell of a brand going.

Then again, why do the most successful brands in the world continue to advertise? Everybody knows what Coca-Cola is and what McDonald's is: why should they bother wasting any money on marketing campaigns at this point? It's because a brand is not a one-and-done proposition. Recall that brands are established through consistency over time, yet brands have to be adapted as the audiences they are being promoted to begin to change. Coca-Cola adds different spices to its beverage on the basis of regional audience, and McDonald's adds (and subtracts) items to its menu on the regional tastes of the consumer wherever the franchise outlet is located in the world.[5]

Once you've identified the attributes of your personal brand, managing that brand must be an ongoing process. You make a commitment to your brand, a commitment to yourself. If you're going to have influence on any group or process, you have to "walk the talk" and lead by example. That means being consistent in your brand and how you represent it, and being consistent in the behavior that creates your brand. And if we're after consistency, then commitment is an imperative. You won't successfully promote your brand unless you have some passion in that promotion, and you can't be passionate about something you aren't truly committed to. Think about a salesman trying to hype something he doesn't believe in—we can all see through the phoniness in an instant.

If self-auditing is about self-awareness and mindfulness and influence, commitment can be measured by how you put practices into place to keep you on the right path—what actions you take to hold yourself accountable and protect your brand. Those actions don't have to be complicated. Any of the following would work:

Set goals for yourself. Sounds commonsensical enough. Keep in mind though that the very act of clearly articulating short- or long-term goals is a tremendous way to keep yourself committed and make yourself accountable.

Write it down. Write down goals, reminders, and encouragements as an accountability measure. Good old cognitive psychology tells us that there's a different level of accountability that takes place when we write something down with pen and paper as opposed to when we just think about something or even type it on a computer.[6]

Check yourself. Take time to be mindful. Some would call it meditating; athletes call it visualizing; others still might call it "getting in the zone." All are equally valid. Take time in the morning to be mindful about how you want the day to unfold. Think through your strategies and goals for each challenge you're going to face. Take time at the end of the day to honestly review how that day unfolded. Where were your successes and what did you do to make them happen? Where did you fail or struggle and why did that take place? Where were there potential opportunities for additional success? What can you replicate and what can you do differently?

Branding may well be a hot topic in business circles. Still, the impact of a well-developed brand is powerful, effective, and undeniable. I demonstrate this point in my programs with a very simple storytelling exercise. Here's the assignment:

Find a friend (no, that isn't the exercise) and (here it is) take two minutes to tell the story of the best meal you ever ate. My framing there is very deliberate: I'm not asking people to describe the best-tasting things they've ever eaten; I'm asking them to give a detailed story, which can include all aspects of the best meal (not just the menu).

And what happens when these stories are shared is remarkable. What makes the stories great has hardly anything to do with the food. A course-by-course description of a four-star meal in Paris may not sound half as interesting as the story of eating the first fish you ever caught, or sharing a bratwurst at Wrigley Field with crazy Uncle Josh. What really makes the difference is not the menu or the setting but the passion and commitment of the storyteller. Language choices, pacing, gestures, emotion, intonation—all of that can make a group feel visceral pleasure, even if what's being described is a bologna sandwich with your child.

The point is that it's the storyteller—the brand—that has greater influence on us than the specific details of the story. And the lesson is, if you want to have impact and influence and want to make sure you communicate effectively with your audience, pay attention to your brand and commit to putting that brand forward with passion.

If you consider that everything you do in the workplace is an extension of your brand, then your brand is something worth developing, maintaining, adapting, and promoting as the situation requires. Once you understand your brand, work to protect it both outwardly and inwardly. Make sure that you are consistent in your behavior and that you are focused on what you hope to project with your brand. Be honest as you audit your brand in real time and evaluate your performance in hindsight. If you can make the small, simple changes necessary to embrace that level of self-awareness, you will always be working toward getting the best out of a given situation, a given environment, the people around you, and yourself.

From divergent versus convergent thinking, to the multipurposed use of "Yes, and . . . ," to the concept of individual brand integrity, we have explored improvisation as a means for personal growth and interpersonal development. In Chapter 4 we will explore improv techniques that show you how to put some energy in your brand.

Chapter 4

ENERGY INDEPENDENCE

WE HAVE TAKEN A LOOK at how improvisation can be a powerful agent for change. We've examined the "Yes, and . . . " philosophy at the heart of improvisation and have seen how improvisation can be a tool to develop the self-awareness necessary for your personal brand. For improvisation to accomplish anything, however, it requires an output of energy—in the same way that a fire requires fuel. In this chapter we focus on the variety of ways energy can be summoned, maintained, and properly manipulated in an improvisational workplace.

I'll give you the big takeaway right up front: Your personal energy and your attitude are both the results of personal choice.

The type of energy that you bring to the workplace—or to anything else you do in life—reflects a choice that you have made. And since your personal energy is inextricably linked to your attitude, attitude becomes a choice as well.[1] The choices you make about energy and attitude have a tremendous impact on both the quality of your work and the effect you have on those around you. Too often we treat energy and attitude as completely beyond our control, like the weather. Yet we do constantly react and adapt to the weather—we check it daily and then put on a sweater, open an umbrella, or reach for a cold drink—that is, we do what is in our power to control our experience of the day. Most people, however, do not put the same amount of thought into their energy and attitude that they do in regard to the weather report. In truth, when it comes to personal, group, or workplace energy and attitude, we should be willing and able to make those same kinds of reactions and adaptations. Indeed with improv techniques we can work to control the "weather" conditions of our own experience in the workplace.

The success of my work with the groups I coach depends on dynamics. I am well aware that while exhibiting too little energy is an unmotivating downer, exhibiting too much of it can feel chaotically disingenuous; further, a singularly sustained energy at any one level— high or low—will turn everything I say into flatlined, white noise. Somewhat in the same way that a symphonic conductor mediates between what an orchestral score asks for and what an orchestra delivers, I adjust my own energy in improv programs so that it remains appropriate for my goals and for the group I'm addressing. I am always looking for the sweet zone of effective communication, and I will make whatever energy choice is necessary to get there and stay there. In that way personal energy becomes a matter of thoughtfulness.

With that in mind I make conscious choices about how to approach each and every class I lead as well. If it is a smaller group, I'll pull them in closer together to create a more intimate, fireside-chat setting (the proximity of people to each other can create energy or dissipate it). If it is a larger group and I have less control over where people sit, I will adjust my personal energy to get my audience engaged. If the group is more gregarious, outgoing, or right-brain dominant, (creatives, marketing folks, event planners), I come out of the gates with big playful energy; if they are more analytical, solution oriented, or left-brain dominant (scientists, engineers, numbers people), my initial energy is conservative and relaxed. I often begin a program in a still or "academic" demeanor, paced and patient (lest I begin too animatedly and scare people away). This allows me time to connect with everyone on a relaxed, personal level. Once everyone is comfortable in the room and at least tentatively committed to the experience, I make a choice to begin ramping up the energy. I build to a crescendo in the classroom and may hit a kind of manic Muppet peak when I know that's what it will take to get people pumped up. Even so I'm always hypersensitive to when I might need to pull the energy down again in response to a question or comment from a workshop participant. Then if necessary I'll pull it down even further or push it back up depending on what the audience is telling me it needs. In essence I audit the audience in real time. I react to them as they react to me, and in doing so I am able to play with the dynamics of the room, much like that conductor manipulating the tempo and volume of the orchestra.

I've learned that awareness and manipulation of energy make me a much more effective communicator in that my energy and attitude impact the message I endeavor to communicate. I could conceivably get through a program by putting up all the usual PowerPoint slides and presenting every bit of program content in the character of a bored and boring professor. If I'm droning on, yawning, just going through the motions, and otherwise acting like I'm in desperate need of a nap, anything useful in the content would be nullified. My low energy would actually challenge the perceived usefulness of my content and quickly make the people in the program feel that they'd signed up for a colossal waste of time. Similarly, if I never left that manic "Muppet Show" state and screamed every line of my presentation, the out-of-kilter energy would alienate the audience and again render the content virtually meaningless. I make a distinct and committed choice to bring a more calm, down-to-earth energy when appropriate—to keep the tone of the class focused on a more serious point or to show respect and thoughtfulness in a conversation. I bring Muppet energy into the room when the time is right for that approach—when I am attempting to get a group excited about the experiential learning we are engaged in (that peak level tends to make an impression because most people aren't used to witnessing it in any work environment). Neither the high or low level of energy is the "natural me" though. Both are the result of my conscious decision to use energy as a technique to add dynamics to my presentation and keep the attention of the audience.

And so I say, energy is a choice.

Why worry at all about something as ephemeral as energy and attitude? Aren't we all just trying to stumble our way to Friday quitting time? The answer is no. The "just make it to Friday" attitude doesn't cut it in today's corporate climate, and if you have any concern with working effectively—with making your time and effort truly count—then the concept of energy and attitude manipulation is crucial. A hefty stack of academic studies have proven what some of us might consider obvious: if you approach your work negatively you're going to perform more negatively, and if you approach your work positively you're going to perform more positively.[2] Positive thinking certainly doesn't guarantee that the final outcome will be precisely the outcome you desire. Yet approaching a challenge with positive energy and attitude definitely does influence outcome and certainly gives you the best possible chance for achieving the best possible outcome.

The lesson here is not "Act happy and everything will turn out OK." Instead, if you take control of your own energy and attitude, you will get your job done more effectively; you will influence the people around you more intentionally and positively; and you will greatly increase your chances for the success you are working so hard to achieve.

Get Personal

Most people don't pay attention to the personal energy they put into whatever it is they're doing; when they do it's usually to rationalize their own low energy. If you're feeling absolutely exhausted and unfocused at work, why spend even more energy enumerating all the reasons you are tired? This is a misplaced negative focus on the past. Focus instead on the present and the future. The truth is, you are probably not as tired as you imagine yourself to be. Think for a moment: if someone stepped in front of you right now and slapped you across the face, smashed your smartphone, or shattered a picture of your smiling family, would your energy perk up a notch or two? If the answer is yes, then your low energy—though physically expressed—is probably more mental than biological. If you feel like you are so tired at work that it's truly impossible for you to focus—even after a slap in the face—then either go home to bed or check yourself into a hospital; perhaps a shot of vitamin B is in order. Assuming that you do not suffer from a physical ailment, you can learn to manipulate your personal energy with just a bit of energy focus.

The very act of self-auditing and honestly assessing where your energy is at a given moment is a first, powerful step toward personal energy awareness. If you don't have a clear sense of the energy you are embodying, there's a very easy way to check: take a look in a mirror and objectively view how your own reflection strikes you. Take a second to truly see yourself. Make eye contact and connect with the person looking back at you. Breathe deep, and be present in that moment to truly see yourself. The "you" looking back will indicate exactly where your energy is. Take a second to assess this energy level, without changing it, and recognize that this is the face and the energy that others see as well.

If you like what you see—go get 'em, Tiger! If not, it's time for some energy manipulation.

Get Physical

If you become aware that your energy at work needs adjustment, the next thing to consider is this: no matter how caught up in our heads we get at work, we never stop being physical beings.

In the same way that positive attitude can lead to positive performance, physical energy can flow into mental energy.[3] In a world of cubicles and Aeron chairs we sometimes forget how important it is to pay attention to our physical state. It's also important to remember a truism of physics that "gravity works." It works really well, as a matter of fact, and the longer you let it push you down in your chair, the more likely your energy will be pulled out of you as well. If you are making the choice to get your personal energy up, one of the easiest ways to initiate the change is to start with something physical. That doesn't necessarily mean the physical act of pouring yourself another cup of coffee and hoping that the caffeine jolt kick-starts the flesh and bones. Get up. Move around. Get the blood flowing. Take deep breaths. Lean. Bend. Stretch out muscle groups. You don't have to find a place to do a full P90X workout. A simple stretch or a reach to the ceiling unleashes endorphins that almost instantly make you feel better, smarter, and more successful. It's remarkable how just a little tweak to your body's physical energy will pay off with a refocused mental state.

Use physical energy manipulation strategically. Summon a bit of extra energy to help you prepare for a particular task on your plate: a meeting, a project, a presentation, a conference call. Extra energy may also be summoned as a refocusing boost in the middle of a challenging and complex (or a completely mundane) project. If you need to refocus, stand up and move around.

One of the most common deflections I hear is, "This heightened energy works great here in the program, but it would not be appropriate in my company." I challenge that: I think most businesses are much more concerned with achieving exceptional results than with trying to keep you from having extra energy at work.[4] I've never been in any meeting with any level executive—and I have spent countless hours working firsthand with senior leaders—in which anyone was upset when someone got up and walked around to stimulate thought. Frankly it's hard to imagine execs getting upset over behavior that has a positive impact in the workplace. Physicality often leads to a much better meeting: the choice to bring physical energy into a room makes it crystal clear that you have every intention of approaching your work with 100 percent of your body, with passion and focus. It would be a very strange situation in which that intention was not appreciated.

If you feel it is truly verboten to get up and move around at work, there are still ways to notch up your physical energy level. Forget about walking around the room and consider some little things you can still do to manipulate your physical energy. Not only will these not be frowned on; they won't even be noticed:

1. Sit on the edge of your seat. Lean forward.

2. Sit straight up without leaning on anything.

3. Get pumped up: take deeper breaths and focus on getting motivated. Visualize what you need to do to nail the task at hand.

4. Bounce your knees on your toes.

5. Make ten fists by squeezing your hands as tightly as you can and then releasing your grip slowly and methodically.

6. Focus on "Yes, and-ing" others to force yourself to be in the moment and involved as an active, vocal participant in the meeting.

Basically do whatever you need to do to stay physically in the moment, which in turn will keep you mentally in the moment. Physical activity can have the added benefit of actually increasing physical energy—you may feel you're too exhausted to make it to the gym, yet if you force yourself to work out, that expenditure of physical energy usually has you ending up feeling energized and happy rather than exhausted and depressed. When the body is energized, the mind is ready to get focused. In our most intense Business Improv programs, participants and I are up on our feet for 33–35 hours of experiential learning over a five-day workshop. At the end of the week everybody is physically depleted. Our minds, however, are fully alert and active and despite the physical exhaustion, everyone in the room feels more energized on Friday than they did on Monday. That is a positive result of energy awareness, positive attitude, and energy manipulation—the decision to be focused and mentally on point even though the body is fatigued.

Navy SEALs will tell you this in no uncertain terms: the human brain is so powerful it can will the body to withstand extreme acts of exhaustion and pain.[5] In my conversation with Navy SEAL captain Jamie Sands, referenced in this book's introduction, we discussed how he stays alert when his body is drained after a long mission. According to Sands: "When I have first watch—acting as security detail to keep a lookout, to keep my team safe when they are resting—and there is a higher need for clarity, I review the day and run through the mission's next steps. I do this to create a sense of anxiety—a fear of falling asleep and letting down my team." This is Captain Sands making the conscious decision to manipulate his energy (in the form of anxiety) to stay alert and not let mental, physical, or emotional fatigue dictate his presence in the moment.

Most businesspeople do not have to endure the type of physical challenges the SEALs go through; we should at least be able to tweak a small part of our brain to get our physical and mental energy bumped up one notch. This often turns into one of the other most useful takeaways I can offer people in my programs: a focused, activated brain will overpower a physically tired body.

Get Fueled

One other physical, decidedly biological concern regarding individual energy manipulation: we need to keep our bodies fueled. Food is our fuel, of course, and it amazes me how many otherwise very intelligent people don't integrate good eating habits into the workday. Food quite literally becomes energy. So make sure you take care of yourself on that level. An eating regimen isn't typically within the realm of improvisation, and I'm not here to preach the relative benefits of carbs or proteins or a particular diet. What I will profess is the continued need for awareness. You must bring your body to work with you; so it's got to be taken care of. Your body knows when you've been giving it enough healthy, nutritious fuel to do what you ask of it, versus food that feels heavy, is harder to digest, and drags you down. Generally lighter, more easily digested foods are going to convert to energy faster and easier than heavy foods (the grilled chicken Caesar salad won't slow you down like the four-cheese lasagna does).[6] The particular menu is up to you—your energy is a choice and so is your entree.

Just be mindful that like the energy you give to a conversation there's a sweet spot for caloric intake to shoot for. You're going to have a hard time finding the appropriate mental focus if your belly is either grumbling with hunger or so overindulged that you find it necessary to tumble into siesta mode. If you want to work hard, eat well.

One extra digestive tip on avoiding post-lunch lethargy: be aware of and avoid the most common thing people do after lunch—sit down (gravity works). After your midday meal move around a bit. A lack of movement will make the body take more time to start the digestion process.[7] It doesn't have to be a lot of big movement or heavy lifting. I am not talking about a full spin class. Keep it simple. Walk around the block or around the workplace for a bit. Deliberately pace a bit in your office or during your first post-lunch phone call. Bounce at your desk for 30 to 60 seconds. Find a simple way to get your heart pumping and your blood moving. Movement will get your stomach into the digestion mode faster, thereby increasing the speed at which the calories you just consumed turn into positive energy, positive attitude, and mental focus.

OK. Let's get out of the cafeteria and head for a conference room.

Team Spirit

Perhaps you feel by now that you have a decent sense of how to assess and adjust your own individual energy and attitude. Few of us work entirely on our own, however. So awareness and adjustment of group energy cannot be ignored. When it comes to achieving and maintaining effective energy levels within a group dynamic, it's all a matter of accountability.

The power of group accountability is showcased in one of my favorite program warm-up exercises. A small group stands in a circle and I ask for a round of New Year's Eve-style celebration applause, just to get a gauge of the group's energy. Invariably a few people clap, hoot, and cheer with great abandon, while a number of people essentially just rub their hands together silently a few times and look around awkwardly. I ask the group to rate the energy on a scale of 1 (low energy) to 10 (high energy). The collective energy of the group usually clocks in at about a 6 out of 10. I tell the group where they stand and that we need to get as close to 10 as possible. Now I instruct the group that the next time I ask for applause, they should all keep their eyes on each other and see who is not buying in to this exercise with the same level of commitment as they are. I remind them not to judge each other; this is about awareness, not about right or wrong. In essence we are asking for everyone to lead by example and simply hold their own equal share of the weight—no more, no less. If some are not carrying out their share of the group task, others need to step in, not to condemn, just to make sure the job is done correctly. We go in for a second round of applause, again with the goal of a New Year's Eve celebration energy level, and once it is done we again rate the applause.

On a scale of 1 to 10 we normally rate ourselves at 11 for round two. In truth, by requiring everyone to simply keep their eyes on each other, we achieve accountability through awareness. We have used conformity pressure as a tool to get everyone on board.[8]

Accountability can be as simple as every member of a group committing to engaging with every other member of the group. When you have your eyes on each other and are aware of the actions of each and every member of a group, it is a lot easier to keep each other accountable as active participants because everyone is aware they are being watched. Everyone knows whether or not they are participating at the same level as every other member of the group. Without that energy accountability, meetings can collapse into stultifying dynamics. The boss speaks, and everyone just listens to the boss. Or a couple of people with the most energy (and loudest voices) dominate the entire conversation and shut out the more introverted people—intentionally or not. People with the lowest energy communicate that they are checking out by leaning back, crossing their arms, typing on their computers or tablets, and declining to participate in any meaningful way. When everybody is asked to be aware of their own energy level as well as everyone else's, and when everyone feels they are responsible for steering the energy of the room, then conformity pressure helps create intrinsic motivation which increases the likelihood of maintaining an energy sweet spot and getting 100 percent participation from every member of the group.[9]

We would all like to think that if we are motivated and talented we can make a difference in what's happening in the workplace. Certainly we can. However, a sad reality is that most humans abandon the talents or perspectives that make them stand out in order to assimilate into a team or group or culture.[10] Conformity pressure can be a negative force when what is being conformed to is dictated by those who huff and roll their eyes in judgment, those who bully and steamroll their way through meetings, or those who opt for texting and Facebook updates over active participation. It is difficult to resist adapting to conformity pressure (negative or positive), and that's why making the choice to establish positive pressure is so important. If buying in to an activity or feeling ownership of the outcome of a meeting is the norm being conformed to, then those who are not buying in—who are not matching the energy of the group—are the ones who feel the pressure. If they want to succeed (keep their jobs), they must adjust their energy to that of the group. That's the point of the warm-up exercise. As soon as the members of the group have been made aware of their energy and have committed to holding each other accountable, and we hit 11 on the scale of 1–10, then I ask them to commit to holding each other to at least a 9.5 for the rest of the meeting. Through group accountability we've found and maintained the energy sweet spot.

High/Low

Generally the challenge within a group is to find a way to manipulate low energy to a higher level. I recognize that energy is something relative—we are all fitted with slightly different power meters. I'm not suggesting that everyone needs to go to "11" or achieve manic Muppet madness. If your natural energy level is set at 3, I want you to understand you have the ability to notch it up to 4, by choice, and then we can get to a 5 or a 6 slowly, over time. And if you're naturally at 7 or 8 on the energy meter, we can likely get you to 10. It is important to respect those differences by starting with an honest understanding of where you are naturally; then you can notch that up to where you are operating at your most effective level both individually and collectively.

A different problem lies at the other end of the spectrum: manipulating high energy down to a manageable, productive level. As mentioned, just as there are people who have inherently low energy and who are more introverted and analytical by nature, there are also people who have naturally higher energy, being more extroverted and gregarious. An easy technique to keep the higher-energy, talkative people from steamrolling the lower-energy, silent folks is to simply refocus their energy. Remember, through our accountability practice we already have each member of the group focusing on every other member of the group. Now let's tweak the focus from basic awareness to support, so that every member of the group is focusing on 100 percent engagement and 100 percent (equal) participation from 100 percent of the group. This wherewithal of team spirit and individual selflessness will help considerably. However, some fellow high-energy Muppets might need additional guidance. Have a chat with them before a meeting and give them the specific focus of helping the meeting itself or even the focus of carefully empowering one or two (more quiet) members of the group—that is, fostering their talent so that each voice is heard equally. This gives your higher-energy folks the feeling of a bit of high status and ownership for the success of the meeting and other people in the meeting.

What if you've got a whole conference room full of Muppets? If the energy of the team becomes too amped up, and all team members are operating at that level without regard to others around them, the energy itself becomes a stressor and a distraction. If a group has the feeling of being outrageously overcaffeinated it stands the chance of losing good ideas, because it is incredibly hard to focus when every idea has got 400-horsepower excitement behind it. The trick is to find what athletes (and improvisers) refer to as "the zone." This is the energy level and mental state that has individuals working at the top of their intelligence and has a group functioning on all cylinders at peak effectiveness. When group members or team leaders become aware that a group's energy is revving too high, the energy can easily be addressed by simply calling it out and refocusing it on the specific task at hand. Remember, high energy should not be without control—you don't want a raging riptide. Rather it is a way for you to create focused momentum to a final outcome, like boating with the current of a river. Another way to seize control of manic energy and refocus a group is through a strict communication policy of "one voice at a time." In improv we call this give-and-take, and here are two easy methods to enforce it:

1. *"Conch shell."* In the classic book *Lord of the Flies* the conch symbolizes social order and deference. When a group of young boys, who are stranded without adult supervision on an island, holds meetings, the only person who can speak is the one holding the conch shell. If you don't have a conch in the office, improvise—have fun—any item will do![11]

2. *Delegation.* One person speaks and that individual delegates who will speak next. The speaker who follows will delegate the right to speak to the next person, who will delegate to the next person, and so on. To help avoid alliances or teaming within a team, you can add the rule that speakers cannot point to the same person two times in a row.

The simple key for finding the sweet spot of group energy is for all team members to be aware of their own energy, aware of the energy of the other individuals in the team, and aware of the energy of the team as a whole. High-energy folks have to come down and low-energy folks have to come up to set the mutually agreed-on energy of the group. Wherever a group's energy happens to start out, if you are in a position to be a group leader it's likely you have a desire to be motivational and inspirational (if for no other reason than that an intrinsically motivated and inspired team is going to produce better results for you). Understand then that "motivation" and "inspiration" should not be seen as ephemera: they are explicit goals that can be reached through enlightened, properly executed energy and attitude manipulation to support the content of your message. When you manage your own energy and attitude—light your own internal fire, so to speak—you influence others to do the same.[12]

Environmental State

A workplace can be an environment that motivates people to do the best work possible. It can just as easily be an environment in which people are demotivated and do the minimum required before they can shoot out the door. The quality of the work environment depends on the energy and attitude of the people in that environment.[13] And even if we're looking at the workplace as a whole, energy and attitude are still choices.

Attitude in the workplace does not have to be angst ridden in order to be productive. Though stress is a serious motivator, it may not be the best motivator 100 percent of the time, and the dynamics of a workplace do not always have to be somber for great work to be done. I try to bring this point home in my programs with some of the group exercises designed specifically to help group members find and maintain an enjoyable energy sweet spot in the workplace at large:

- A simple physical warm-up is "Eights," a process in which each limb is shaken one at a time, first counting up to eight and then from eight counting back all the way down to one, picking up speed as numbers decrease. That simple physical activity not only brings the energy up but tends to bring a smile to faces as well, and those smiles—smiles of connection with the group— always pay off when the group uses this newfound bump in energy and moves on to the task at hand.

- To dial in the appropriate mental focus, a quick exercise I use is "One-Word Story": a story is told in which each member of the group supplies only one word of the story at a time. This classic short-form improv exercise can seem a little daunting at first, and quite often the first few sentences that get constructed are very simple, if they make any sense at all. As the group buys in, though, sentences get more coherent, word choices get more daring, and more interesting stories can be constructed. This exercise requires intense listening, full-group focus and participation, a positive attitude and willingness to make anything work, and the ability to postpone judgment and make sense of ambiguous data. It often produces some very funny results. The laughter doesn't make the group less likely to take their work seriously, however—it makes them more focused and excited to take on whatever I task them with.

- Another, less classic and more intense exercise has two people face each other, count to three together, and then try to say the same word at the same time. Though the two participants always start out with a pair of random, completely unrelated words, they continue counting to three and saying words at the same time until, eventually, they realize what the other person is thinking and finally end up landing on the same word at the same time. This is a difficult challenge, though it's amazing how quickly people get into the zone and start taking cues from each other to try to say the same word simultaneously. They are fully engaged—listening and thinking, and also speaking—to have a specific impact. I don't think I've ever run this warm-up where there weren't a ton of laughs and excitement as participants were approaching the "shared" word. The point is that what comes out of the exercise and into the proceeding work is not just the laughter; it is also the engagement and the focus and the group mind (group mind is different from groupthink, a concept we'll break down further in Chapter 9).

I've seen some of these warm-up techniques put into practice by some very non–touchy-feely managers (military commanders, National Cancer Institute scientists, elite financial planners, rocket scientists, radiologists, to name a few), and the feedback is always the same. Loosening up a workplace with a bit of laughter does not squander workplace energy or send work ethics spiraling downward. Instead that levity helps us to relax and reengage in the moment. I would not advocate for nonsense in the workplace, but a bit of laughter is a valid outcome of workplace contentment and an encouragement to be fully present for the work at hand. An invitation to have fun at work is an invitation to maintain the most effective energy and attitude of the workplace.[14] That's an invitation most of us enthusiastically accept.

Energy Exchange

Individual, group, and workplace energies are very similar forces. In all three cases the key to successfully manipulating energy and attitude is to understand that awareness of your own energy is only a fraction of the equation—you must also be mindfully aware of the effect that your energy has upon another individual, other members of a team, or your workplace environment. Energy and attitude, like laughter, are contagious. I think we've all seen the energy contagion in action: some people can walk into a room and suck the energy right out of it, while others can lift the energy up and spread motivation. This is in great part due to what behavioral psychologists have labeled the "chameleon effect"—the fact that we tend to subconsciously mimic or mirror each other's behavior by reading a variety of physical and emotional cues, which can range from blatant to extremely subtle.[15] The premise is that if you're in a meeting and lean forward with elbows on the table, eventually others will begin to lean forward with elbows on the table without even thinking about it. Similarly a smile is often answered with a smile—if a person smiling at you is focused and in the moment it actually takes a strong physical effort not to smile back. In my experience the chameleon effect can be extended to energy and attitude. If you walk into a meeting super excited about something, there's a pretty good chance that through the simple bio-physics of the chameleon effect, other people will begin to subconsciously mirror your energy level. I don't claim this to be any kind of revolutionary breakthrough. Social psychologists J. A. Bargh, M. Chen, and L. Burrows published articles about this back in 1996. It simply serves as a reminder that we should always make the cognizant decision to be aware of our actions, knowing full well that our energy, attitude, and actions are going to have a direct effect on other people.

As we know, most people follow behavior over words, so another easy way to wrangle the wild horses is for the leader of the group to model the behavior he or she wants. A small bump of energy and at-titude creates intrinsic motivation in yourself that yields tremendous results in the way you affect others, and in doing so, you lead by ex-ample. Others then mirror you and follow your lead. Taking time to become aware of the energy and attitude of a team and making the cognizant choice to move team members in the direction you want them to move does not waste time or cost a dime. It simply leads to adjustments that allow for better work and better business.

Remember too that our energy levels not only send physical and behavioral cues; they also reshape any verbal message we are attempt-ing to communicate. Energy changes the tone and cadence of our communication, which in turn subconsciously affects our actual word choice. This changes both the message and the perception of that message. In a nutshell, our energy changes the whole package being delivered in a communication.[16]

It's not hard to get a handle on how this works. Think about receiv-ing a simple message from a coworker, perhaps a green light on some part of a project. If that coworker is slumped back in a chair with arms folded and looks away from you while he mutters, "Yeah, you should go ahead and do that," you hear the message one way. If he is on the edge of his chair, looking you straight in the eye, and excitedly says, "Yes, you should go ahead and do that!" you hear the message another way. The basic content in both situations is essentially the same: it's a "Yes." The message received, however, is very different. One supports and motivates, and one clearly does not. It's the energy and attitude put into the message that makes the difference.

Long-Distance Buzz

In an era of distance communication, distance learning, and telepresence, some of the most vital workplace connections we make do not happen in face-to-face settings; they happen virtually. However, the fact that your interpersonal communication may be taking place via phone or screen does not alter the importance of energy and attitude awareness—if anything it makes that awareness even more important. Your energy and attitude have just as much impact over long-distance means as they do when you are speaking with someone face-to-face.[17]

A very simple and powerful example of just how much our energy and attitude impact our vocal communication can be seen online in any number of video clips that show voice actors at work. Voice actors are the artists hired to perform roles that primarily require the use of their voice. They are behind every line spoken by a character in an animated project, such as *The Simpsons*, *Family Guy*, any Japanese anime program, and the animated films of Disney and Pixar. What you find when you watch them work is that even though they're in a booth with a microphone and their vocal performance is the only thing being captured, they still act with their body and their face. If they are speaking a line that projects happiness, they smile. If they are speaking a line that communicates excitement, they gesture with their hands. Conversely, if they are conveying sadness or boredom, their faces have a more melancholy expression and their hands have much less movement. They physically project everything they want to communicate, because they know that even though their hand gestures and facial expressions will not be seen, their physical energy is communicated through the microphone and has an impact on the vocal communication that is captured. They are absolutely aware that energy and attitude are a choice, especially when the means of communication might seem limited. In other words, energy and attitude, in combination with physicality, affect the "package" of communication that gets delivered, even when the package is limited to what others can hear in your speech alone.

For example, when a speaker alters his or her physical energy and attitude with a simple facial expression, it has a direct effect on vocal rhythm, speed, intonation, cadence, and subconscious word choice. This not only changes how a speaker delivers a message; most importantly it changes how the listener perceives the message.[18] In other words it changes what the listener walks away understanding from the message. We spend a lot of time thinking that we are in control of our message because we are wording things the way we want to word them. We assume that we know how our words are going to be heard and understood. We forget that our choices in terms of energy and attitude greatly affect the way our message is interpreted.

You don't think that energy and attitude matter in, say, phone conversations? Test it for yourself:

- Get on the phone and have a work-related conversation in which you're up on your feet, moving around, and using your hands in an animated way. Then have a conversation where you're slumped in your seat or leaning back with your arms crossed. Ask the person on the receiving end of the call if he or she can hear the difference.

- Have another pair of phone conversations in which you're smiling versus frowning or holding a look of anger. Ask the person listening if he or she can hear the difference.

- Tell a story to a friend or significant other, in which you ask them to sit and listen to you with their eyes closed. Tell your story for three minutes with a frown on your face (or even no facial expression at all) and your arms folded. Then continue your story for three more minutes with a smile on your face and your hands moving wildly. Ask your friend if he or she heard a difference and if so, what was heard.

The differences that energy and attitude can make in delivering verbal-only messages are certainly clear every time we make a call to a customer service number. You know from the moment a random representative answers the phone whether this is going to be a good experience or a tough slog. It's all in the voice. I instruct all my Business Improv client relationship reps that there will be no phone calls made sitting down; they need to be up and moving around when talking to clients. The reps' work spaces are also plastered with Post-it notes reminding them to "Smile"—a direct order from the boss to keep the energy and attitude up. What's interesting to me is that these kinds of instructions are rarely seen as an imposition. My reps quickly figure out that the positive energy they bring helps them to be more successful at their jobs, so standing and smiling become less and less of a conscious choice and more of an automatic adjustment in the workplace.

Branded Energy

Energy is also a powerful tool for conveying one's personal branding message. One of my favorite ongoing Business Improv programs is the five-day intensive at Duke for MBA students. This winter program usually coincides with the students' interviewing for positions and internships. What I've observed again and again over the years is that before taking the program, many MBA students head into their interviews feeling nothing but nervous. They approach the interviews as if they were weather events—that is, something they know they have to endure, over which they have no control. They feel they have no choice but to cede all authority to the process they are stepping into. They are operating with an overwhelming fear of not getting everything exactly right to get the internship, even though they may not be quite sure what "everything" is. This state of mind in effect quashes the personal energy they might otherwise bring to the interviews. All their energy is going into a fearful reaction to a hypothetical about what they feel they need to do, as opposed to what they can do.

Students who make the choice to refocus their energy during the interview experience find they are able to set aside fear as the major motivator and instead react nimbly and honestly to the real situation they encounter. By simply reminding themselves that they have a choice of what energy to bring into the room with them and how they focus their energy, they step into the interview properly focused, and adaptable, and what they find is that by bringing the right energy and attitude, they connect with the interviewer.

The ability to make that kind of connection is a very big deal, because "connection" is one of those crucial intangibles that have become a big differentiator in the business world. If an employer is looking at two resumes from equally qualified candidates—solid schools, solid grades, solid experience—more often than not the person who gets hired isn't the one who just looks like a good fit on paper; it is the candidate who actually is a good overall fit for the team. In fact for some employers the attitude and fit may be even more important than the resume.

Think of it like this: if you were assembling a team and had the choice to pick a slightly less talented person with a great attitude, a willingness to learn, and a desire to be part of a great team, versus a person with great talent, huge ego, and stubborn arrogance, who would you choose? Many would choose the person with slightly less talent and a better attitude. Why? Because the person with the better attitude is teachable and will be a good fit on the team.[19]

Or we might consider the age-old question of the business traveler: On a long layover whom do I want to be stuck in an airport lounge with? The answer quite simply is someone you like being with; that is, someone with the right energy and attitude—someone you can connect with. Energy awareness and manipulation are all about making that connection with your coworkers, your team, and your workplace.

Riding the Waves

The maintenance of peak personal energy can be thought of in terms of physics and momentum: it is easier to keep a ball rolling than it is to stop it and start it again. However, what keeps our personal momentum up is more often a matter of motivation than physical force. A child may need to be coerced out of a warm bed early in the morning to get ready for school. That same child will spring eagerly from the same cozy bed early on a holiday morning when presents and celebrations await. The kid, the bed, and the clock are, in science-speak, constants, while the intrinsic and extrinsic motivations are completely different, which affect the observable shift in energy and attitude of the little tyke. In the workplace we are constantly subjected to a similarly shifting spectrum of intrinsic and extrinsic motivations, which cannot help but impact our energy and attitude. The purpose of becoming aware of your energy and learning how to manipulate it is not to sustain a certain energy level just for the sake of sustaining it. The goal is to be strategic with this knowledge in order to react most effectively to shifting circumstances and motivations.

Thinking strategically means that energy manipulation should not be an end in itself—it has to be used thoughtfully as a means to get to a desired end. If you open the throttle of a boat tied tightly to a dock, you are generating a tremendous amount of energy, and you aren't going anywhere. You have to untie the boat, put it in the correct gear, point the boat in the correct direction, and move with purpose. And most importantly you don't automatically go full throttle and rocket off as fast as you can—you have to know when to accelerate, the effects of your acceleration, how long you should accelerate, what you want to do with the trip, how much fuel you have in the tank, and (perhaps as importantly) when and how to slow down.

To stay in the water for a moment, there are some people whose energy is like a current—a steady force that can move them at a steady pace for as long as necessary. For many more of us, energy comes in waves. If you are one of the wave people, there are always going to be peaks and dips in your workplace energy and even times when your energy flattens out, like water finding its own level. Effective energy manipulation by necessity entails an awareness of your peaks and dips. Energy awareness should lead to energy manipulation, which in turn should lead to energy control. If you can't sustain a certain energy level throughout an entire day, or even throughout a long meeting, look to create little bumps and waves of energy when you need them.

When it comes to idea sharing, collaboration, or creativity (on a team or even a personal level), momentum is hugely important. You want a smooth flow of productive energy, not a lot of stops and starts. To underscore this point, let's rely on one of the great minds of the 17th century, Sir Isaac Newton. Physicist, mathematician, and philosopher, Newton created three Laws of Motion, and the first—sometimes referred to as the Law of Inertia—is the one that will help us here. It states that "a body at rest will remain at rest unless an outside force acts on it, and a body in motion at a constant velocity will remain in motion in a straight line unless acted upon by an outside force."[20]

Channel a bit of Sir Isaac and be that outside force. A little pop of energy—a warm-up, a smile, a laugh—can increase the energy in others, which will affect the kinetic energy of the group, which you can then use to create momentum, a momentum you can ride, like a wave, to increase engagement, collaboration, and productivity.[21]

Maintenance

When elite athletes get into a "game state" before a competition, they put themselves into a mental place that allows them to focus with laser-like intensity on whatever needs to be accomplished. This also allows them to summon the appropriate level of energy they will unleash and maintain to achieve success. They know that it's unwise to get so excited in the locker room that they lose focus or burn up all their energy before the game begins. Any seasoned improviser knows what it is like to have a really energizing warm-up, but warming up too early and expending too much energy before the start of the show burns out the energy of the performers before they even have a chance to light up the stage. The result: a performance that is low energy and unfocused.

Starting strong is only one variable in the energy equation. Seasoned athletes know they have to play hard from the start of the competition to the end. They must have some juice in the tank for the fourth quarter, third period, ninth inning, or the last round. They know how to mentally draw on energy and how to control it. They know it is unwise to try to sustain energy at the most manic levels; rather, they have to sustain at a level that will allow them to perform throughout a game at the highest possible caliber. A baseball pitcher who is working on a no-hitter (a game in which no opposing batter gets on base because of a hit) is a perfect example of game-state thinking. No-hitters are rarely accomplished by pitchers who simply attempt to hurl 100 mph fastballs with every pitch. Instead, the pitcher is using strategy, pacing, and a controlled expression of energy. And his mental focus is sustained even while he is sitting on the bench as his team is batting. The pitcher does not allow himself to get distracted by anything. His focus is on the game and he is in the zone. His teammates respect this and leave him alone to stay focused. Everyone on the team is aware of the mental state of those playing the game.

It can be considerably harder to achieve a game-state approach to energy throughout an entire workday in the workplace (for one thing we usually don't have a stadium of 50,000 people cheering our every phone call). We greatly improve our chances for success, however, simply by reminding ourselves that this is the focused mental state we are after.

Before your next meeting take just two minutes to check where your energy is, and then make the decision to do something about it with either a bump up or a bump down. Create a wave of energy if you need it—something you can pump up, build momentum with, and then ride out. Get yourself into the state of mind that this meeting means something and that you are going to contribute to its meaning. (Otherwise, why are you attending the meeting? Seriously.) Make the choice to take charge of your own energy, and then see if you have a better experience for yourself and what kind of impact you have on those around you.

Even if your moment of focus results in the conclusion, "I'm not focused," you are way ahead of the game in that you have accurately diagnosed your mental state. You are aware that a personal adjustment needs to be made. If all the members of a group are checking the collective energy, it's important for each individual to be willing to show a little vulnerability. Admit that you are a little unfocused and ask your team members to have your back. Create group accountability and empower the team to admit when the energy of the group has to be adjusted. Meetings become especially deadly when no one (tactfully) admits that the productivity of the meeting has stalled. Acknowledge obstacles so that they can be eliminated; otherwise energy seriously sags, passion plummets, morale decreases, and ultimately it becomes incredibly difficult to be productive. Each member of the group must be responsible for the entire group if it is to succeed at its highest level. To that end be careful not to confuse "looking busy" with sustaining energy: having everyone simply attempt to look like they are doing something is as unproductive as having everybody slumped in their chairs ready to go night-night. Be focused, be aligned, and hit your targets.

Make the Choice

In facing down real-world workplace situations, be forewarned that energy maintenance and manipulation aren't always as easy as a quick self-audit and a couple of deep breaths. Energy and attitude can slump for any number of legitimate reasons, and there are times when it seems almost impossible to get your energy where you want it. You have a newborn who sleeps in a crib in your room and awakes every two hours for feedings. You were out late the night before and are feeling it today. You are disengaged because you are overwhelmed by the sheer volume of work you have to do. You are down because a project isn't going well. You may actually be ill, and it's not impossible that you could be so physically exhausted that your body might have trouble responding to requests for mental energy. You may feel your low-energy, negative frame of mind is a rational response to the circumstances you find yourself in—and you may in fact be evaluating those circumstances with absolute accuracy.

However, if you allow your reasons for not performing at your top level to dictate your emotional and psychological response to your peers, your team, and your work environment, you are unnecessarily ceding the power to manipulate your energy and attitude. It can be extremely difficult to make adjustments in your energy at times, but it's important to remember that it is possible to try. Even in difficult circumstances you are the one in charge of your attitude and energy. You have control over them, and you can always decide what to react to and how to react to it.

Understand too that energy can be fabricated—not fabricated as in "faked" as much as in mindfully constructed. Adjusting your energy up doesn't mean you force yourself into a good mood. Sometimes you can't authentically be in a good mood: the pipes have burst at home; you left the house angry with your spouse; your phone was eaten by your neighbor's angry alpaca. There are a thousand valid stresses and distractions, but they are only excuses to let crappy non-work-related events dictate the way you behave in specific, work-related circumstances. You can make a concerted effort to refocus, check your attitude, and get in the right mental state to work, especially if the outside stresses won't help you get a positive outcome at work. Emotional dips happen to everyone, but there is a very thin line between an excuse and an abandonment of choice. Always make the choice to get your job done the way you want to get it done. For individuals or groups the point is not to force a fake level of energy; it is to recognize the current energy level and decide whether that level is going to get the job done or whether it needs to be adjusted. Some people do function better at a low simmer, and some are at their best in roiling boil. Whatever the case, respect energy and understand that you can do something about it.

Prime Choice

Let's look at this from a different angle: creativity. Think for a moment about your workday and about your peak time to be creative.

Where does it fall in the day? Are you creatively at your best at seven o'clock in the morning, before the coffee has kicked in? No no, you say. That's too early for you; you haven't quite gotten into your groove yet. Well, how about a little later, right before lunch: is that the best time to be creative? No no, you say. At that point you're too distracted by the things you need to get done before lunch, and by the thought of lunch itself. OK then, how about right after lunch? No. Lunch lethargy has kicked in. You need some time to get back in the groove. So how about toward the end of the day, right before you head for home? Absolutely not, you say. By that point your mind is probably already one hemisphere out the door. To review then, if you scan an average day looking for the peak times to be creative in the workplace—early morning, late morning, early afternoon, late afternoon—the conclusion might be that in fact there is no good time.

The truth is, there is also no bad time. My advice is to turn the dynamic around. The day itself is not going to consistently offer up the perfect time to be creative, or productive, or effective. You have to create that time for yourself by making a choice about your own energy and attitude. You can make the choice to have a productive meeting, whether it's just before lunch or just after. You can make the choice that the 5:30 p.m. phone call is going to be the most effective of the day. Again, you may not always get the outcome you're after, but you will put yourself in a position, by choice, from which that outcome is achievable. You can choose to be as creative, productive, communicative, and motivated as you wish to be at any given time.

From the outside perspective of a fan, we have no way of knowing whether LeBron James plays his best games on the days when he has no outside worries. We can't know, because he usually performs at an incredibly high caliber. Chances are, though, that there is always something other than basketball that he could be worried about at game time. In fact we know that he has had some phenomenal games when he was sick or injured or was going through events in his personal life that could have easily given him reason to be unfocused. Yet he prepared mentally, before the game, and stayed in the zone.

You can make the same choice. Don't stare at the computer screen with your mind on the annoyance of estimated taxes right up until the moment you need to join a conference call. Step away from the things not relevant to the job, and when needed look at your notes to get back on point. Check your energy. Check your attitude. Get yourself focused. Stand up and shake your limbs. Give yourself a goal—tell yourself you are going to say one thing that has a positive impact on the next meeting you attend. We're not all going to end up being the LeBrons of our chosen fields, but we can all learn from him and other elite performers and make the choice to apply the right level of energy and the right attitude to our work when we need to—which just might be every day we show up.

Now hold your energy at a steady 8 out of 10 and we'll move ahead to take a more in-depth look at the dynamics of teams.

Chapter 5

TEAMING UP

HENRY FORD WAS CERTAINLY NO SLOUCH when it came to running a business, and he famously assessed the importance of teamwork this way: "Coming together is a beginning. Keeping together is progress. Working together is success."[1]

Those words still count as wise and I think even Mr. Ford might be surprised at how difficult it can be to get through that three-step process in today's business environment. The chief complicating factors, which we touched upon in previous chapters, are speed and unpredictability. To a great extent teams in today's workplace cannot be thought of as static, established units that always have the luxury of a lengthy developmental timeline. These days teams can be brought together and taken apart in an instant, and the circumstances and challenges facing such teams can shift on a project-by-project basis.

A further complication lies in the misguided notion that simply throwing a team at a problem will take care of it—that is, the act of assigning a task to a group ensures that the task will get done faster and better. This idea was shot down pretty well 40 years ago by pioneering software engineer Frederick P. Brooks, whose Brooks's Law states that "adding manpower to a late software project makes it later."[2] The point here is that teams don't get the job done well; good teams get the job done well. And what makes a team good? Respectful communication and collaboration and great chemistry. Enter improvisation.

In this chapter we'll take a look at how improvisational thinking can facilitate the trust, support, and commitment necessary for great teamwork; how it can level status within a team; and how improvisational leadership can effectively guide a team. Concepts that have been discussed in earlier chapters—ways to apply improv personally, in one-on-one conversations, and in small-group situations—will be taken to the next level as we explore the causes and pitfalls of poor team dynamics and examine how the use of improv techniques can build successful, adaptable teams in the workplace.

First allow me to jump back up onstage for a moment. Theatrical improvisation is by nature a team effort, and we improvisers take pride in our teams. Tremendous pride. So much so that there is an active phrase that improvisers use and truly live by: "Go out of your way to make somebody else's idea succeed." As members of an improv team we each make a dedicated effort to support every other member of the team and drive their ideas toward success, even if that means we sacrifice our own ideas. In a smoothly running group this rarely feels like sacrifice because there is a shared purpose. Look at it like this: if team member Marion is focused on making the ideas of teammates Sean and Cesar succeed, and Sean is focused on making the ideas of Marion and Cesar succeed, and Cesar is focused on making the ideas of Marion and Sean succeed, then nobody is working to drive their own agenda. What happens is that the team becomes more important than any single member in it. The process becomes more important than any one person and the product (the outcome) becomes more important than any one person. When every member of a group understands this and buys in to it, the collective consciousness of the team outweighs that of any individual, all while allowing and even inviting every individual to fully express his or her unique perspective. (Remember, there is a huge difference between individual perspective and individual agenda.) The magic is that by putting every other person's ideas ahead of your own, the team, the process, and the product are each significantly elevated.

This directly links to an old adage of improv guru Del Close: "The worst idea with great support will go much further than the best idea with no support."

Teams in a business setting may employ a variety of processes and may be assembled to create a wide range of "products." However, the core concepts of every successful business unit are exactly the same as the concepts embraced by an elite improv ensemble: trust and support. Trust is an unwavering confidence that things will unfold the way intended, and support is a desire to help achieve the desired outcomes. Trust and support are inherent in great improv teams because they are the law of the land and are ingrained in us from our first Intro to Improv class: that every member of a team will unconditionally trust and support every other member is explained, understood, and protected—with passion and vehemence. Every team member is a centurion charged with guarding these particular "gates" to team success, and those who attempt to breach these gates in pursuit of their own agenda will either be battle-axed from the team or doom the team to dysfunction if not failure.

For a team to succeed in the business setting, trust and support have to be fostered and protected with just as much passion and vehemence. Teamwork is where all the principles of "Yes, and . . . " come to the fore. In a successful team each member has to listen to and react appropriately to other people. In any successful team, no one member always runs 100 percent of the game. Members have to support the decisions other people are making, with the knowledge that other people are going to support their own ideas. When members are only interested in driving their own agenda and achieving individual success, they are attempting to assert themselves by force rather than by the higher motivations of trust and support. When a team is built on trust and support, members actively elevate and even celebrate each other's ideas, and the chances of team success skyrocket.[3] If someone has no interest in offering that kind of support to team members, it's going to be crystal clear very quickly to the others. The team should not stand for it.

This isn't an argument that every team should function as a perfect democracy in which every idea from every member is considered to be great. Successful teams can indeed be meritocracies in which the greatest of ideas rise to the top. The crucial point here is that the improv model increases the chances of that great idea being discovered and driven to successful outcomes, because everyone is being heard. The by-product is that individual and group buy-in is increased. Following the improv model, any great idea is supported as a team idea.

To be a member of such a supportive team, one has to have developed the ability to focus and concentrate on something other than one's self, and to be practiced in a heightened state of observation and the postponement of judgment. Above all one has to be adaptable—a team in which support is given out in all directions and received from all directions requires constant adaptation.

While it's important to support what everyone else is doing in a team, it's also important to understand that if one's only role in a team were to offer support to others, one would have limited value on the team. Each member must make initiations and declarations and take responsibility for making connections and catalyzing forward motion. To that end supporting people is not necessarily doing the work for them. Support can take shape in a number of different ways, including morale boosting, motivational encouragement, granting of freedom and responsibility (without micromanaging), granting of time (to struggle, discover, learn, and invent), and yes, even giving physical assistance. Teamwork is what makes a team work and what helps an overall project succeed at a higher level.[4]

One bit of pushback I hear consistently on this topic centers on the matter of choice. It's a valid concern. Any elite, professional-level theatrical improv team is composed of members who have chosen to be a part of that team. A great improv team has the agency to include whom it wants to include and expel whom it wants to expel. It's certainly a little easier to foster trust and support when every member of a team has explicitly chosen to be a part of that team. Obviously that kind of choice is not always present when business teams are put together.

Quite often people are in situations in which they've been assigned to a team, and those teams may not have the freedom to adjust membership. The Darwinian evolution of a team can't always take place.

This would seem to be a major obstacle to fostering the kind of trust and support I'm talking about. However, I'd call to your attention any number of teams that function beautifully even though members haven't come together by choice. Navy personnel who wish to serve on a submarine can volunteer for that duty, but they do not choose their mission or their fellow crewmates.[5] Every member of a sub crew can assume that every other member possesses a certain level of competence, and every member understands that their very life depends on every crew member doing his or her job. With rare exceptions players on pro sports teams don't pick who their teammates are, but all those players understand that victories are only attainable if the team agenda is put ahead of personal agendas. The truth is, the overwhelming majority of brand-new improv teams are assembled by the leaders in the theater, and beginning improvisers do not have a choice on which team they are placed. They are forced to play on the team they have been assigned to. The team fails or eventually becomes elite on the strength of every member buying in to the same philosophy, having the same goals, and following the same rules.

The point is that you don't have to pick and choose your team for that team to be successful. Whether members have actively chosen to be on the team or not, success is made possible when every member understands the purpose of the team, buys in to and follows a set of guiding principles, and commits to a common goal for the team. Nobody is asked to surrender their own critical perspective—in fact it's mandatory that you bring your voice to the team. Yet that unique perspective must serve the group rather than the individual.[6]

Get Committed

All right, let's say you've been assigned to work with a team. The team members seem committed to making the team work. There's no startlingly obvious reason why this team can't accomplish whatever it's been tasked with. And yet as we all know, as teams begin their work, it's very easy for the team dynamics to slide sideways or southward. Let's take a look at some of the things that go wrong within team dynamics, and at what improv-based solutions to those problems might be. About a half dozen years ago my colleague and great friend Kate Duffy introduced me to two great questions, which we now ask in every Business Improv program.

Question 1. Have you ever been in a meeting that is supposed to be 100 percent collaborative—everyone is supposed to be involved— and you got through that meeting without once participating or speaking up?

Normally just about everybody raises a hand—that is to say, 100 percent of the people admit they have not participated at least once when 100 percent participation was required.

Question 2. Have you ever *led* a meeting that was supposed to be 100 percent collaborative and participatory and in this meeting you knew of at least one person who did not participate?

Again, just about everybody raises a hand. The conclusion: what a waste.

If team members aren't committing to a team or a process, such as a meeting, and leaders are not holding those nonparticipants accountable, then what a squandered opportunity. What a waste of time, of energy, of morale and trust (the last ones are a deficit that is particularly hard to recover from). And for those keeping an eye on the bottom line, what a waste of money! (You are paying someone to be in that meeting who might have mentally checked out.) Look at it this way: if you consistently do not participate in any meaningful way in meetings, you serve the same purpose as a penguin on a pirate ship.

If a team is supposed to be collaborative and every member is supposed to participate, then every member should consider that to be a personal responsibility. Every team member has to have a stake in the team's success. Active participation—ownership of the fact that you are a part of this team—has to be a baseline requirement. Simply showing up in the room where the team meeting takes place is not enough. The leader of a team has to be explicit about the rules of engagement—for this period of time you will be held accountable for these duties and responsibilities and this is how you will be held responsible—and then protect the team by making sure those rules are enforced. Team morale is a delicate thing to establish, and like an eggshell, once it is broken it's incredibly difficult to put back together. A team that starts out with members who are not committed is undermining morale from the start, almost guaranteeing that it will be wasting its time rather than gunning for success.[7]

As a member of a collaborative team, if you do not want to participate you should leave. If you don't have the energy or attitude to commit to a team and contribute to it, then get up and go do something you actually want to do. I'd much rather endure the momentary sting of seeing someone leave than have to put up with the deadweight burden of someone who does not want to be part of the team and whose negative attitude undermines the process for weeks on end. This is an approach that I embrace. It extends from my improv teams, to my classrooms, to my business dealings, and it is an approach I often encourage others in leadership positions to adopt. In laying out the rules of team engagement, I make it clear to any potentially anti-team player: I *want* you to stay and I respect your choice to stay and participate, and if you cannot follow these rules, I also respect your decision to leave and not participate in the team. However, you must understand (and here's the kicker!) that if you choose not to be a part of this team and this process, you are also choosing to give up the right to judge whatever the team does, as well as the right to judge the final outcome of the team's work. You are not allowed to remove yourself from the process and then claim ownership in any capacity once the process is completed. If the team succeeds you're not a part of it, and if the team sinks you're not on board. If this team seems like a wrong turn to you, then go do something else that will make you happy and proud.

Life is short—you should create a practice of happiness. Life is also a long journey, so you should do things that can contribute to your happiness. In my experience one of the greatest problems with teams in a business setting is that the team members are not committed to the team. This signals a lack of leadership, a lack of accountability, and a team headed straight for the dumper.

Start with yourself. Check your attitude to make sure you are active and engaged in meetings. Understand that it is not your birthright to sit around and be a wet blanket 100 percent of the time. No one values the curmudgeon who thinks it is his or her job to say no to everything—the business equivalent of the old man yelling at the kids attempting to retrieve a ball off his lawn. Understand that if you consider it your primary job to be the one who always says no, you are sending the message that you consider yourself more intelligent and more important than everyone else in the room. You send the message that only you have the right answer, no matter what the question. If that's true, congratulations—you are the smartest person in the world and you do not need a team to collaborate with you. Otherwise, a persistent "No" attitude has no function on an effective team.[8]

Get Connected

As discussed in the first chapter, some of the barriers to collaboration within a team are virtually the same as the barriers to creativity: fear of being wrong, fear of being judged, fear of making a fool of yourself. If these fears are not acknowledged, the result could be a team in which people feel afraid to speak up, fearful that what they might say won't be valued. If team members are afraid to attempt to have an impact on the team, talent gets suffocated and unique, risky, great ideas never get expressed. This is where the establishment of trust and support is so critical. Too many times people assume that once a team is pulled together the team is ready to go. But a great team is never automatic—it has to be created, curated, and cared for. It takes active effort to establish trust and support.[9]

By active effort, I'm not talking about "trust falls" or a ropes course or even going out for pizza together (though that can be fabulous). I'm talking about team members communicating with each other. On a very basic physical level this means talking openly, honestly, and making eye contact. Each team member needs to make it clear to the others that they are valued and respected on the team.

What teammates personally communicate to each other matters as well. People need to get a little deeper than a Twitter bio (160 total characters) to know who their teammates are. When I bring a designed program to a company that is seeking help with dysfunctional teams, one of the things I encourage right off the bat is for team members to take a wider view of the people they are working with. Nobody is simply a job title or a Twitter bio. We encourage people to talk to each other about things that would not be found on their resume. (This is an exercise that my great friend Scot Robinson has shared with me and that you can do easily over a team lunch: "For the next 30–60 minutes, no shop talk. Just talk about anything other than work.") As always the point is not to get team members to hold hands—the point is to get them to connect in a more personal way so that trust can be established. There are going to be times when a team has to coalesce for the clear purpose of getting something done right now. However, if team members have bonded in a more personal way, then tighter, better teamwork under pressure becomes easier to achieve.

Team bonding can be a tricky process. It requires trust, and trust implies vulnerability. Many people are not used to making themselves vulnerable in a work setting. When every member of a team allows for a controlled level of vulnerability, however, it's amazing how quickly a team can come together as a unified force.[10]

Status Shuffle

Another perceived impediment to effective teamwork is the way status is recognized within a corporate climate. Even when a team is composed of members who want to be there, are committed to the process, and are willing to communicate openly with each other, a team's progress can be hobbled by the simple fact that team members are at different levels within a company hierarchy. Once a team gets working, that initial willingness to communicate can go right out the window if nobody feels comfortable disagreeing with the VP at the end of the table or nobody considers that the new junior salesperson might have something worthwhile to say.

I like to think of our positions within a company as a combination of rank and status. Your job title is your rank and responsibilities within an organization. Your status is given to you by other people, or taken away by other people (either to your face or behind your back). In most cases someone with a high rank is going to be granted a great deal of status by coworkers—that's the nature of a corporate ladder. Status isn't just granted in regard to rank however; it depends on competence, communication, work ethic, leadership, personal relationships, and any number of other workplace variables. When a team is assembled of members who hold different ranks as well as differing status levels, it's very easy for it to collapse under the weight of all the ensuing deference to hierarchy.[11] If a team is to succeed, rank and status must be leveled—at least for specific, strategic periods.

You don't think status matters? Test it for yourself with this exercise:

- Get a normal deck of 52 playing cards. Divide the deck in half so that you are working with only two suits: one red suit (either hearts or diamonds), and one black suit (spades or clubs). Shuffle these cards.

- Assemble a team of six to ten people.

- Everybody in the group selects one card from the deck, keeping it secret from the group. At this point no one knows what their card means. Put the card face down, to the side. It will not be used in Round 1.

  Round 1. Have the team huddle to come up with as many ideas as they can for a holiday party. The ideas should be detailed and cover all bases including specific foods (appetizers, main courses, desserts), drinks, entertainment, decorations, prizes, locations, and so on. This is a numbers game: the group must come up with as many ideas as possible, and you are to give them only 45–60 seconds total. Stop the ideation exercise after that time.

Round 2. All team members take their card and place it in front
of them face up so that the other members can see it. Now
explain to the group that the rank of one's card represents one's
status in the group: ace is the lowest status; king is the highest
(the suit does not matter). Again, the rank of the card is that
person's status in this meeting. Once each member knows the
status of the other members, the group continues the conversation, this time each member playing the status that is on his or
her card. As members interact with each other, remind them to
be aware of the status of the person they are talking to. Give
them three to five minutes for this conversation. Note: Do *not*
remind them that their task is to come up with ideas for the
holiday party! Allow them to take natural ownership for the
progress of this meeting.

Very often people fall immediately into the trap of using the three
to five minutes to emphasize their rank, drive their own agenda, and
undercut every idea that isn't theirs. The group almost completely
loses sight of the point of their time together, which is to come up
with ideas. They become singularly focused on their own agendas and
where they are on the ladder.

Round 3. Now the color of one's card matters. If one's card is a red
suit, the player aligns and agrees with other red-card holders only;
if a black suit, he or she aligns and agrees with other black-card
holders only. Encourage the group to interact with one another
and to actively form teams within the team. Have them fight for
their team's ideas and put down the other team's ideas; in other
words, lower the other team's status in the group while actively
raising their own team's status. Give them three to five minutes
for this portion of the round. Again, do *not* remind them that their
task is to come up with ideas for the holiday party! Allow them to
take natural ownership for the progress of this meeting.

By the time those final three to five minutes are up, a number of people are usually shouting at each other and group ideation has devolved

into attacks and accusations. No matter what anyone has to say, no matter what ideas are being presented, everyone is fully consumed with proving their rank, working from their own motivations, and driving their own agenda.

Which round generated the most ideas? The answer is always clear: Round 1. Even though the group had only 45–60 seconds to work with, they got the job done. More ideas were generated in that round than in the second or third rounds of three to five minutes, and usually more than in both of those final rounds combined. The most notable thing about this exercise is how fast people slip from divergent thinking into convergent thinking without realizing that they had the power of choice. They had a choice to use their rank as motivation to inform both individual and collective perspectives, and they had a choice to use it to drive their individual agendas. The team with a focused goal—a team in which every member was an equally valued participant—got the job done splendidly. The minute that individual agenda became more important than the mission, and teaming within the team took place, the mission failed.

When I run this exercise in my programs and ask participants which round felt more like the meetings everybody is used to going to, just about everybody votes for Round 2 or 3. Those rounds exemplify what happens so often in real-world business situations: goals get knocked sideways by a room full of rank, status, emotions, personal agendas, and personal alliances.

These can be difficult traps to avoid, though again, not every team in a business is going to be—or needs to be—a perfectly egalitarian democracy. There are certainly situations in which the status and company hierarchy is appropriate within the team. However, we're looking at what goes *wrong* within teams, and if your team is struggling with communication, teamwork, trust, morale, creativity, risk taking, or adaptability, there's a fair chance that its troubles are related to how status is being played out within the group. If a person is speaking as a job title rather than as a team member, the team is going to be negatively impacted.[12] Few things squash open communication faster than a higher-up speaking from on high. There may be times when people need to marry themselves to a specific agenda that is based on their rank and job title; yet if that agenda doesn't fit with a team's agenda, the team suffers as do the individuals within it. Alignment is imperative.

All of the outside measures of status that we bring with us to a team are much better set aside when a team begins to work together. Exhibiting your own status is not synonymous with achieving a team goal, and if you're mostly concerned with the betterment of your own position rather than that of the team, you are working against the team (and quite possibly lowering your position outside the team).[13] If cliques—teams within the team—form around perceived status of members and begin to undermine each other, that works against the team's success. If you are concerned with giving credit to an idea because you happen to like the person who comes up with it, or discrediting an idea because it comes from someone else, there's little chance the best ideas will get the support required from the team (recall Del Close's improv adage: "The worst idea with great support will go much further than the best idea with no support").

In the fall of 2014 in a Duke Fuqua Exec Ed program, I had the experience of running a "status leveling" exercise similar to the one I described above with a group that included a U.S. Navy captain who had been one of my biggest improv skeptics. Time after time as we ran through exercises, he didn't feel he was getting any usable takeaways ("I can't imagine going back to my superiors and suggesting any of this. We don't have time for this".) In the status exercise his group had fantastic success coming up with ideas in the first, 45-second round; then it promptly imploded, generating zero ideas in ten minutes from rounds two and three combined. The impact of this destructive meeting and the idea of setting rank aside—for a brief period, even within a hierarchy such as the military that functions on rank—hit the captain like a torpedo. Status leveling was now something he could make time for, and from that point forward the captain became the biggest improv advocate in the class, creating strong links to real-world applicability and discovering places to use a variety of improvisational tools and techniques, even within the ranked hierarchy of the military.

That captain's "conversion" always puts me in mind of the team dynamics of an exceptionally high-functioning military team who know how to level status very effectively: the Blue Angels. The Blue Angels squadron is the United States Navy's premier flight demonstration team, performing all across America. These flying aces are famous for their precision formations and coordinated, split-second maneuvering—a thrilling sight to anyone who's ever watched them in action. What may be less known is how the team conducts postflight team debriefings, in which they beautifully demonstrate status leveling. At the beginning of debriefings the members of the Angels literally remove their rank, pulling off their varying stripes and insignias and setting them aside: rank is not useful in getting the most honest assessment of what went wrong and right with a flight, so—for the meeting—it is suspended. The only moment in which rank matters comes at the start of the debriefing, when the team captain speaks first and lets the other pilots know what he did wrong and how he could improve. With that example set, everyone else in the room is compelled to speak just as freely about what they can do to improve their performance. Every Angel ends his contribution to the debriefing by saying "Glad to be here"—a simple credo that powerfully puts the team and the operation above the individual.[14]

Lead the Leader

For a team to work well, we need awareness, accountability, engagement, commitment, full participation, and a leveling of status. Simply knowing all this, however, is rarely enough to make an impact on how a team functions. For such concepts to be put into practice, someone has to oversee the process. Thus, the possibility of excellent teamwork increases as a result of excellent leadership.

To emphasize leadership right after we've just asked everyone to surrender their status may seem somewhat paradoxical, but then what is life without the beauty of paradoxes? In real-world business settings the role of "team leader" is often made explicit to the team. The presence of a "ranked" leader does not necessarily undo the positive team dynamics we've been speaking of; however, care and thoughtfulness must be taken. A leader's style of leadership must instill and protect positive team dynamics.[15] Leaders have to know when to lead from on high, when to lead from within, and when not to lead at all—to let the group self-regulate.

For people in positions of leadership within a team, status is something to be very mindful of. Some "persons of rank" are understandably proud of their job titles and cherish the status they have been endowed with by others. The pitfall is that as soon as that title begins to dictate the style and quality of collaboration in team efforts, the chances for the team's success may be greatly compromised. As a leader consider how you do or do not foster creativity, risk taking, and talent. Are you suppressing ideas with your style of leadership, or do you make the decision to create environments in which status is leveled and communication is open?

A leader, even the strongest of leaders, has to realize that it can be counterproductive to dictate the tone and pace of every meeting. If you as leader want the people on your team to be engaged and committed to the work of the team, it will be counterproductive to micromanage and steer things directly to the outcome you want. I recently worked with a V-level exec who was tasked with running the South American branch of a high-powered financial firm. He was wondering why he couldn't get more out of the people he worked with, and the problem turned out to be exactly this: he assumed that the only way to be a strong leader was to constantly remind his teams that he was the strongest man in the room. If a group he was leading started off on a tangent, he would pull back too hard and too quickly. He did not demonstrate the trust to let the group have the freedom to move anywhere other than where he wanted to go. He kept a tight hold of the reins and felt that any time the discussion drifted, the team was off track and not focused.

What this particular VP came to see was that if he wanted optimal work out of his groups, he had to allow them to become their own entity with their own voice. The individuals that made up the groups had to feel they had value and that their voice was a part of the group, while also understanding that the group itself had a greater vision and a greater voice that everyone was there to serve. Without instilling and protecting this concept, the VP found himself not leading true teams—instead he was simply giving orders to a bunch of people who had less status than he had and who were not connected to each other.

The improvisational solution in this case was to introduce the concept of distribution of leadership. I've seen again and again that leaders get the most out of their teams when they position themselves not as a leader of underlings but as a leader of leaders. This is accomplished through very practical means. For example, a leader can assign two other people the duty to run a particular meeting. Or the nominal leader insists that leadership be rotated each meeting so that a different team member leads a meeting every week. Specific leaders can be assigned by topic or project. Seats can be moved around and rooms changed by type of meeting so that the physical workplace setting doesn't develop into a reflection of hierarchy ("That guy's always at the head of the table"). To that end be deliberate about where you sit, so that you are not at the head of the table. When meetings are allowed to include different voices, different energy, and different input, they become more dynamic, increasing the level of interest, engagement, and collaborative buy-in. When every member is given responsibility to lead some part of the team and is accountable to the overall team, then everybody has a stake in the team. Team duties become a matter of respect and responsibility rather than mere assignment. The team dynamics will improve almost instantly.[16]

For any nervous leaders wary of surrendering the reins to the group, this doesn't need to be a zero-sum game. Team leadership is not a simple choice between maintaining complete control or letting things run wild. Distribution of leadership means the team's leader must know when and how to lead as well. The leader has to be aware of what he or she wants out of the team and has to figure out how best to get there. At times a leader must keep the train on the tracks and make sure all scheduled stops are hit. The power to command that train doesn't ever have to be surrendered. However, a leader must be open to the idea that strategic risk taking—letting the group drive the train—may result in the discovery of an excellent shortcut, a more efficient route, or a new track altogether. Leaders have to allow themselves opportunities to discover that there may be other ways to get where you want to go other than the one path you have charted.

A leader should always step into a team meeting with a firm agenda. That same leader has to possess a great sense of observation and awareness as well. If you want a team to flourish—to do the work you're asking of it at the highest level—you have to approach the team with mindfulness. If the group needs a moment to digress, or dive into details, or even goof off (connect with each other), an enlightened leader should recognize the benefits of allowing the team to have that freedom.[17] That doesn't mean the leader has completely surrendered anything. This is a "multi-tool" style of leadership, adaptable to the voice of the team and getting the best out of individuals within it.

If pressed to PowerPoint what we've covered so far, I'd suggest the following four ways to build great team dynamics:

1. Establish buy-in by getting 100 percent participation from every member of your team in the development process. The buy-in will turn into "build-in" as each member contributes more equally to the success of the team, the process, and the product ("build-in" is a term I've heard the great professor Iris Firstenberg use many times in UCLA Anderson Exec Ed programs).[18]

2. Level status by distributing leadership. Groom others to lead a meeting or two, or three, or every other meeting.

3. Loosen the reins. Come to meetings prepared with your agenda and then be flexible to allow the group to take control. Keep your agenda on your map as your final destination, and be open to others finding alternate routes to get there.

4. Talk to your team. Be vulnerable. Find out what can be done to do better or at least be open to learn from whatever they have to say about the team.

This was a very hard lesson for me to learn in the early days of my business—ironically enough a business predicated on the power of improv. When I was first getting Business Improv started and finding my voice as a leader, I was very concerned with improv's reputation as being a "soft," pleasant, yet otherwise ineffective way to create business teams. I was passionate about proving that improv had a place of value in business-centered decision making. With that in mind I was going to run my business like a business—not like an improv group that also happened to do corporate gigs. If I had a half hour's worth of agenda to cover, I scheduled a half-hour meeting. I thought I was valuing everyone's time by punching items out from the first minute to the last. This felt great to me—the budding young CEO of my own venture. Meetings were right on time and I always got to say everything I needed to say. My agenda was presented fully and explicitly. However, the results became counterproductive. My team felt I was a drill sergeant, just barreling through talking points. They continually felt like they didn't have any say in the outcome because they were not part of the process. Consequently they didn't feel motivated to follow an agenda that had been imposed on them.

Fortunately I was working with elite improvisers with whom I had performed hundreds of shows for many years. They were (and still are) experts at using the tenets of improvisation to communicate, and one day a few of them pulled me aside and honestly communicated the team's frustration to me. Very quickly I realized that the individuals in my teams needed time to be who they are as people, and not simply collections of people assembled to listen to a particular boss. In large part the solution was very practical. I simply built 10–15 minutes of extra time into meetings so that the people in my teams could connect, joke around, and talk in a more personal way. Those extra minutes were at the top of each meeting and could be spent "off track" on whatever the group deemed worthy. To some clock-watchers those 10–15 minutes could be viewed as wasted time. Internally though, that brief period of time became an incredible asset: not only did the meetings accomplish everything they were supposed to accomplish;

the individuals in the meeting were much more vocal about how to actualize the agenda. People left those meetings with a strong sense of being part of a team. They were intrinsically incentivized to be part of the success of the program because they cared about each other and felt their voices were heard. Further I became a member of the team and not just a boss. I still had the ability to pull the reins—there were times when things needed to get done quickly and I couldn't allow the group to take over and wander at will. Now though when I pull the reins the team falls in line without complaint and follows my directions to the letter. They do this because I consistently show care and respect to each individual in my team, and I only bark orders when there is an actual need for such urgency.

This successful adaptation was not the result of a grand vision. Rather it took place because I also employed the tenets of improvisation. I empathetically listened to the individuals in my team. I considered what they had to say to be important, was humble enough to realize there was room for improvements, and adapted their thoughts to what I needed to do so that meetings—and my business—could run as effectively as possible. That small investment of time continues to be a tremendous investment in human capital and their trust and support continue to pay off, hugely.

Team Practice

Introducing a style of teamwork and team leadership is one thing. Making it work on a day-to-day basis is another. From a leadership point of view simply giving people permission to contribute to a team rarely creates the positive dynamics we've outlined above. People don't respond to just hearing the new rule—they respond to seeing it put into practice. People have to be convinced that as part of a collaborative team there is no right answer that will win them status. They have to understand that their value is in their voice—the act of simply participating—and that they need to make contributions to the team without fear. People really have to feel that status has been set aside before they will loosen up and let things flow. So it becomes an additional responsibility of a team leader to make sure that people are both involved and protected. This not only requires leading by example; it also requires that a leader become the great protector of every person in the team. Personal attacks, petty jockeying for position, and outright bullying are deadly poison to team morale. The leader has to make sure that while a team's communications are open and honest, they are always based on mutual trust and support.[19]

Time is really the X-factor here: we're talking about diligence and consistency. A memo announcing a new approach to teamwork is fine, yet it's only by having that new approach work over time that people will train themselves to become better team players. As with any element of corporate life people must have the opportunity to put best practices into action over and over again so that they can become "business as usual" workplace habits. From the simplest elements of good teamwork—eye contact, active listening, focus and concentration, postponing judgment—to the bigger issues of "Yes, and" communication and collective ownership of ideas, all of these work together over time to allow a team to function at its highest level. If the foundational architecture of a team is solid and well thought out, it's actually very easy for trust and support to happen naturally. If poor team architecture is either erected or ignored, it's going to be very difficult to suddenly get a team to function well when the next crisis hits.

Therein lies the beauty of the cost-benefit equation for teamwork. Perhaps worrying about such soft-sounding things as "trust" and "support" appears to be an indulgence when things are easy and the quarterly reports look rosy. At some point, though, when the excrement hits the oscillator and everybody is under pressure, you're going to need a team that can execute perfectly, and at that point having spent a bit of time curating your teams will turn into the wisest of investments. In times of risk, uncertainty, and crisis, people fall back on their overpracticed behaviors.[20] If you want people to rise to the occasion in times of crisis—and we all know that in the business world there will be occasions—then you have to prepare them for that. Give a team a chance to get used to doing its best when things aren't too hard, and that team will know exactly how to do its best when the challenges get tougher.

So, How Is the Weather?

A final point, which ties in with something that came up in the last chapter: it's all right for teams to have some fun. In 2000 when my company was just starting and improv was not as prevalent either in the public consciousness or in the business mind, the very idea of "business improv" seemed like something goofy without any hope of tangible outcomes. Why? I think primarily because improv was associated with comedy, laughter, and—gasp—fun. Now, with EQ and behavioral psychology becoming ever-hotter topics of corporate conversation, "fun" is not entirely taboo anymore. This is further illustrated in the evolution of the dress code of corporate America. Just 20 years ago most business executives showed up to work wearing a business suit. Then, as the dot-com companies grew, high-powered leaders like Bill Gates lost the tie and wore a dress shirt, blazer, and dress slacks to work every day. That then morphed to dress shirts and nice jeans and dress shoes. Now, in 2016, some billionaire leaders wear hooded sweatshirts, T-shirts, and shorts to work.[21]

The corporate dress-code evolution coincides with the rise of Gen-Y and Millennials, who demand a different type of corporate culture than baby boomers did. Many of corporate America's future leaders want a relaxed work environment and fun is a mandate! Remember, having fun does not mean you are not productive or successful. Look at any current listings of "the best places in America to work." Twitter, SAS, Google, and Facebook (to name a few) are all incredibly successful, powerful billion-dollar companies, and they are also fun companies to work at. People—serious people—can see a measurable business benefit to workers enjoying a bit of levity, connecting on a more human level through laughter, and otherwise relaxing a bit within the workplace. Not every business day involves the heaviest of lifts, and not every job has to be approached as if lives were on the line. Even in jobs where lives *are* on the line, there has to be a balance between stress and relaxation. Firefighters have family barbecues, and navy fighter pilots play volleyball. That's all part of building the team chemistry that becomes crucial when there is a heavy lift.

The bottom line: being part of a team shouldn't feel like a burden. Your team should be a place where you can work just as hard and smart as you would on your own, with the added benefit that you are supported by others working just as hard and smart. If your job involves teamwork and you want to do well at your job, then knowing how to commit and contribute to a team is simply part of getting your job done well.

Next, with your exceptional team assembled, let's put it to work at one of the most common collaborative team endeavors: a brainstorming session.

Chapter 6

MUST BE SOMETHING IDEATE

ONE OF THE KEYS TO SUCCESS in any business lies in the ability to generate a tremendous amount of ideas, because when it comes down to it, almost every organization is at heart in the idea business. This is not a revolutionary concept. However, what is often overlooked—or simply misunderstood—is that the generation of great ideas is a numbers game. Businesses are ostensibly always looking for killer ideas that will boost profits and cut costs; ideas that streamline processes and maximize investments; and ideas that will have significant impact in the marketplace. To get to those killers, though, a business may have to cough up a mess of ideas that are ridiculous, budget-busting, unusable, or simply awful.

I would contend that these loser ideas are not merely waste products—they are indicators of an extremely healthy brainstorming and idea-sharing process. This chapter will take the concepts that have been discussed in earlier chapters—"Yes, and . . . ," postponement of judgment, EQ, divergent and convergent thinking—and make them practicable through the step-by-step process of leading successful collaboration sessions.

A business that runs on the assumption that it will come up with a great idea exactly when it needs one is severely limiting if not deluding itself. That business is most likely achieving "greatness" by simply lowering the standard of what counts as great. The fact is, to get to unimpeachably great ideas—sharp, innovative, outright brilliant ones—you have to come up with an ugly pile of horrible ones too.[1] By way of analogy think about the old process of gold panning. As you might remember from elementary school studies of the California Gold Rush, panning is the art of extracting gold from a river by scooping up sediment with a large pan. Panning is a sloppy, difficult process, and it can get results.

Jebediah, a hungry prospector on a quest for gold, might try to speed things up by avoiding the pan altogether and simply sticking his finger in the river in the hope that when he withdraws it from the water it will be sporting a perfectly polished gold ring. But with that approach ol' Jeb is probably going to end up with nothing more than a wet finger. If he takes a slightly more ambitious approach and grabs a fistful of river bottom, he's probably going to end up a little wetter, and not much richer. Instead, if fortune-seeking Jeb knows his business, he'll understand that he is going to have to use the biggest pan possible and invest some sweat equity, sieving through as much river muck and goo as he can to boost the probability of success. As Jeb pulls his pan through the water, he will not expect to come up with a panful of sparkly gold nuggets every time he sifts what he's dredged up. He knows this is a longer process and he's going to have to work his way through a heck of a lot of mud, slime, weeds, foul-smelling detritus, and even fool's gold to find the small flecks of real treasure. He also knows that those raw flecks aren't an end in themselves—all gold has to be refined to become truly valuable.

So it is with the process of group ideation, which we commonly refer to as brainstorming. Brainstorming is a process of communication and adaptive problem solving, and to the improvisational way of thinking, great brainstorming sessions are only possible when failure is not just tolerated, it's welcomed.[2] Such sessions require everyone in the room to understand that sorting through clumps of mud and muck is a necessary part of the process in order to get to the prized gold. The fostering of failure is perhaps a bit counterintuitive in most corporate cultures, and failure itself is of course never the explicit objective. The point is that if a business truly encourages a "Yes, and . . . " approach to open communication and if the culture also embraces the possibility that great ideas can come from anyone and anywhere, then failures—dead-end ideas—are actually an indication of a very vital and vibrant corporate culture.[3] Just as in life outside the workplace, you can learn more from failure, and failure allows you to learn more from success. Even the most naturally talented musician does not first pick up a violin and instantly sound like a virtuoso. We understand that the young fiddler is probably going to sound fairly crappy for a while. There will be wrong notes and muffed passages—failures—on the way to musical excellence. A surfer who has never fallen off his board is either preternaturally gifted or has not actually put his board in the water. It is falling off the board (or the bike) that helps build technique and develop ability. A beautiful ride will be better appreciated when we are fully aware of the falls it took to get there. Within the improvisational workplace, failures can almost always be framed as steps toward success.

We've examined why improvisational skills and tools should be used in a business setting, and we've examined how those skills and tools can be used by an individual, between individuals, and within a group. Now we're stepping into the "when," looking at a very specific, common, concrete part of the workday—the ideation meeting, collaborative conversation, idea-sharing chat, and brainstorming session—in which improvisational techniques can improve process and facilitate success. I've stressed that one of the most powerful blocks to overcome is the very basic, primal emotion of fear, and this is perhaps never truer than in the creative process. In a workplace permeated by a fear of failure, it's virtually impossible for anyone to feel comfortable offering up a new idea, let alone an unusual idea that might in fact make all the difference in a marketing strategy, a product development plan, a customer-focus drive, or a new in-house bookkeeping system. When the fear of failure is eliminated and the participants in a brainstorming session are encouraged to fail early and often, they have the greatest chance of succeeding at whatever task they've been asked to handle. (Keep in mind, we are talking about strategic failure protected by a specific time and place, and not about thoughtless, repeated failure.)

Before we get deeper into how a successful brainstorming session should be run, let's take a look at the dynamics of business meetings in general. If you were suddenly pinged by a coworker right now and were told that it was necessary for you to put this book down and head off to an ad hoc problem-solving meeting of some sort, would you bolt out of your chair with enthusiasm? If you're anything like millions of other inhabitants of the corporate world, your response to such a request might not be a hoot of unbridled enthusiasm but instead a good deal of sighing, slumping, eye rolling, and muttering along the lines of "Another &$*!@ meeting?"

Why should this be the case? The answer is simple: most meetings are run terribly, and for a great deal of businesspeople meetings have become the bane of their existence rather than a boon to getting the job done.

Much too often the actual purpose of a meeting is just to say that the meeting took place, and participants end up in a highly frustrating and morale-sapping *Groundhog's Day* loop of inaction: they end up having a meeting that covers the meeting they had last week. Then they need to schedule yet another meeting to discuss what hasn't gotten settled in previous meetings. The downside of poorly run meetings isn't just measured in annoyance and frustration, however. Bad meetings waste time and energy, which means that they waste money. Bad meetings are bad business.[4]

If a meeting consists of a group of smart, dedicated people around a conference table and that group is open and willing to take on whatever challenge is at hand, how is it that things go in the dumper? There are two typical trajectories. First, as we discussed in Chapter 4, there's a question of energy and energy maintenance. If the meeting leader doesn't accept responsibility for setting a level of energy that invites people to stay engaged, that meeting has as much chance of sparking great ideas as a warm blanket and a sedative. If attendees feel they have the ability or even the right to disengage and allow their own energy to plummet—again, good night, Irene.

This doesn't mean that the person running a meeting has to crank up the karaoke machine, put on a goofy hat, and belt out "Born in the USA." It's more about being aware that every room and every group has an energy, and that energy can—or must—be manipulated (see Chapter 4 if this doesn't ring a bell).

The other big problem with meetings is a basic matter of communication. A huge part of what's not working in a lousy meeting is that people don't feel comfortable contributing. There may be some great ideas inside the heads in that conference room and they don't ever get expressed because people don't feel they have a stake in pitching in. There are a number of reasons why people don't feel they have buy-in at meetings. Some folks think that by simply showing up they have fulfilled their workplace obligation. Some meeting leaders may fail to communicate the focus of a meeting or may pedantically overcommunicate, in either case shutting down the opportunity for real engagement. Then there's that most common obstacle to communication, our old friend fear—fear of judgment, fear of rejection, fear of being wrong, fear of looking like a fool. A climate may exist in which people feel that if they speak up they'll be judged harshly, perhaps by people who are of higher rank or status in the corporate hierarchy. As we discussed in the previous chapter, a roomful of meeting participants can be so acutely aware of the status of everybody around the conference table that everyone plays defense: whatever the most powerful VP in the room thinks, that must be the right way to go, so let's all just nod and get on with it.

Sometimes these fears are not simply the result of "climate." They may be based on real experience. If somebody has had a hand figuratively slapped at a meeting for saying something that didn't fall in line with a boss's or a company's philosophy ("That idea is too far out there. Let's stay focused on the problem. Remember our budget parameters"), that person is going to remember the sting of that slap and will be reluctant to speak up again. Further, others who witnessed this negative reaction to a voiced idea aren't going to want to speak up either, because they do not want the same thing to happen to them. A reluctance to expose oneself to negative consequences isn't just a matter of workplace habit; it's a survival instinct deeply rooted in brain science.[5] If our core reactions reduce down to two basic instincts—fight or flight—this reluctance to speak up is the mental equivalent of fleeing, or curling up into a ball in the corner of a room. With fear and status at the front of everyone's thinking, a meeting can become so dispiriting that it suffocates any sense of intrinsic motivation. Nobody feels they have any skin in the game, so they see no point in giving their best effort.

The solution quite simply is to create a culture in that meeting room in which communication is open and everyone wants to contribute. Of course that kind of culture can't be ordered up along with the office furniture; it's the result of choices made and efforts expended to make those choices a reality. The choice to utilize improvisation in the workplace is primarily a choice to make real, honest communication a top priority. That choice can help create a culture in which people want—passionately want—to contribute and to succeed, as opposed to a culture in which people do not even want to try because they are taught not to try.[6]

When it comes specifically to ideation and brainstorming, that culture is created through a focused application of some of the techniques we've already discussed: "Yes and-ing," postponing judgment, choosing a constructive energy and attitude, and designing a well-managed process of divergent and convergent thinking based on accountability. These techniques can make all the difference in getting the individual members of a collaborative, brainstorming team to feel they're being talked with rather than talked at—something that may sound small but can actually be the difference between a session that gets serious results and one of those meetings that merely creates the serious need for another meeting.

As I've stressed repeatedly and emphatically, effective improvisation is not some abstract, touchy-feely, let's-hold-hands-and-skip-through-a-field-of-poppies philosophy, but is instead a simple, honest, results-driven approach to communication. This is especially true for ideation, during which the application of improv techniques should result not just in a roomful of smiley people but in a roomful of smiley people who have worked together to generate a usable, profitable, killer idea. How do you get to that great idea? I humbly submit the following guide for successful ideation—the Laws of Effective Brainstorming:

1. Participate (or go do something you want to do).
2. Embrace "Yes, and . . . "
3. Postpone judgment (for a specific period of time).
4. Suspend critiquing and overanalyzing.
5. Have fun and celebrate ridiculous ideas (remember, it's about the number of ideas here).
6. Stay energized and focused.
7. Support every person in the group (100% participation, 100% engagement).
8. Give and take the right to speak.
9. Remain positive.
10. Hold each other accountable to follow the rules.

Of course some of the above may be easier said than done, so let's go a little deeper into the river to pan for gold.

If there are indeed "laws" of effective brainstorming, then someone has to administer those laws. That would be the leader of the ideation session. Perhaps it goes without saying that successful brainstorming begins with effective leadership, but I'll say it anyway: successful brainstorming begins with effective leadership. The dismantling of cognitive blocks to creativity must come from leadership. The freedom to ideate and openly share ideas begins with understanding that the dynamics of a room are established from the top down. Why? Because the leader is in the position to demand that everyone commit to the process, and in the position to guide the team to success. The leader needs to mentally and physically embody the spirit he or she wishes to see reflected in a team.

It is a wrong-headed assumption that simply calling a meeting and having everyone in one room together for a certain amount of time is actually accomplishing anything in and of itself. Additionally it's a terrible mistake for a leader and for participants to assume that since everyone in the room got the memo calling for the meeting, they all know why they're here. If you as leader want the meeting to actually work, lay down the law. A leader needs to state explicitly and simply what the meeting needs to accomplish, and what is expected of all participants. A clear time limit needs to be set so that people know how to pace their energy (great brainstorming can be done in as little as 10–30 minutes). Technology should be banned—the meeting is about presence, engagement, and connection.

The "laws" governing an improv-based brainstorming session are specific and need to be restated at the top of each session. The guidelines I favor are simple and clear. Everybody in the room is expected to participate and come up with ideas. To not participate is not an option. Team members should not let self-editing prevent them from expressing ideas. Fail early and fail often. Members who are stuck in their heads are making a selfish choice to only think of themselves and will bring limited value to a group. If brainstorming is panning for gold, then don't psych yourself out thinking about the cold water. Don't try to tiptoe into the river either; go for the cannonball. Get in the water fast and get those ideas out and splashing around. Once everybody's in the water, every idea that is tossed around will not just be accepted, but be accepted enthusiastically as if it's the best idea anyone's ever heard. Support of every team member by every other team member is mandatory. You are panning for gold here, so it's about the amount you can pull out of the river (the number of ideas) rather than trying to pull a single pinch of dirt out of moving water. Keep individual and group awareness and respect high: have one voice speak at a time and encourage every member of the group to participate.

Keep in mind that the collective consciousness of the group is greater than that of any individual, including the leader. Participants need to commit to the process, then, and keep their energy level high—and so should the leader, equally. Everyone should be encouraged to make eye contact with other team members to engage the team. When the majority of people in the meeting buy in and participate following these rules of collaboration, a level of pressure for positive conformity will be created so that no one would feel comfortable being the person who is not committed to the process, and who is not in the river having fun.

Presence

Presence doesn't simply mean you fill a seat at the table. For ideation to work, every participant has to be mentally present and in the moment. Perhaps that phrase has become a bit clichéd, but it does address a real solution to a very common problem. A basic pitfall of human communication is that we think about what we're going to say next as opposed to being focused on what's being said in the moment and then reacting honestly. This leads to the strong probability that we will miss content and subtext being communicated to us because we're too busy thinking ahead rather than thinking in the present. A brainstorming session requires that participants speak and listen in the moment, free of distraction.

This starts from the top down. In my experience nothing is more deadly to ideation than a distracted leader. If the person ostensibly running a brainstorming session doesn't seem willing to commit to it, then why in the world would anyone else in the room be willing to commit themselves? Cognitive psychologists tell us that our bodies send out messages all the time.[7] If a leader has arms crossed in a defensive bit of body language, or keeps looking at a watch or a phone, the message being sent is that the leader would rather be somewhere else. Why shouldn't the rest of the team feel the same way? The enlightened leader understands that a huge part of the leadership role is to actively acknowledge that this session is happening here and now with this team and with this particular task at hand. The effective leader must be able to make a conscious effort to focus on nothing other than what is happening right here, right now. This skill can be developed in the same way that one might work a muscle group: as a conscious effort to focus is made more and more often, less effort is required and one's focus becomes sharper. A good workplace habit is created.

For members of a brainstorming team, being in the moment means being ready to participate fully. At a nuts-and-bolts level this means banning the external distractions of technology from the rooms—no smartphones, iPads, or laptops. The only databases in the room are a bunch of human brains. Internal personal distractions should be set aside as well.

Before a leader or member heads into a session, it's remarkably helpful to take one or two minutes to get one's head in the right space (game state) and make the conscious decision to be a productive part of the team. People get flustered and frustrated for all kinds of reasons in the workplace; however, it's self-defeating to carry a headful of problems into a meeting that's not designated for solving those problems.

Once a brainstorming session is underway, it is important to stay in the moment. Everyone in the room needs to maintain a productive level of energy and a positive attitude. Don't forget that energy and attitude are choices. It's okay to feel tired or to be caught in your head or even be negative sometimes. However, it is dangerous to assume that you are not affecting people negatively. If every team member makes the choice to affect the session and the people in the session in a positive way, the stage is set for a great, productive meeting. People can certainly have natural dips in energy and attitude, and no workplace can expect everyone to be a high-energy Uncle Smiles all the time. However, it is also unfair to play the part of Aunty Poopy-Panty every single meeting. The point is to accept that you can make the choice to affect energy and attitude in any direction you want.

The Scribe

Once the laws of the land are established and everyone is fully present, you're off to a great start. On a practical level though, it is the team's job to come up with the ideas, not to record them. Add one or two people to the mix, whose sole job is to record ideas. We'd all like to believe that we are expert multitaskers, but it is actually very hard for people to listen, write, think, and speak constructively all at the same time.[8] Moreover, for some, writing can become a kind of defense mechanism—a way to cash out while looking like you're doing something important when in fact you're not contributing anything to the team. If everyone is writing, everyone's head is down and everybody is connecting with paper rather than with each other. (When eyes are down, energy goes into the paper. When eyes are on each other, we give each other energy and feed off of the energy of others.) Relieving a team of the task of keeping track of what they brainstorm will have a tremendous impact on the session and is a way to encourage active (vocal) participation, promote group accountability for engagement, and increase buy-in. This also further eliminates the need for technology. And scribes can come from anywhere; the leader can pull someone off another job to serve as scribe for the length of the brainstorming session.

Prepackaged Mix

When it comes to effective brainstorming, the techniques of improvisation are applied at even the most basic level—they begin with the real-world, real-time physicality of the room and the meeting participants. Simple adjustments to the physical space and the way participants inhabit that space can make a huge difference in the quantity as well as quality of ideas that get generated (memo to the accounting department: making these adjustments doesn't cost a single cent).

What's the first thing most people do at a brainstorming session? Probably the same thing they do at the start of any other meeting—they sit down. And when they sit down they usually sit in the same seat they always sit in, across the conference table from the same person they always sit across from. The space a brainstorming session takes place in, and the way that space is inhabited, should reflect that a premium is being placed on the energy needed in the generation of fresh ideas. Rigid structure leads to rigid thinking, and lazy routines lead to lazy ideation. A leader who wants energy, focus, and interaction to be at the highest possible levels should shake things up. Get rid of the table and the chairs. Fight against gravity by keeping the team on its feet. If the table can't be moved, remove the chairs and stand around it. If it's too difficult to get the chairs out of the way, at least insist that people sit in different seats or keep changing seats during the session. (If technology has been eliminated and no one is writing anything, then there should be minimal baggage to be carted from seat to seat.) Physically altering one's perspective helps to keep minds alert and the energy in the room elevated.

Next, reduce the temperature in the room to 20° C, or 68° F. This may seem cold, but look at it this way: if you go into an improv theater one evening expecting to see some comedy and you have an alcoholic beverage and you sit down in a dark room with white lights focused on the stage and the theater is warm—what do you think will happen? If you are like most people at the end of a long day, you will fall asleep right away. We keep the theater cold, because comedy is a dish served cold. If you are cold, your skin reacts to the chill in the air; your body starts compensating (you bounce, rub your arms, etc.); you are mentally stimulated by the cool air, in contrast to being sedated by air that's too warm. Besides that, we are aiming for physical movement in the rooms, which will naturally increase the temperature of the room. A cool room is another simple, inexpensive way to inspire activity and engagement.

If a problem could easily be solved in a traditional, straightforward fashion, brainstorming wouldn't be necessary. If the point of the meeting is to come up with fresh ideas and get team buy-in (or build-in) for the ideas, the leader and participants must make the strategic decision to make sure the room is crackling with fresh energy.

Warm It Up

Before a roomful of minds becomes engaged in the task at hand, get that roomful of bodies active. Once team members are out of their chairs, they should be encouraged to move around. A meeting can begin with some sort of small, fun, unexpected physical activity—a group stretch, a game of musical chairs, or even a "wave" around the room. This isn't deep neuroscience; it's simple biology: the human brain works best when it's pumped full of oxygenated blood, and physical action gets that blood pumping. This step may encounter a little more resistance than some of the others at first, but it's a cost-free way of fostering team bonding and setting a desired energy level. If the energy or focus wanes during the session, add another warm-up to shake things up as necessary. Physical warm-ups also reinforce the very concept of team: team members who shake together are more likely to be present, supportive of each other, and committed to the process.[9]

Protect the Team

To the team leaders or execs calling for a brainstorming session in the first place, when you find the teams that take to this process and make it work—protect them. If you've got a team that embraces the whole process, from warm-ups to follow-through, and is dedicated to making a difference, treat them as prized, go-to thinkers, an elite Special Forces Idea Squad. Give them these tools and the training they need; put them in the best position to succeed; and then protect the environment you've created for your team to work in. Respect the process that's been established. Make sure that team members remain clear about expectations and the rules of the room, and get the people who don't want to be part of that team out of there (before they can make the forces less special).

This ties directly to that all-purpose tool of improvisation: postponement of judgment. We've seen that the postponing of judgment is crucial to the "Yes, and" approach to personal creativity and interpersonal communication, and it is especially crucial as a leadership tool to facilitate productive ideation. Within the specific dynamics of a brainstorming session (the divergent thinking side), postponement of judgment ensures that a team member's role is simply to contribute and support, not to critique. This concept is expanded a bit during brainstorming to include individuals' judgments of their own ideas. For ideas to flow as freely as rainwater, people must turn off their internal censor and allow themselves to be both vulnerable and spontaneous. This can be a very difficult dynamic to instill in a roomful of thinkers who are not used to it, though once the ideation session is effectively established as a safe zone—a divergent thinking arena in which everyone is asked to speak openly and in which no particular position needs to be defended—it's amazing how productive the communication becomes.

Remember that a postponement of judgment simply means that judgment must be deferred to the appropriate time. Let's be honest here: to drive raw ideas to productive use, the judgment process is insanely important. Moreover team members' critical decision-making abilities may be in large part the asset that earned them a spot on the team in the first place. However, when people revert to employing their critical-thinking skills too quickly, they miss the chance to recognize opportunities in the unexpected. They also miss the opportunity to show that the ideas and input of others are valued. Leaders of a brainstorming team as well as all team members must remain disciplined about exercising a postponement of judgment and must insist that the team stay equally disciplined. Don't inadvertently throw out the gold just because it's covered in mud. Pan gold like ol' Jebediah and then later sift out the sand and the muck and the mud.

Brainstorming sessions must be energetic, fun, focused, creative, inspirational, and ultimately productive. Leaders and team members should not allow any negativity to impinge on that. Cognitive psychologists have proven that moods are contagious and positive moods facilitate creativity.[10] Keep the attitude positive and the energy high. Remain supportive and protective of the team. Celebrate the last great idea thought up, and look forward to the next.

Stay Divergent

The heart of improvisational brainstorming is a well-managed flow of divergent thinking. As defined in the Introduction, divergent thinking allows ideas to radiate from a single point of origin (a problem, a challenge, a question, a need) and leaves those ideas free to head in any direction. The goal is to see how far away from the point of origin you can go and how many ideas can be listed. Such ideation is not to be hampered by self-judgment in the person thinking up an idea, or by a fear of judgment from other participants. An embrace of divergent thinking means that the mud and muck in the water are accepted as part of the process right along with the flecks of gold. In the divergent thinking phase failure is encouraged, even celebrated, so that failure (just like risk taking) becomes irrelevant. Again the point here is not that a business is better off seeking ideas that fail, but that truly great ideas emerge when people feel free to fail.

For divergent thinking to succeed, the creative process must be clearly separated from the urge to edit, analyze, question, and refine. Ideation is a creative process, and creation is always messy (no matter how elegant the oil painting, you can be sure there are dirty brushes and spattered paint in the artist's studio). The participants in a brainstorming session must allow for this and accept that there is no one single correct way to create. (Paint-by-numbers creation will give you a lot of safe, less-messy, "inside the box" ideas—that someone else actually created.) That said, creativity is still a defined process. When a session moves into divergent thinking, this is the time to be fearless and bold and to actually celebrate mistakes. There's no tally of failures and success; it's all about participation. There's no "best answer" but simply an effort to pile up as many answers as can be thought up. By focusing on the sheer number of ideas (quantity over quality), success in the divergent thinking phase increases the probability for success in the convergent thinking phase. The bad ideas inspire the good ideas, and vise versa. The editing process (convergent thinking) will come later and will offer plenty of time to focus the ideas, remove the "bad ideas," find the "best answer," and fine-tune the raw concepts into productive, utilitarian ones.

Remember that the divergent/creation process is completely different from the convergent/editing process. Maintaining a disciplined approach to divergent thinking in a roomful of talented people, especially critical thinkers, can be tricky. Humans have a tendency to adopt mental framing, and in a corporate setting we are quick to think about the parameters, the cost, the logistics, the rules and regulations, and even the people that would prohibit us from doing something differently—why we can't do it. Have you ever been in a brainstorming session in which an idea that's presented is almost immediately rejected because somebody deems it too costly or not likely to be successful ("We tried that before and it did not work")? All of a sudden this session switches from one of free-flowing ideas to one in which there are right answers and wrong answers. The conformity pressure to commit to the group and the task becomes inverted; now, instead of each member not wanting to be the one who isn't participating (not wanting to be the last one in the river), each member is thinking that he or she doesn't want to be the one to speak up and risk looking foolish (to get in the river at all).

When divergent thinking is truly embraced the notion of "risk taking" actually disappears. When everybody in the meeting enthusiastically accepts every idea, then nobody is really taking a risk and everybody is free to contribute. Oddly when the notion of risk taking disappears people are emboldened to take tremendous risks. The assessment of all that risk taking is really only a consideration in the next process, when convergent thinking and judgment is (re)applied. In the divergent phase the concept of risk doesn't exist—it's all about participation and generating the greatest number of ideas. This is a prime area for the leader of a brainstorming session to lead by example and intentionally submit "bad" ideas that would never work. The leader should be willing to present truly ridiculous ideas early in the process to demonstrate that it is acceptable to "fail" this way at this time.

There is some common and very dangerous corporate conventional wisdom concerning idea creation: that editing in real time, while we are creating, will actually speed up the process and save everyone time.

Like a reverse epidemic, this obstacle to divergent thinking can spread from the group to the individual and manifest itself in the form of self-judgment and self-editing. For some it is a choice to censor their ideas in real time and try to fine-tune them into great ideas before they voice them—the assumption being that thinking and talking more "realistically" (negatively) is a sign of seriousness and intelligence. Others have made a less cognitive decision and have fallen into the subconscious habit of judging their own ideas while they are trying to create. Whatever the case, the idea is that we will reduce the overall time spent on a project by pulling convergent thinking into the divergent phase. In truth this misconception creates huge blocks to creativity and collaboration and is counterproductive. You actually end up spending significantly more time straddling the two processes—judging on the fly—than you would by clearly separating each process and respecting the different focus of each. To sum up, people in any business setting will save significant amounts of time by keeping creativity and judgment as two very separate processes.

Get Convergent

I have passionately argued that the practice of creation is completely different from the practice of editing, and we should honor and respect both processes as two unique and imperative approaches. I hold this truth to be self-evident. So, let's look now at the very important second half of brainstorming: convergent thinking.

Editing, analyzing, critiquing, and fine-tuning are necessary. Without this process there are no books (like this one), no movies, no songs, no commercials, no advertisements, no proposals, and no focused, strategic mission. After all, if you do not take time to sift the pan and toss out the water, the mud, and the fool's gold, all you have is a pan full of muck. Failure is part of the process; failure is not the point of the process. After a prescribed period has elapsed, the wild collection of ideas accumulated through divergent thinking must be sorted. This is the time to begin questioning, analyzing, and critiquing (notice I did not say "criticizing"), always within the respectful and supportive rules of "Yes, and" communication.

The divergent phase of a brainstorm can take as little as ten minutes and may also last many hours if a particular challenge requires that kind of focused time investment. Once the great pile of ideas has been amassed, it's time to enter the convergent thinking phase. For me the first step in convergent thinking is prioritization. What is the top tier of ideas that look incredibly promising and even like low-hanging fruit; what is the middle tier of ideas that are promising but problematic; and what is the bottom tier of ideas that are unworkable and should be dismissed? If this is a solo project, the prioritization should be thoughtful and relatively quick at this point. However, if team buy-in and ownership (build-in) are needed, the process may become convoluted and devolve into the realm of disrespect. Here is an effective way to keep the "Yes, and" mentality even when you are in the convergent process of judging ideas:

> If this is a group decision-making exercise, an incredibly easy way is to "bucket" the large master list of ideas into the three categories by voting for them. For this first round of convergent thinking you and each person get as many (or as few) votes as you want. However, you only get one vote per idea and you are only voting for the ideas you like. (There is no reason to focus energy on the ideas you don't like.) What you will see is that the best ideas will receive more votes from the group. The result of this approach is almost a Darwinesque natural selection of ideas, wherein the strongest ideas rise to the surface to survive, and the weakest ideas fall to the wayside relatively quickly. Focus now on the top tier(s) and prioritize once more, from the best idea down. Pick one of your top ideas as a project and enter back into the divergent thinking phase to blow it up. Once that process is done, prioritize the ideas for the project in another round of convergent thinking. Depending on the detail needed for your project, you may need to practice the divergent/convergent approaches several times through. Thoughtfully bounce back and forth from divergent to

convergent thinking, fleshing out and developing the project until ultimately an action plan for the execution of the project begins to fall into place.

It's amazing how quickly a consensus on what's "best" can be formed in a group that has established a climate of open communication and positive focus. Maintaining that climate is crucial. It's important here to reinforce the idea that brainstorming is a team event. No one owns a particular idea. No credit is going to be given to or taken away from individuals because of a single idea. All the ideas that are collected during the divergent thinking phase are group ideas, and in prioritizing those ideas in convergent thinking the group still functions without regard to the status or rank of the people who contributed any particular idea. During the prioritization phase the group is separating the obvious muck in the pan from the possible flecks of gold.

In convergent thinking judgment is no longer postponed. Members of a team now apply critical thinking to sort out the bad ideas, discuss the okay-maybe doable ideas, question the ideas that need clarity, determine the most workable ideas, and bring that wide range of initial thoughts back to a single, productive conclusion. If divergent thinking is the time for unbridled creation, convergent thinking is the time for driving to innovation—the development of new ideas to a productive use. In convergent thinking the biggest, brightest ideas are finally refined into shiny, singular bars of gold.

Divergent thinking is Jeffersonian: all ideas are created equal. Convergent thinking is Darwinian: only the strongest ideas will survive and evolve. This is the editing end of the creative process, in which ideas are whittled down, debated, critiqued, and tweaked with an eye toward a final product. Perhaps there really is no budget for an otherwise great idea (an elephant parade). Perhaps what sounded like an intriguing bit of thinking outside the box would actually result in a PR nightmare. Perhaps, after being fully explored, what was once thought of as an inspiring idea simply cannot work at this time. This type of discussion can and should come up freely now. However, as suggested, convergent thinking should not suddenly give license to destroy the goodwill and spirit of creative collaboration that's been established. Reinforce that nobody owns an idea individually; the team owns all the ideas and will handle all ideas with respect, even when—in this phase—some ideas are being dismissed. Cling to "Yes, and . . . " here as well. It will help protect the team, manage conflict, and keep communication paramount.

Support the Big Idea

A couple of times now I've mentioned Del Close's wisdom that "the worst idea with great support will go much further than the best idea with no support." I'll point out here that Del was not giving a shout-out to terrible ideas. Quite the opposite. He protected the art of improv and the quality of performance in his classroom as fiercely as a lion protects his pride. Rather his words were a strong reminder that the great idea needs the full support of the team. That support is created when every member feels their participation is valuable and valued, and that the ideas they generate are valuable and valued. If someone comes up with that great idea and gets no support, nothing is going to happen and the whole point of idea sharing has been defeated. You need a team to support the great idea, with the understanding that "greatness" is not always evident right from square one. By creating a team environment in which there are initially no bad ideas and everyone has to participate, intrinsic motivation to recognize and support greatness emerges from each individual.[11]

It is in this environment where we should once again take advantage of the opportunity to embrace diversity. Though race, gender, religion, ethnicity, and age are all ways to measure diversity, what we are talking about here is a celebration of diverse perspectives. These perspectives are informed and influenced by unique circumstances: education, background, family, habits and rituals, and general life experiences. In creating a culture of acceptance through divergent thinking, we have a true opportunity to dive into the nuances that make each of us unique and to peak inside the heads of each person in our team.[12]

Repeat as Necessary

Brainstorming can and should be part of the infrastructure of a company—its "idea factory." Along those lines I recommend that improvisational, creative, idea-sharing sessions be made a regular part of the business week, perhaps something that happens every Monday morning for (only) 15 or 30 minutes. Look for opportunities to practice, practice, practice. If decisions need to be made about how to present something to a client, how to reorganize a department, or even how to plan a company party, collaborate and brainstorm when appropriate opportunity arises. The more the process is practiced, the stronger the team gets at it and the easier it is to get to great ideas. The process is incredibly difficult to develop during a crisis, when it is needed most; a business's ideation team should not be instantly stressed out every time a session is called because they know something has gone terribly wrong. Keep your elite Special Forces Ideation Team trained and in shape!

It's understandable that people who are not used to an improvisational approach to ideation are at first going to feel constrained by it. When I'm confronted by status quo bias ("We can't do that because it's not the way we're used to doing that"), I like to evoke the challenge of learning to ride a bicycle. The first time any of us got on a Schwinn minus the training wheels, the challenge of staying upright, moving forward, and steering around obstacles was completely awkward and daunting. It's highly likely that a maiden ride ended with a fall, a skinned knee, or a collision with a tree. However, it's almost universally true that this challenge was not anxiety filled at all the 50th or 500th time you mounted the bike. Experience, managed expectation, and muscle memory made riding a bike a pleasure rather than a challenge. (For those who grew up without getting on a Schwinn, think of the act of typing: was your very first time at a computer keyboard different from your 500th time?)

The "conscious competence" learning model in psychology was originally developed at Gordon Training International in the 1970s and is a good way to frame the learning stages to get to muscle memory.[13] Originally chronicled as "Four Stages for Learning Any New Skill," the development paradigm shows the arc of mastering a new skill (muscle memory) through four psychological conditions in the course of growing from totally incompetent to completely competent in a skill, like riding a bike, learning new software, or using improv techniques. In a nutshell:

1. *Unconscious incompetence.* You do not know what you do not know. You are blissfully ignorant.

2. *Conscious incompetence.* You know that you do not know how to do something; however, you choose not to learn. You are intentionally ignorant.

3. *Conscious competence.* You know how to do something. You are no longer ignorant; however, it takes concentration and a concerted effort to accomplish the task.

4. *Unconscious competence.* You have mastered the task and you can execute it flawlessly, without thinking about it.

Practice makes collaboration something important. If a business wants a team to be working at the highest possible level, the process deserves time and attention. If you make the decision not to practice this process, you are assuming that whatever you come up with when you need to brainstorm will automatically be the best idea you can come up with. In other words you are saying that you can stick your hand in the mud anywhere along the brainstorming river and pull out a gold ring. Given a choice, I'd rather work with an expert, find a precise location on the river, take a large pan, and pull up as much as I can from the river, and thereby increase the probability of finding gold. Practicing "Yes, and" and divergent thinking is about increasing the probability for success when you need it most.

Sometimes you need a little encouragement to take a first step, a first bike ride, or a first dip into the river. So I would encourage you to begin practicing improvisational ideation by using this pair of simple guidelines for two initial brainstorming meetings:

Meeting 1. Review the concepts above, then assemble your team. Be honest about what you're doing ("We are going to try a new way of coming up with and sharing ideas"). Lay down the laws of the room as necessary; be clear about your expectations for the meeting and for each and every participant. Assign somebody the role of scribe, whose job it is to record all ideas, postponing judgment about what he might think is a "real" idea or just a goofball joke. Everything gets captured. If the meeting room doesn't feel conducive to a new way of thinking, move the damn chairs around. Set the proper energy level; use a warm-up when necessary.

State your real and specific challenge to the group ("We need to shift to a customer-focused sales strategy").

Diverge (15–30 min.). How many odd, inventive, wild, improbable, even crackpot ideas can your team come up with to address this challenge under brief time constraints? Everything is game and must be captured by the scribe even if it does not directly address the challenge you've presented. Lead by example by occasionally saying the craziest ideas that would never work (there's that elephant parade again). With that in mind maintain a balance between getting wild and staying on task. Coming up with ideas that are not directly relevant does not mean going on a tangent and losing your way for 15 minutes. Loosely guide the team rather than forcefully confine them. Each idea is stated and captured, and then you move on to the next idea without exploration, explanation, examination, or even consideration.

Converge (15–30 min.). Prioritize, organizing like ideas into tiers if necessary. Discuss and deconstruct the ideas at the top of each tier, and prioritize those. Talk about the plusses and minuses of ideas. When a number one idea (or at least a top tier of ideas) is agreed on, the meeting is over.

Meeting 2. Assemble your team and repeat the brainstorming set-up initiated in Meeting 1. Keep your team focused on the end goal by restating your mission to the group ("We need to shift to a customer-focused sales strategy").

Diverge (15–30 min.). Using your previously established number one idea (or one from your top tier of ideas) as a starting point, direct team members to freely explore ways this idea might be strategically executed. Use simple, critical questions (who? what? where? when? how? why?) as a way to flesh out every important detail of the idea. Diverge on specific parts of the number one idea to help figure out possible best action plans for success. Think big, fail early, and fail often—and reach for the stars here! Budgets, timelines, and other constraints can be postponed to get the greatest number of ideas.

Converge (15–30 min.). Put on the serious thinking caps. Now all ideas must be judged against real-world constraints (budgets, timelines, personnel, etc.). Critique, edit, discuss, debate, and fine-tune, quickly reentering the divergent phase when ideas need to be fleshed out more fully, until the team has settled on an action plan for executing the number one idea.

I hope this approach to brainstorming sounds easy, because it is. However, I've been a human being long enough to understand that simply asking a group of people to be better, more supportive communicators in no way guarantees better, more supportive communication. In the brainstorming process one of the common obstacles to creativity occurs in the convergent thinking phase. People will generally embrace the idea of being divergent—of being free to speak and supporting everyone else's freedom to speak. When it comes to getting convergent though, the same people can get nasty: you've been sitting there for 20 minutes working hard to be accepting of wild ideas; now's your chance to shoot them down with extreme prejudice. In the convergent phase you want the strongest idea rather than the strongest personality to dominate.

Here are some additional tips for fostering successful convergent thinking while being respectful and protecting each and every member of your team. If you are trying to lead a group discussion of each idea that was raised in the divergent phase, you may be up against faulty memories and a blurring or forgetting of details. Instead of talking through the ideas, write each of them down in simple form—a one, two, or three-word bullet—and post them on the walls (sketches are welcome!). Then have the group vote for them anonymously (Post-it notes, stars, a ballot box, Hello Kitty stickers, etc.). If this project is large and affects the entire company or a larger group than just the team brainstorming, send out the big, messy list of ideas (or at least the top two tiers) to the larger group via e-mail, and ask the masses to vote for the ideas through a free polling software (such as Survey Monkey). This will allow the larger, more objective group to vote anonymously, thereby promoting honesty and at the same time increasing company ownership of the change, direction, decision, or ideas. Here are the voting rules:

1. Only vote for the ideas you like; there is little need to discuss anything you do not like. This keeps the focus on the positive rather than the negative.

2. Mob rules: the group mind makes the decision. You are not trying to create meshing cogs in a groupthink machine. Rather you want to facilitate the ability of intelligent people to exercise their individual right to make choices in a group setting (especially when anonymous). Whatever the results, they will be shared and mutually supported.

As I've said often enough by now, improvisation is a tool and not every tool is right for every job. Undoubtedly there are times in every business when "good enough" truly is good enough. There are times when it is simply not necessary to reinvent the (bicycle) wheel or brainstorm through a simple idea; or when there just isn't time and "No" is the only right answer (Get those elephants out of here!). As always, it's up to every business and every leader to decide when this particular approach will be useful and effective.

The trick to making use of improvisational ideation is often a matter of mental framing: think about where this approach to brainstorming might really work as opposed to all the situations in which it definitely won't. You will find that you'll be able to apply it much more often than you thought. If you can't utilize improvisational brainstorming for every decision the company needs to make, then don't. Use it when it will be of value. Just remember that "good enough" isn't much of a business plan. If you're truly interested in getting to great ideas, then don't be afraid of panning through the muck to get to the gold.

And don't forget: gold needs to be invested, not simply hoarded. With that in mind, let's explore how poor team dynamics can lead to wealth being siloed rather than shared, and how that siloing can be avoided in a more open, improvisational corporate culture.

Chapter 7

BUSTED

I THINK BY NOW I HAVE MADE IT CLEAR that while the critical first step in changing a corporate culture is to commit to initiating positive change (first on an individual basis, then on an interpersonal and small-group basis, and then on a larger team basis), the even more critical follow-up step is to put in the effort to sustain those changes. If you have taken steps to instill "Yes, and . . . " communication, developed habits of self-auditing and mindfulness, become aware of how to reach energy sweet spots, assembled (or begun to assemble) elite teams, and encouraged open ideation among colleagues, then all of these changes must be continually developed, practiced, and fiercely protected.

Sometimes, though, that protection can itself become a problem. If individuals, small groups, teams, or departments within a company become self-protective to the point of becoming insulated and isolated from the rest of the company, the company might suffer—no matter how many best practices have been put into place in the isolated group. This is familiarly known as siloing, stove-piping, or chimneying, and it remains one of the problems I am most frequently asked to deal with in ailing companies. Let's blow up some silos.

Back in 2003 the American Management Association published a survey in which 83 percent of the respondents acknowledged that there were silos in their companies, and 97 percent of that group said that siloing had a negative effect on their company.[1] In the years since then the trend in business has been for management to become less hierarchical and more team oriented. One might assume that a lot of silos have been toppled. In fact the problem is still with us and in some ways has become even more prevalent. The classic silo problem might have been envisioned as something that happened in the largest companies when one department just refused to play well with others ("Those slick marketing guys don't ever tell anyone in sales what they're up to"). Turns out that silos can be put up just about anywhere, in any size company, even within the teams and departments of a company. It's not just a problem for behemoths with 50,000 employees—even small businesses at the 50-employee level can run into siloing trouble.

Just to be clear about terms, picture for a moment a real silo on a farm. The silo is an individual structure and primarily does one thing: stores corn or other grain. It is vertically oriented and is designed to do its one task no matter what else is happening on the farm. In that setting the silo is not a problem: the farmer is perfectly happy with a silo that is insulated and isolated, as long as it accomplishes its one task of containment.

In a business setting the separate, single-minded silo is rarely an asset. If we get a little more metaphorical and think of the workplace silo as something that contains communication rather than barleycorn, the containment of that communication usually works against a company's overall interests. When groups, teams, or departments begin to act as their own independent entity and don't allow communication to flow inward from or outward to other people, teams, projects, and departments, a company is going to suffer from competitive turf wars, sagging morale, and poor relationships (internally within the company and externally with customers and clients). That suffering will eventually impact profits.

The solution to silos is, logically enough, silo busting. That's the process of letting all the elements of a company know that there will be no independent entities allowed to function on their own.[2] No matter what team you're on or what department you're in, communication with other people in the company—horizontal communication—is required. Teams must share with other teams, not only to learn best practices but also to learn about pitfalls and challenges. To mix the metaphor (while staying on the farm), when we bust silos we are proclaiming that no one gets to be the corn that stands alone.

There are rare times when siloing would fit the nature of the work being done (note that in the AMA survey cited above there were a whopping 3 percent of respondents who didn't feel silos were a problem). Such positive silo scenarios might include things like government work in which classified information is being handled, military operations in which secrecy is required, or medical research in which a study must be conducted independently and must stand on its own. Sometimes a very strict division of labor is required to get a job done, and if you have strong teams with specific expertise working toward a specific goal, that division of labor makes sense. The classified government work ostensibly has the nation's welfare in mind; the military mission is part of an overall strategy; and the medical research aims to benefit the public at large. A thoughtful, strategic approach to a division of labor is not the kind of siloing that produces problems.

However, what we do in the business world rarely rises to the life-and-death matters dealt with by SEAL Team 6 or doctors working toward miracle cures. The chances that a given silo is a good thing are pretty slim, especially over long periods. Even in the realm of top-secret data and classified information, recent history has shown us that silos can be counterproductive. Probably the greatest example of governmental silo busting over the last couple of decades occurred in the wake of the September 11 attacks with the establishment of the Department of Homeland Security (DHS) and the Director of National Intelligence (DNI).[3]

The DHS was established to facilitate communication between 22 separate federal agencies from the Coast Guard to the Secret Service, and to make sure that all these agencies, each with their own culture and history and communication channels, worked together toward common goals: keeping America and Americans safe on our home turf. Similarly the position of DNI was created to oversee the 17 agencies of the U.S. intelligence community (CIA, FBI, DEA, etc.) and to ensure that information relevant to national security was not hoarded by any one agency. We can leave it to historians and political pundits to decide whether the DHS and DNI truly busted silos or just created one humongous, better-fortified silo in which to store a group of smaller silos. The point, though, is that both were created because the perils of noncommunicative teams and departments could not be ignored.

Siloing naturally exists in organizations that have recently merged with other companies and have yet to consolidate into one organization. Silos also exist in organizations that have different departments in which there is limited perceived benefit to sharing information. And silos are inherent in organizations that have multiple branches that operate autonomously from each other with their own sets of problems. In each example, however, there is a real need to unify the company, establish trust, and have people talking and sharing best practices with each other.

Why Go Bust?

The breaking up of silos isn't just something that needs to be done when things go wrong. Even within a company that appears to be functioning well, the presence of silos precludes greater success. When you break down silos you are opening up intracompany communication, which means that ideas, opinions, and perspectives get shared between and across divisions. When that happens everybody has a chance to hear the ideas that are working best for everyone else. The actual practical details of changes made by the folks in the marketing department may not be directly applicable to the accounting folks, yet learning about those changes might influence conversations in accounting that ultimately lead to an aha discovery saving the company tens of thousands of dollars. And maybe this knowledge leads to the accounting folks instituting changes in their department that stream-line a process and make life easier for the marketing guys. Maybe just hearing that the IT folks took care of a problem in their department will spark other departments to spot and take care of similar prob-lems. If communication is shut down and siloed, there is little likeli-hood of this kind of cross-pollination occurring.

Another tremendous benefit from busting up silos is an increase in the diversity of perspectives based on occupation, background, edu-cation, relationships, and experience—that is, the differing points of view that relate to what an employee does for and brings to a com-pany. As employees each of us represents a unique bundle of back-ground, training, skills, and responsibilities. It's good to hear each other's voices because those voices have value whether they come from the next cubicle over or from a department two floors away. In breaking down silos we are essentially asking individuals, teams, and departments to "Yes, and" each other and open themselves to the pos-sibility that somebody else has something valuable to say.

If I don't have your background or your job, your education, or your life experiences, then I must acknowledge that I don't see things the same exact way you see them. How can I possibly assume that I know what you're going to say and why you're saying it, or that what you have to say is incorrect or irrelevant? It is my obligation to stay open minded, to postpone judgment, to listen carefully, and to think about what you are saying before making a thoughtful decision on how to react. (Remember, there is more than one way to hit a piñata, and you never know which crack of that bad boy is gonna get you to the good stuff inside!) The point of busting silos is to make it clear to everyone that we are one company and that this company runs at its best when all employees are committed to supporting and learn-ing from each other through clear, open, and honest communication. With silos gone the greater good of the company, project, team, and collaborative process can be more readily achieved.

Breaking down silos encourages sharing, and sharing is caring.

Too cheesy for you? Me too, because it is not necessarily true. It's not just the sharing and caring that matter—it's *what* gets shared in an open, siloless company that makes its corporate culture a healthy one. On the most practical level, facilitating the sharing of information should be a top concern because if one group has information that might be pertinent and helpful for any other group, there's absolutely no benefit in having that information sequestered. Additionally if a team within a company has collected evidence of a pitfall, or figured out ways to troubleshoot a tricky unanticipated challenge, there is absolutely no reason other teams should not learn from that same evidence.

It all comes down to the point I've made before about the difference between individual agenda and individual perspective. Align the two. Every team, group, department, and division within a company should be heartily encouraged to have its own perspective. That perspective and the skill sets behind it are exactly why any specific team has been given its own responsibilities and challenges. A company cannot succeed though if every team develops its own agenda. The mythical, monstrous Hydra was probably proud of its many heads, but those heads served the purposes of a common body.

Even if those private agendas happen to fall within company goals, they are almost certainly going to create problems of unhealthy or unnecessary competition within a company. Certainly company leaders want all teams to strive to be their best. However, if teams are measuring their own worth strictly on the basis of team success and disregard what they're doing to serve the greater company, communication will break down. In a workplace where people are ensconced in silos, why would any department share information if they believe another department's success puts their own bonuses at risk? To return to the more serious example of 9/11, a lot of coverage was devoted to the difficulty that the NYPD, the fire department, the Port Authority, and the EMS teams had communicating with each other in the wake of the crisis; each department had its own communications system and not enough thought and planning had gone into the interoperability of those systems.[4]

In a business context the overriding agenda of any company is the company's success. Success may be defined by annual profits or by a mission statement. Either way, the company's goal represents the "greater good" and is the ultimate trump card. A company is in trouble if personal, team, and department agendas are at odds with company goals. Silos foster these private agendas. When silos are broken down, the ulterior motives inherent in private agendas are broken down as well. Without silos every employee of a company will likely feel they have equal buy-in and ownership of a company's success.

Conversely, when the workplace is free of silos employees may become openly aware of a company's overall struggles. (Employees often hear about the struggles anyway; the hamsters powering the rumor mill rarely rest.) There is no benefit in having employees feel that a struggling department can just sink on its own independently of every other department. With silos gone a departmental problem is recognized as a company problem and best practices can aid in creating success out of a struggle. And when the whole ship is going down, all hands have a stake in doing what they can to right it and get it back on course.

I would also contend that silo busting is not just necessary for optimal internal communications within a company. It also opens up and improves the communication a company has with external agents—most significantly clients and customers. As business author Daniel Pink has pointed out, the U.S. economy has transformed from one of "buyer beware" (caveat emptor) to one of "seller beware" (caveat venditor).[5] Customers are smarter than ever before and now have the ability to access enormous amounts of information about any company they do business with or any product they consider purchasing. A brief Google search of a company or a product can lead you down the rabbit hole of virtual communication and information sharing. Facebook groups, chat rooms, and even Twitter hashtags are examples of arenas in which anyone can quickly find a wealth of information, opinions, and guidance that strangers freely share around their learned experiences. It's very easy to cross-check customer/client experiences, so easy that customers and clients cannot be thought of as individual entities—they make up an integrated, well-informed virtual community. To put it another way, the customer is no longer siloed from your company, your competition, or even other customers.

More importantly silos within a company have zero value to a customer. A client doesn't care that a standoffish, siloed human resources department thinks it's doing a great job if that client's ultimate experience with a company is a poor one. That customer may do some silo breaking of her own and join a social media group to communicate her dissatisfactory experience. If the silos in your company are getting in the way of a great experience for the customers and clients your company is supposed to serve, you had better get moving to knock those silos down.

Getting Busted

Sometimes silo busting requires structural change in a company. Sometimes the busting can be achieved at a more practical level. One prominent U.S. business school found a very logistical solution to siloing. When it became evident that the administrative processes of the school had become unnecessarily inefficient because of a lack of communication between departments, the answer was not to bring in communication coaches or to send staff off to executive education programs. The solution was to simply scramble the layout of offices so that almost no one had an office that was next to someone in the same department. All of a sudden somebody in finance found themselves in between people in international law and integrated marketing. Through the brute force of physical proximity, people in different departments were forced to interact with each other—which led them first to feel more curious about each other, then to communicate more with each other, and then to the great cross-pollination of ideas and open communication that silo busting always seeks to achieve. When people had to see each other in the halls and spend time around the same coffee station for their afternoon cup of java, silos started to tumble.

We are just beginning to see some of this type of silo busting in of all places the automotive sales industry. Some car dealerships have begun to do away with having salespeople work on commission, so it no longer benefits a salesperson to be competitively territorial, to hoard information or hide it from a colleague, or to undermine anyone else to make their own sale. The act of eliminating commissions sends the signal to the entire organization that "we are one company and we are all in this together." A certain amount of commission can work as personal incentive, but if people are working on 100 percent commission they are likely siloed. Any of us who have ever felt uncomfortable when a car salesperson swoops in the moment we step onto a car lot knows that this kind of siloing does not serve the customer well. Knock down the silos and the customer is in for a much more pleasant experience. Business Improv worked directly with one of these companies, Sonic Automotive, who not only did away with sales commissions but made it mandatory that employees from all departments in all stores—from the salesmen to the mechanics to the cashiers to the GMs—communicate openly and often, with everyone sharing the responsibility for a successful customer experience.

Technology can also become an ally in the fight against silos. A prominent consultancy agency created a common web portal on which project information could be shared. Teams in various cities— Boston, Chicago, Los Angeles, etc.—posted slide decks, strategies for dealing with various challenges, ways to avoid pitfalls and quicksand, ways to handle conflict, and troubleshooting techniques. As a result of sharing this material in a virtual community, people from various departments in a number of cities established relationships with each other and even picked up the phone and talked to one another.

Here are some ways to bust organizational silos:

- Make communication an imperative and hold people accountable.

- Create the architecture—a bridge for consistency in communication. A weekly meeting is the perfect opportunity to share pitfalls, struggles, and best practices and to learn from others. This can also be done in daily, fast, touch-base meetings, and if you operate remotely from each other a shared web page is a great way to post and share information.

- Encourage people to actively look for and communicate opportunities for improvement outside of their direct duties.

- Encourage people to take ownership of an issue, even if it is not their job. "If there is a problem you can fix, then fix it. You don't need permission. Just tell me, after the fact, what it was and how you fixed it, so we can avoid the same problem again in the future."[6]

- Hold people accountable when communication slips or opportunities that are ever present are not communicated.

Checking Out

Some structural silos are the almost unavoidable result of the way work-related hierarchies have been developed and maintained (an example of this would be those 22 government agencies that stood alone before being integrated into the Department of Homeland Security). They can also be "structural" due to geographical challenges. For example, some organizations—like the various departments of the UN—may not have each division located in the same building or even the same country, and the logistical challenges of working in a different location or culture may create silos.

Much more often, though, silos are self-developed and self-imposed. They reflect conscious and subconscious choices made by employees and managers. Breaking down silos is a matter of opening up communication, which is why the techniques of improvisation are useful in resolving the problems created by silos. I think the best way to explain exactly how improvisation can destroy troublesome silos is to take a look at a case history—a luxury hotel in Dubai.

The hotel was an iconic landmark and had received praise for its beautiful design, fantastic service, and excellent food. The property included a convention center and had great appeal as a high-end, all-inclusive stop for business travelers. The hotel had achieved excellence in everything it initially set out to accomplish. What it lacked was an ability to adapt.

Since the dawn of Dubai's oil economy in the 1960s, change and development have happened at a dizzying pace. In the early 2000s, when Dubai positioned itself as an increasingly important business destination, there was a rush to develop luxury hotels. The newer hotels recognized that while the existing hotels served businesspeople well, they offered minimal services to family members who might be traveling with the businessperson. If a traveler did bring the family along to the older-model hotels, it was stuck with the less than exciting choice of hanging out in a hotel lounge or figuring out something to do in Dubai's 115°-plus Fahrenheit heat. The newer hotels had fabulous family attractions—incredible water parks, ice rinks, and indoor ski slopes, and even access to what still ranks as the largest mall in the world, all while providing adequate space to hold business meetings and conventions. Competition had changed Dubai from a business destination into a legitimate family destination.[7] If a business traveler was going to travel that far around the world and wanted to be with his or her family, the newer hotels would offer the ability for the traveler to conduct business, the family to have a blast, and everyone to get back together in the evening. All of a sudden that fancy older hotel went from a five-star booking to a place that was simply not the best overall option.

This older hotel had been one of the first into the market and had run hard to establish itself. And while running hard, hotel management had spent more time maintaining its own success rather than looking over its shoulder. Now they were up against brutal competition, and the bottom line was that the bottom line was affected—money that had at first been easier to make was now drying up like water in the desert.

With business sputtering and occupancy down, the hotel had to trim fat. Departments were streamlined and people were let go without much explanation, which led to a morale problem for those who remained. As the hotel's future became more and more unknown, management struggled to understand and address the problems that its own staff were painfully aware of. Management promised again and again that change would take place and business would soon be booming again. When change didn't happen and more cuts were made, morale seriously sagged even lower. There was a lot of grumbling among employees, who had lost faith that they could make a difference in the overall success of the hotel. One result of all this discontent was that the separate departments of the hotel—25 of them in this case—unintentionally fortified their silos and stopped talking to each other.

The hotel business is no stranger to structural siloing. Classically the departments within a hotel tend not to communicate much with each other. Though the laundry may dialogue a bit with housekeeping, it has next to zero contact with security or the food and beverage team; guest services may not talk much with the engineering department; and of course no one wants to hear about accounting's problems. Every department essentially runs its own business with its own budget, reporting upward to a general manager. Hotels can easily end up with a series of vertical hierarchies—silos—in which everyone answers to two or three people above them but does not communicate laterally to any other division. That system can certainly function well if top management makes an ongoing effort to hear, address, and cross-pollinate every division's concerns. However, most top leaders (C-level, V-level, and GMs in this case) are incredibly busy and simply do not have the time to act as a bridge between every department, every day. They should make the time to be bridge-builders, so that each department knows that crossing the bridge from one part of the guests' experience to the next is not only wanted, it is a necessity.

When a system that doesn't naturally encourage cross-communication is in place and morale drops, the divisions between departments start to run even deeper and become tougher to bridge. A business in the process of changing is a business that needs more open and honest communication among departments, yet if the framework for that communication hasn't ever been created, people will respond to the difficulty of change by reverting to their most overlearned and overpracticed behaviors (such as shutting down).[8] While the heads of departments may continue to talk to each other, most employees hunker down in their insular silos and wouldn't think about building bridges or coming up with solutions for anything that falls outside of their own immediate responsibilities. Room service may see a way to solve a food and beverage problem, but that idea never gets communicated because there is no architecture for communication in place. Employees even start to limit their communication upward to their own department heads. A "That is not my job" attitude prevails, and the overall lack of communication gets shrugged off by way of status quo bias: "That's just the way it is."[9] All this marks the beginning of the hospitality-industry equivalent of an alligator death roll.

At the older Dubai hotel I was called in to work with, the management—to its credit—recognized that all this was happening. The people in senior leadership positions, rather than having a management-tilted bias, were honest about what was going wrong. They knew they had fallen behind their competition and they were taking steps to upgrade the hotel and its services. However, while they acknowledged that staff morale had plummeted and that interdepartmental communication was practically nonexistent, they weren't sure what to do to correct that. They had made an accurate self-diagnosis without an idea of what the prescription should be. I was brought in to begin treatment.

What I saw right away was a heck of a lot of silos. This was an element of the problem that management had not been aware of. From what I learned of the way the company was run, the morale issue was largely due to an accountability issue. People had stopped taking the initiative to fix anything, not just in other departments but even within their own departments as well. However, employees would talk to friends within their own department about the problems, thereby creating silos within silos. An attitude of "It's not my problem" had taken hold to such a degree that company growth was paralyzed. Solutions to problems were not being pursued because it was assumed that getting permission to make some positive change was not worth the effort. This attitude had gotten so bad that even little positive changes that could be made—changes that didn't require any permission from higher-ups—were left unexplored.

I saw one glimmer of hope in the fact that even as the business was struggling, the hotel was still very good about communicating guest experiences to all the departments. That showed me that cross-communication was possible; it just had to be opened up and encouraged. I realized I was looking at a large staff made up of people who wanted to do a good job and felt they had no voice and no support. They had come to feel that being successful at their own individual jobs was the only thing they could do to contribute to the hotel's overall success.

Checking In

My plan for silo busting at the Dubai hotel began by bringing together all 25 department heads and getting them to open their minds and be ready for some change management. That act alone turned out to be a powerful silo buster in itself. This was not the first time the leadership team had come together. In fact they met quarterly to discuss the problems of the hotel and how to succeed. The problem lay in the fact that the meetings would inevitably degenerate into defensive posturing, wherein the leaders would focus so single-mindedly on their own department needs (individual agendas) that they never shared best practices and how to help each other succeed for the greater good of the organization. They knew hotelwide change needed to take place. They just did not know how to embrace that change; they did not know how to model this change in their actions and they had no architecture for successful communication and collaboration. They sensed they were in silos, and they did not have the tools to bust out of them without help.

The Business Improv team proceeded to put these department heads through a one-and-a-half-day program in which there was a strong emphasis on how to make change happen and how to put accountability practices into place. All the basics of "Yes, and" communication were laid out in lectures and readings and reinforced through exercises and discussions. Small-group work was done with exercises in group decision making, adaptability, leveling status, divergent thinking, and developing focus and concentration. Again and again I emphasized the concept that a diversity of ideas was to be sought out and celebrated, and I was happy to see that this concept itself was cherished. The simple act of telling people that their voices were valued and that they needed to find value in others' voices had the effect of changing the energy and attitudes of the leaders. Gloom began to dissipate and a bit of optimism began to bubble up.

As the program progressed, I pushed the heads to find ways of communicating more effectively, not just with their staffs but with each other. I encouraged them to lead by example and to take on the real work of silo busting. Again there was great enthusiasm for this. In divergent thinking phases the participants put a tremendous amount of effort into coming up with ways they could let other departments know about pitfalls and obstacles being encountered, while also finding ways to marry successful solutions across departments to demonstrate how the change initiations were taking hold. The exercises I led for this program followed an arc, building from self-audit and individual accountability, to interpersonal communication, to small-group communication, to department communication, to intercompany communication, to creating an improvisational company culture.

Here's an example of one of the more effective silo-busting exercises:

Assemble a small team of six or so people from one department that is taking on a real work challenge. Add to the team one or two people from a completely separate department in the company, who have absolutely no idea of the challenge or any knowledge of struggles or successes the team's department has had in the past. Using both the "Yes, and" language and overall philosophy, have all members participate in an idea-sharing session (divergent thinking). In order to do this there must be an agreed understanding that

1. The outside person(s) entering the team will dive in fearlessly and participate to the top of their intelligence.

2. The group will work collectively to accept the new member(s) and incorporate them into the team as quickly and effectively as possible.

In divergent thinking the group should not deny, negate, or discuss restrictions or "how that did not work in the past." Rather they should accept every idea that the new members suggest.

Now enter into convergent thinking with the shared commitment to go into the judgment phase with minds open to discovery and thoughtful understanding. In other words enter into the convergent thinking phase with a divergent thinking attitude. Rather than purely judging ideas as "good" or "bad," talk with the new members about what they were thinking that led to their suggestions. Look to create a greater understanding of their unique perspective. For example, what you might find is a best practice that created a stop-gap measure in an approach that you tried but that "did not work in the past." By keeping an open mind to understand the new members' perspective, you learn that the stop-gap measure they used to deal with a previous challenge will actually work to solve a current problem for your team.

Wherever possible I stressed accountability and transferability in the Dubai hotel—the idea that the open communication we were establishing in the program wouldn't amount to much if it didn't find its way back to actual workplace practices. In silo busting at the hotel a part of the transferability depended on getting the heads to recognize the usefulness of manipulating status. They had to learn how to shatter entrenched hierarchies and siloed communications by lowering their own status within each of their departments. (As we discussed in the last chapter, if a boss's title is getting in the way of open communication, that boss needs to create an environment in which his or her own status is lowered, temporarily, so that open communication and a meritocracy of ideas can emerge.)

The department heads and I worked hard to come up with ways that the improvisation exercises could be translated into the workday, and some of the specific, practical takeaways they developed were inspiring. The head of laundry came up with a plan to use "Yes, and" techniques at the laundry staff meeting on Monday mornings. A security head decided to have one meeting a week with staff in which everyone would be free to raise issues and problems without any pressure to work toward a solution at that particular meeting; solutions would be worked out at a separate meeting. Other heads embraced plans to work out staff problems through wide-open ideation, making full use of divergent/convergent thinking techniques with other departments.

After a day and a half of very hard work, the department heads were revitalized, refocused, and primed for success. Silos looked ready to tumble. I would love to take personal credit for that, but it would do a disservice to the motivation, drive, and intelligence of the great leadership team in that hotel. I supplied these folks with tools and techniques they could use to bring back a natural flow of communication. Simply getting people together in a room and giving them improv techniques to postpone judgment and speak freely went a long way toward busting silos.

I would be remiss if I did not point out that this particular program did not happen without my coming up against a fair amount of resistance and skepticism. The accounting head was a particularly hard nut to crack. He was good at crossing his arms and rolling his eyes and did not think that anything I was doing would help his ailing workplace. Throughout the program I looked for opportunities to do some one-on-one work with him, during which I asked him to reframe his thinking about his role in the hotel. While it was entirely understandable that he should be concerned with the numbers, it was not his job simply to say "No" to people. He needed to see that his job was to help everyone else accomplish what they were trying to get done, even while keeping an eye on the numbers. Sometimes those numbers might dictate that "No" was the proper response. However, he occasionally had to consider that "Yes" was a possibility as well. By the end of the program it clicked for him. He could find ways to hear and support his colleagues while still protecting his balance sheets. And he understood that a hotel with a staff that felt it was being heard and supported would probably have greatly improved balance sheets in the long run.

Let's Jam

When silos are present in a company that I've been asked to help, one of the elements that I like to include in a multiday program is an improv Jam session. These are usually evening events—sometimes after very long days of a scheduled program—at which attendance is voluntary and the atmosphere is much looser. It's at the Jams that we embrace some of the classic short-form improv games that people are familiar with through TV shows like *Whose Line Is It Anyway?* Those Jams have a great value though, especially as an extension of a silo-busting program. The Jam is a demonstration of people stepping up to do something without any idea of what they're getting into, now in front of an audience of their peers! What feels like fun—because it is fun—is actually giving people a real opportunity to learn that they can operate in the unknown, can embrace the unexpected, and can benefit from the offers made by peers and collaborators.

While the Jam works as a pleasant decompression point at the end of a long day, it is also tremendously beneficial in developing all sorts of crucial intangibles that are necessary for silo busting: camaraderie, commitment, vulnerability, respect, unconditional support, heightened listening, heightened focus and observation, flexibility and fearlessness. These are precisely the things that are missing in a siloed workplace, and to have them introduced in a no-pressure, enjoyable context can actually turn this into one of the most memorable take-aways of the program. This was definitely the case in Dubai. After only one full day of improv the program participants used the Jam as a way of solidifying those first crucial, wobbly steps (that we had worked on all day) toward much better communication and company unity.

If the lessons of "Yes, and" can get some positive spirit and communal energy behind people, as in the Jams, then morale can change for the better very quickly. The more people learn about other coworkers, other teams, and other departments, the more they feel a connection with them.[10] The more they feel listened to and understood, the more they feel that they have value and will want to know about what is going on in other areas of the workplace. If a few leaders set the example of open communication, it shows that "this is the way we run our business" and others will mirror and mimic that behavior. Then when more people are performing that specific behavior, the more positive peer pressure (conformity pressure) is put on other leaders to communicate what they're doing in their departments. Once enough people feel they have permission and encouragement to communicate and once they have the tools to do so, there's just no point in being in a silo anymore.

Up, Down, and Sideways

There is one other important aspect of the "how" to consider when one is busting silos. Whether in physical or metaphorical form, a silo is a vertical structure. If you're going to break the metaphorical silo down, it's likely the vertical chain of command within that structure will have to be reevaluated and maybe even repositioned.

Vertical hierarchies are familiar to most of us, often charted out in pyramid or ladder form. When silos get busted the result is often a flat hierarchy—a horizontal chain of leadership. Keep in mind that moving from vertical to horizontal doesn't take away from the importance of leadership. In fact leadership skills are necessary to maintain an environment in which everyone is welcome to share fearlessly and openly. And there will be a point when the group will need direction and guidance (i.e., they will need to be led, which I will explore more fully in the next chapter).

Leaders have to understand the benefit of leveling status and may find it necessary to lower their own status—to flatten rank—at least for periods in order to develop an open atmosphere. That doesn't mean that rank or status is arbitrarily given away. Part of the culture of open communication is that everyone acknowledges that rank exists and knows that even if it is set aside it can be reasserted when necessary. If we consider that your rank is your job title within an organization, and that status is something that can be given or taken away by other people, then your rank is not actually affected when status is manipulated. So if rank is getting in the way of communication, set it aside. The bonus of allowing a hierarchy to be flattened is that even when rank comes back into play, open and honest communication continues because you have led by example and already shown that not only is this wanted; it is needed. You have created the routines and rituals of manipulating status to reinforce stellar communication, and as we've discussed, employees will revert to their most overlearned and practiced behaviors!

In early 2016 I had the extreme pleasure of interviewing Alex Gallafent, a design lead at IDEO's New York studio. IDEO is one of the most successful global design firms around—it helps organizations create new products, services, ventures, and more, from medical devices to entire school systems. I was fortunate to get a firsthand look at their collaborative workspaces and at what has been called IDEO's "culture of helping."

IDEO New York is an environment built for collaboration: it is open and playful. In some of the shared spaces guidelines for interpersonal engagement are posted on the walls (such as the lighthearted "Rules of the Makespace," which include a reminder to teach others). In individual project spaces teams are encouraged to redesign space to uniquely fit their needs. Alex said, "The more we're able to create spaces that fit the work styles, personalities, and interests of the team members, the more likely that team will feel creatively confident as their project proceeds." Minicultures within the larger culture! IDEO project teams are intentionally multidisciplinary too. People arrive at IDEO with an enormous variety of skills, backgrounds, and educations. Collaboration between those distinct points of view and approaches to work is baked into IDEO's value proposition. Success comes from individuals taking ownership of their work and being individually responsible for the health of the studio's culture; it also comes from the collective, collaborative sum of those individuals working together. The physical layout of the studio supports these behaviors: at one moment designers may be in their own project space, heads down in concentrated work. At another they may be present in the wider studio community, getting inspired by other teams, asking them questions, or—when invited—offering critique.

At IDEO a sense of grounded professional vulnerability is perceived as a strength rather than a weakness. Not only do IDEOers actively offer help to teams that might need a little support or some fresh eyes; they also actively communicate when they themselves need assistance. "We learn from failure," said Alex. "Getting things wrong is a signal that we're making progress." Because failure is celebrated and not feared, the studio's culture is grounded in a sense of serious play.

IDEO understands that the overall success of any project is owned by every single member of the organization. And in understanding this, they know the collective consciousness of the company is far greater than that of any one individual. Egos are set aside and the whole company operates as one giant, openly communicative team!

Silo busting not only promotes horizontal communication within meetings and departments; it also promotes such communication upstream and downstream and cross-stream—upstream to higher-level executives, downstream to customers and clients, and cross-stream to (and through) other teams. If communication is flowing in all directions, management skills have to flow in the same directions. Tearing down the restrictive, vertical hierarchy of a silo is a positive action. However, once that familiar hierarchy is gone, people have to know what to replace it with. Depending on the structure of the company, the removal of silos may require some time to understand how to use the skills needed for managing up, managing down, and managing sideways.

Managing up refers to the management of those of higher rank than you; managing down, to the management of subordinates; managing sideways, to the management of peers. I find that a lot of people assume that the easiest of the three would be managing down, because that implies a dynamic in which you've got status and rank working for you. That assumption often proves to be faulty because if you let the rank and the status do the work, you are in effect relying on a silo rather than breaking it down. Simply asserting rank will not likely open up communication and create any intrinsic motivation in subordinates.

To manage down effectively, you have to embrace the somewhat paradoxical idea that ruling effectively from above sometimes means being willing to lower your own status, lead from within, and even let others of lower rank lead. There's an old improv phrase that I first learned from my mentor, Martin de Maat. That phrase is "Follow the Follower." In improv this phrase means that no one is the leader. We are all followers. And if we all follow each other, something organic will emerge that we all created and that we all have an equal share of. I introduced this phrase to the U.S. Naval Academy in the 2014 Leadership Conference when I was on a panel titled "Change from Below: Creativity, Dissent and Reshaping." I explained "Follow the Follower" as a means of lowering your own status to listen to the newer members of your team (in this case midshipmen and women). It is a way to not only learn their perspective but to "think outside of the box" and even develop a reverse mentorship.[11]

Managing across turns out to be the easy one when the environment is set up correctly, like the New York office of IDEO. In dealing with a colleague of equal rank, there should be a naturally relaxed dynamic that allows the "managing" to feel more like collaborating on a team. Personalities aside, when all things are equal in peer-to-peer relationships, it is not so hard to level status.

The key to managing up, down, or across is fairly simple. Don't think of them as three different management tactics; rather, think of them as one smooth method of communication. Respect the rank and even level of status that each person has garnered, and speak to them respectfully. Rather than worrying about tailoring a communication to go up or down a chain of command, communicate with clarity of purpose and a high level of self-auditing—be aware of your own behavior as well how you are affecting others. Be consistent whether communicating up, down, or sideways. Allow for some humility and vulnerability—whichever way you're managing, it's okay to show a need for help and to request guidance (it takes strength to recognize your own weakness). That kind of openness shows care for the greater good and can create buy-in at all levels. The point of doing away with silos though is to allow people to start caring about what others are doing, and to be agents of each other's success. Honesty, candor, and openness are keys to strong relationships whichever way the communication flows.

Conflicted

It would be so nice to conclude our talk of silo busting by telling you that once communications are open and once you have an environment in which honesty and candor are in abundant supply, your workplace will run as smoothly as a freshly waxed Mercedes. Unfortunately humans seem to suffer from something called human nature, and in the aftermath of busted silos, open communication may be accompanied by interpersonal and interdepartmental conflicts.

Not to worry. Changing behavior is hard, and this is a natural part of change. Being forewarned is being forearmed. If you go about the business of silo busting, you may be pushing people outside of their comfortable safety zone and you need to be ready for some conflict management.

I very specifically use the term "conflict management" rather than "conflict resolution" because in some cases conflict is a good thing. Sure it needs to be guided and focused, but not necessarily immediately extinguished (resolved). In the next chapter we'll take a look at a variety of leadership techniques. As far as silos are concerned, let it be said that when communication is opened up, people in leadership positions need to be cognizant that "open communication" may now sound like something closer to debate, especially when different departments with different jargon, acronyms, and subcultures are forced to work together. Let's explore the nature of a debate.

We can think of a debate as a clash of opposing points of view, of pros and cons, in which the ultimate aim is to "win" the argument. However, as you may recall from Chapter 2, if you think about the rules of debate followed by school debate clubs, you start to get closer to something that is surprisingly "Yes, and"-ish in nature. Whether in the high school multipurpose room or around the conference table, to debate your opponent you have to be present and in the moment, to postpone judgment, to listen intently, and to be adaptable. When silos tumble and people find themselves free to speak up, there is almost a guarantee that everyone will not be in agreement on every point. This is as it should be. When a culture of acceptance is set up correctly, there should be opposing views and the diversity of thought should be celebrated. Opposing views (perspectives) are not the same as opposing agendas. Debate can be constructive and conflict can be good. Again, though, for conflict to be a positive it needs to be channeled properly.

Here are a few simple techniques someone in a leadership position can employ to channel conflict correctly:

- First of all it must be clearly established that arguments in favor of one point or another can never become personal in nature, which doesn't benefit anyone.

- Conflict can be encouraged as long as the parties with conflicting points of view accept that they have a common goal, something greater than self.

- A leader must lead. A leader has to set a tone for debate in which it is clear to everyone that what is being sought is a problem-solving consensus, not a win for one side or the other. The dynamic cannot be "Here's why I'm right and you're wrong." It has to be more along the lines of "Yes, and you've got that problem. I've got this problem. Let's punch this out from all angles and figure out how we can work together to solve both issues and create less headaches for both of us." Further, if you see emotional investment from any party (frustration, anger, resentment), then the parties are not aligned on the overall mission.

- Once the debate is done, realign the team, especially if the debate got heated. The last thing you want is for a person to harbor resentment and carry (or bury) negative emotions back into the workplace.

It's amazing how often framing a conversation or debate properly makes seemingly intractable conflicts disappear. Once conflicting opinions have been stated and a work-appropriate level of emotion has been vented by all sides, reframing the central question from "Whose idea is better?" to "What can we do to help each other?" has tremendous impact. As always the point is not to get team or department members to feel so good about each other that they exchange foot rubs—the point is to get the team or department to do their work in the most effective and efficient way possible.

Once silos are busted individual perspectives can flourish. An improvisational workplace can be a place that encourages dissent and expects issues to be explored as richly and as deeply as possible. Yet diverse perspectives must always be expressed within a culture of acceptance and respect toward the same overall agendas. Opposing views can be a tremendous asset to a business as long as they eventually come together to support a common good. On the farm, silos work just fine for wheat and rye. In business they're just not necessary. Open communication is a much better means to success.

Now we'll leave the farm behind to look at how leaders can lead the way to that success.

Chapter 8

TAKE ME TO YOUR LEADERSHIP

AT FIRST THOUGHT and perhaps even at second thought, "improvisational leadership" might seem to be an oxymoron. Improvisation by nature is a team endeavor, in which no one individual is more important than the ensemble and consequently no one leads. If in the art of theatrical improv I was forced to recognize a leader I would have to say that the improvisational performance itself leads. The piece being performed influences each performer's role and responsibilities just as any good leader would, and every individual performer in the piece is there to serve the needs, wants, and demands of the overall group performance. In improv this is known as the improvised performance taking on a life of its own—a creative process that is both semimystical and quite practical, in which the natural talents and heightened communication of the performers come together to serve the ultimate "boss": a great, audience-pleasing performance.

The leveling of status I've spoken of is crucial to a theatrical improv troupe. However, behind the scenes there are leaders organizing warm-ups, scheduling rehearsals, and taking care of all the show business logistics. Up on stage there are no VPs of Wordplay, no Chief Farcical Officers, and no C-level scene-stealers—are all equal. Part of embracing improv as a theatrical art form is accepting that the group must always come before the individual. I've mentioned an old improv phrase that I first learned from my mentor, Martin de Maat: "Follow the follower."[1] Onstage, we all follow each other as a way to facilitate organic discovery in the group. We focus so intently on the other individuals in the group that no one can become the leader; we work in service to that which is bigger than any individual: the team, the process, the show.

This is the crux of "Yes, and . . . " and as we've seen in discussing everything from branding to brainstorming, from status leveling to silo busting, this "Yes, and" philosophy can be easily and effectively adapted to the workplace. Obviously, though, when improvisation moves into a corporate setting the dynamics of leadership also have to be accounted for. Though we may all be equals as humans who put pants on one leg at a time, a lot of us have job duties that tell us otherwise. And whether or not your job title labels you as a leader, in general terms the corporate workplace might be broadly defined as "an arena in which somebody is trying to get somebody else to do something." In other words if work is going to get done someone needs to be a leader.

Given that theatrical improvisation is more rooted in group harmony than in individual solos, do improv techniques have to be discarded with extreme prejudice when we focus on the corporate environment and excellent leadership? Absolutely not. After a bit of quiet contemplation (and energetic head pounding) in the early days of developing Business Improv, I came to an aha moment: even though there's no "leader" on an improv stage, the same skills and mind-set that make an excellent improviser make for an excellent leader in the business setting. This chapter draws on all that has come before it in examining how improvisation can be used as a means of effective leadership. By analyzing traits of great and horrible leaders, we will show how, through improv, leadership skills can be developed so that one has an understanding of how one's energy, attitude, and communication style affect others.

Lead Story

My introduction to the benefits of improvisational leadership was a very personal one. Back in 2001, in the very first year Business Improv became incorporated, my company was hired to run the afternoon sessions of a four-day intensive executive education program being presented by the Fuqua School of Business at Duke University. Business Improv had already run many successful programs for MBA students and professors and had gotten great feedback from our participants. This particular program presented a new challenge in that it was the first time we were addressing a group of top-tier executives—sixteen VPs, presidents, and CEOs representing large, well-known companies from all around the country.

We were riding high on the tremendous success of the MBA programs and went into this new one confidently. After our first three hours of workshops on the first of the four-day "Creative Leadership" program, the participants took a dinner break and over the course of their meal decided that Business Improv had failed utterly in providing them with anything useful in either creativity or leadership. These top executives felt that our attempt to blend improvisation techniques with corporate skills was a complete waste of time, and they were not interested in seeing any more of what we had to offer in the remaining three program days to follow.

Their decision was no doubt influenced by a number of factors, including what I would later deduce to be a bit of ageism and some culture clash. I was only 29 and considerably more fresh-faced than I am now. I dressed like a very business-casual improviser in khaki pants and a short-sleeve polo shirt and often played awkwardly with my name-tag lanyard when I talked. To a room of gray-haired corporate titans I may as well have been wearing rainbow suspenders and a propeller beanie. I speculate that to them I didn't look like I had the experience to lead them to any insight. So at the end of day one—a day ironically themed "Suspension of Judgment"—they simply stopped listening and judged, harshly. My age and demeanor did

not explain the entirety of the failure though. The course was supposed to begin with an introduction to improv techniques (postponing
judgment, loosening of inhibitions, and introducing "Yes, and") and
then gradually, over our four days of workshops, make clear how and
why these techniques could be relevant in the workplace. That sort of
approach worked perfectly well when I was leading a "team" of MBA
students through a program. This audience was very different though,
and in not letting them know exactly what we were doing, why we
were doing it, and where we were going right from the start, I failed
them as a leader.

The morning of the second day of the program my coteacher and
I were fired. Sort of. Rick Staelin, the wise, steady associate dean of
executive education at Duke, informed us that Business Improv's services would no longer be required in the four-day creative leadership
program. This was a horrible professional gut punch—the first time I
had ever been terminated from a real job. It was an awful feeling that
something I had taken so seriously and had put so much effort into
could result in rejection. However, I say I was "sort of" fired because
Rick Staelin engaged me in a way that I have come to recognize as a
tremendous life-changing moment of leadership.

Instead of instructing us to pack our bags and get the hell out of
the lovely R. David Thomas Center on the Duke campus, Rick told
my coteacher and me to stay. He informed us that we would be paid
for our time at the rate we had agreed on in our contract with Fuqua,
and instead of facing the C-levels again we were to spend the next
three days rethinking and revamping and redesigning our program.
We were grateful for that chance to redeem ourselves and consequently
worked our tails off over those next three days. We gutted the program,
transforming every aspect of it—from preprogram communication to
dress attire to our language to our exercises and course materials to
our learning outcomes and business links to our wrap-up discussions—
and ending up with an immensely improved program that is still the
basis for all our multiday executive education intensives. Rick met with
us on the final day to talk through the changes, and what resulted was

a new program for Duke Exec Ed: a three-day, Business Improv intensive called "The Workshop in Managerial Improvisation."

More than just influencing the content of our program, this experience was a huge lesson to me in the power of positive failure—a lesson made possible by Rick's improvisational approach to his own leadership role. On a strictly strategic level we had not delivered to his "customers" what we had promised, and he had every right to send us packing without pay. Rick was thoughtful though and saw enough potential in what we were doing to take a small risk and invest some time and money in us. He provided us an opportunity to fail and challenged us to learn from that failure. We answered that call to action. We created a much better program on every level and completely redefined my company's (and my personal) mission. The real kicker came a year later when one of the executives who had watched us die our long, painful "Creative Leadership" death returned to Fuqua for one of our three-day, Managerial Improv intensives and ended up raving about how much he had learned in those three days.

My point is that it took enlightened, improvisational leadership to turn a rough failure into an eventual success. Our terminated program was Business Improv's very first step into executive education, and if we had been summarily dismissed by Rick I'd say the chances of my company's going on to become what it has become would sit somewhere between nil and no way. Because of Rick's leadership in that moment of crisis, not only has Business Improv had a chance to thrive; we've also been able to maintain one of our strongest, longest-lasting academic partnerships. Today, as a leader of my own business, I endeavor to create the same opportunities for the people I work with that Rick created for me.

Follow the Follower

In theatrical improv the goal and the means to that goal are always clear: a group of improvisers is performing to explore their art, having fun and entertaining their audience. In the business world goals are

constantly shifting and new teams are being assembled every workday. Even if the members of a team are capable of working together
beautifully, the team is pointless without a leader to articulate its goals
and process. That's not to say the team is pointless because it can't
do anything by itself. It can, and left alone it might just find its way
toward a useful goal. In most situations, however, someone has to step
up and give a team direction and focus and deadlines, or things don't
get done. Parameters have to be put into place for a team to function—and to know how to function—and someone has to set those
parameters and police them when necessary. In business settings any
work being done by two or more people working together will require
leadership.

From a sort of business-feature headline perspective the term
"leader" is sometimes defined in the grandest sense: a leader is a visionary, an innovator, a game-changer, an iconoclast. Henry Ford.
Richard Branson. Steve Jobs. These kinds of leaders are measured by
the size and success of their big ideas, or perhaps simply by the size
of their market share. However, in a day-to-day business sense when
we talk about leadership we're really talking about the ability to work
with people. There are of course many different ways to lead, that is,
to get people to achieve at their highest potential. In business the current leadership trajectory combines emotional intelligence (EQ) with
rational intelligence (IQ)—relationship building that is based in empathy as much as in rational, analytical, strategic intelligence.[2] Beyond
vision, leadership is about connection and engagement, so all the skills
required for engaging with others are crucial whether one is guiding a
team, heading a department, or managing a crisis.

In improvisational leadership the concept of "Follow the Follower"
shifts a bit. The "following" doesn't imply a surrender of authority.
Instead it refers to a leadership state of mind in which a leader is
capable of leveling status and fostering talent. The improvisational
leader is still a person in charge; however, that person is also open to
ideas, opinions, interactions, and actions from his or her subordinates.
The most enlightened leaders I know actually pay very close attention

to the people they lead and are inspired by them. That doesn't mean that leaders need to be dismissive of their own vision, goals, drive, tenacity, and motivation. It simply means they operate with a heightened awareness of exactly whom they are leading. The required level of awareness in leaders has evolved significantly over the last 15 years or so, at least partly in response to the prevalence of social media (Twitter, Facebook, Instagram), crowd sourcing, and the internet and the evolving ways that we communicate with each other. The younger generations are dictating how we communicate with each other like in no other time in human history. "Follow the Follower," to an enlightened leader, means that by focusing on the people you lead, they will focus on you in return.

We are all in people businesses, built of personal bonds and personal connections. We know there is a basic human desire to be understood and the thing that connects us in all the great relationships in our lives is that somebody "gets" us. Of the "Six Domains of Leadership" created by Duke Fuqua School of Business professors Sim Sitkins and Allen Lind, the attributes of great leadership most closely aligned with improvisational thinking center on the need to share your personality and authentic voice, build relationships, create a team that will serve a greater purpose, lead with passion, support and protect the team you create, and lead with integrity.[3] When you can actually turn that around to the people that you lead—when you get them as much as they get you—you have a great opportunity to demonstrate a freedom from status bias and a willingness to learn.

There's no perfect equation or foolproof formula for creating a great leader (if there were we'd see a lot more great leaders out there). There are a lot of x variables in every leadership opportunity, variables that can range from the nature of the goal being pursued to the dynamics of the team being led to the natural leadership style of any particular individual. Whatever those variables may be in any given situation, though, improvisation can become a pivotal piece of leadership strategy. The very nature of improvisation is awareness and adaptability, and any leader has to be aware enough to recognize what he or she has to work with in a given team, and adaptable enough to manipulate circumstances toward a desired outcome. A leader must constantly make sense of the shifting pieces of a shifting puzzle—exactly what an improviser does—and an improvisational leader knows how to blend EQ and IQ.[4]

An improvisational leader must have fully developed the improvisational skill set we've discussed in previous chapters. A leader has to live in the moment (truly the essence of improvisation). A leader has to be in a state of mindfulness, aware of his or her actions, and make pivotal changes in the moment to influence, inspire, and engage others. A leader has to be prepared to listen and observe with focus and concentration. A leader has to postpone judgment. A leader has to allow for some humility and vulnerability, accepting a willingness to be wrong and a willingness to ask a team for help. An improvisational leader understands that it is not the job of the leader to always come up with the "right" answer—the job of the leader is to get a team to a desired outcome.

I want to stress most emphatically that the "desired outcome" is really the whole point here. I would never argue that the techniques of improvisation should be seen as any kind of cure-all or replacement for actual strategy. In a business sense effective strategy is the road map by which you will travel to execute your mission. That mission might be an expansion of territory, a new marketing campaign, a way to streamline operations, a new customer-focused approach, or a new way to generate profits. Every bit of logistics, analytics, and practical thinking that goes into your mission is a matter of strategy. A new phone system needs to be set up. Temps need to be hired. Office space needs to be converted. Budgets need to be drawn up. Teams need to be assembled and headed up. All of that finely considered strategy stays in place. The introduction of an improvisational style of leadership and teamwork is not meant to replace the thoughtfulness required for the day-to-day execution of a job. The point of improvisation is to complement such strategic thinking. In fact improvisation thrives at the pivotal intersection where planning and strategy meet execution.

This ties directly into the improv myth we busted a long time ago—that improvisation is making up something out of nothing. For any decent improviser and most especially for an improvisational leader, improvisation is creating something out of every resource available. A truly scatter-brained performer would soon bore an audience, and a scatter-brained leader will struggle to guide a team. Onstage as in the corporate workplace there's a lot of structure required for improvisation to appear to be as free flowing as it looks when it succeeds. Embracing improvisation as a leadership technique does not demand any weakening of structure, nor does it demand any sacrifice of strategic awareness of mission, goals, and deadlines. What improvisation adds to the picture is an advanced approach to how you complete that mission and meet those goals and deadlines. Improvisational leaders improve the chances for team success because such leaders do not limit themselves to a single plan of action in order to achieve a desired result. Improvisation allows a leader to see a variety of opportunities for success with every challenge, within every plan.

New Management

Leading is not managing. Managing is not leading. To some this is a pair of seemingly obvious truisms. Others lack clarity on the difference between leading and managing. I'd suggest that the act of managing focuses strictly on strategic thinking at its most practical—on execution.[5] Managing is taking care of logistical and practical details. Every team-related task needs to be managed to some extent, and the quality of managing can fall anywhere on a spectrum that runs from well-oiled machine to gear-grinding nightmare. The real problem arises when anyone confuses the managing of job-specific details with actual leadership. One does not need to be a visionary to qualify as a leader, but leadership does imply vision from a position of oversight.

Managing is a part of leading, and a great leader can and should be an excellent manager. The skill of managing, though, is only one part of leading, and managing in and of itself is not leading.

While a good manager needs to effectively communicate data and details, a good leader communicates on a broader, higher level. A leader drives for results, leads by example, and develops talent—actions that may not readily show up on a manager's spreadsheet (but which will engender results that make that spreadsheet a lot better looking). A great improvisational leader promotes teamwork and cooperation, values and respects the differences of team members, connects with others in empathetic ways, and leverages the talents of others to get the best possible results out of a team, all while hitting the strategically targeted bull's-eye.

Being There

One extremely critical aspect of leadership is "presence," physical and otherwise. The way in which a leader's presence is felt dictates the leader's ability to command the respect, attention, and devotion of a team.

Leaders need people to follow them because, on the most basic dictionary level, you can't define yourself as a leader if nobody is following. There are of course many ways to get people to follow you. In some workplaces—probably way too many—leaders lead through fear. Sure, fear can be a powerful motivator but when you've got people doing what you ask them to simply because they are afraid of being fired, you might be severely limiting the type of success you can achieve. When people are afraid of failure they do not take risks, and without risk there is limited chance for adaptation, innovation, and great discoveries.

Other leaders might allow status to provide all the leadership they desire. Such leaders can give orders in military style and assume that others will obey. If a leader's position is codified by rank—job title—it's a reasonable assumption that people of lower rank will follow the orders of leaders of higher rank. Within the military itself this kind of leadership via job title is needed to maintain structure and avoid chaos. In business, however, if people are following a leader only on the basis of his or her position in a hierarchy without any inherent trust and respect, it is likely they will never feel intrinsically motivated to do anything beyond executing simple orders. In improvisational leadership the emphasis is put on communication and connection rather than hierarchy. The appeal of this approach is that people come to feel they are appreciated and valued for what they can contribute, and they commit to a project, process, or person more fully. When a proper relationship is built between a leader and those being led, people feel good about doing much more than the minimum required for a job. Those good feelings are a fringe benefit—the real benefit is the return one achieves with a small investment in human capital (i.e., the job gets done better and valued employees want to stay with their leaders, who care about them—remember, people don't quit jobs; they quit people).

For an improvisational leader presence begins with mindfulness. As discussed in Chapter 3, mindfulness is a state of active, open attention in the moment. When you're mindful you observe your thoughts and feelings from a distance without judging them good or bad. When you are mindful you are living in the moment and completely engaged with the experience around you. Mindfulness is always a key element of improvisation, and in a position of leadership a mindful level of awareness becomes even more important. To be an effective leader you have to know how others perceive you and how to control and adapt yourself if those perceptions need to be manipulated. You also need to know how to perceive others—how to "read" them—and you have to be fully prepared to interact with all sorts of people in all sorts of situations. In reviewing how you see others and how others see you, you should have a strong sense of the kind of leader you are (which may not always line up with the kind of leader you aim to be). How do you respond in real time to a dynamic environment? Are you angry? Frustrated? Stern? Passionate? Cool and collected? Withdrawn? The more honest you are about how you are truly perceived as a leader, the better the chance you can influence those perceptions in a positive way.[6]

It doesn't cost much in time or money to achieve mindfulness. About two minutes' worth of thoughtful self-auditing can do the trick. That small mental refocus, however, can be the difference between improvisational thinking focused toward success and flying by the seat of your pants to get the best result you can at the time. And again, the purpose of putting in that two minutes' worth of self-auditing effort isn't to get a team to like you. The purpose is to become a thoughtful leader who gets the best possible work out of your team, and out of yourself. I would add though that those two minutes really have to count. Improvisation requires real focus and concentration and it never helps to go through the motions of being focused without really getting into the mind-set. A lot of people think that concentration works like a light switch—"I'm going to switch this switch on, and now, poof, I'm focused." What I've found is that focus and concentration—like the ability to postpone judgment—aren't switches. They're dials, which can be turned up or down. If you want to get into the game state of mindfulness, make sure you're turning up the appropriate dial to the appropriate level. Further, you have to practice turning the dial often. Once you achieve a level of muscle memory turning the dial, you will be able to shift from "unfocused" to "focused" as quickly as if you were hitting a switch.

Mindfulness makes you present in a mental, intellectual, and emotional manner. Once that's achieved, there is also a practical, physical aspect of presence that needs to be considered. This is where the self-audit comes also into play. It's extremely important that a leader be seen. However, presence is not simply the physical act of being in a room. There is mental presence and the act of how you hold yourself while in a room. Like energy and attitude, moods are contagious.[7] A great leader leads by example, and when it comes to intangibles like team focus and team energy if the leader is not around to model the example, it's not going to get followed. A leader's physical presence is a guiding force when things are running smoothly and becomes even more important when something goes wrong. In a time of crisis a team needs somebody to step up and say, "I'm the one who is accountable. I'm steering the ship, and given what's happening around us, we're going to follow the course I set." That holds true for the leader of a small team, a whole department, or an entire company. Think about how motivated and inspired Apple employees must have felt when Steve Jobs took to the MacWorld stage in 2007 to introduce the game-changing iPhone—after he had gone public with the fact that he was suffering from terminal pancreatic cancer. Or how those employees must have felt when Jobs returned to the stage in 2009 after a months-long medical leave to introduce the original iPad. An effective leader should always remember that physical presence speaks volumes.

A few tips on getting physical:

- *Observe.* When you first arrive in a certain situation, take a moment to observe and take in as much as possible. If you are aware of your environment then you put yourself in a better position to recognize opportunities as they unfold, to set up contingency plans on the fly, and to react instinctively in the environment, in the moment.

- *Listen with your entire body.* Most of us think about what we are going to say next as opposed to being focused, present in the moment, and simply reacting honestly. This is a basic human communication pitfall and leads to misunderstandings, misdirection, and conflict. Commit to the person talking with you and give that person your undivided attention. Make sure that attention is made clear through both mental focus and physical posture.

- *Lean forward.* If you lean forward, which way will you fall? (And if you lean backward, which way will you fall?) This is another way of saying be active and on your toes. Develop habits like mentally leaning forward, and strengthen the skill set needed to react thoughtfully.

Don't Go Micro

Being present shouldn't be confused with micromanaging. A leader should always be more than a manager and should certainly avoid the temptation to control every aspect of every single duty. Trusting and supporting your team means trusting and supporting them to do their job without hovering over them like a creepy drone-cam. Improvisational leaders have their presence felt both directly and indirectly—that is, when they're there and when they're not there. Don't be afraid to empower a team by stepping back and letting them initiate. A leader who functions as a supportive mentor has just as much authority as a detail-obsessed dictator. You can still guide a team and keep them on task and focused on strategy, and by encouraging the individual members of a team to take active roles in projects or meetings, you create buy-in through build-in by giving them a stake in achieving the goals you're after.

A military term that is rapidly gaining popularity in the business world is VUCA: volatility, uncertainty, complexity, and ambiguity.[8] As neatly as this acronym sums up the "you can't control much out there" reality of present-day life, it really encapsulates four unique issues. As such VUCA is a call to action—a command to create greater depth of knowledge, a directive to develop new approaches, and an edict to erect new architecture for dealing with unexpected and dynamically shifting situations.[9] In any leadership position you know that VUCA is coming your way in one form or another. Improv thrives in a VUCA atmosphere because it creates nimble, flexible, adaptable mind-sets in individuals as well as in teams that can function well through times of crisis.

Don't squeeze so hard then. The 90/10 rule for decision making states that as leaders only 10 percent of decisions we make have to be right 100 percent of the time. The other 90 percent of decisions just need to be made, and there is room to react and adapt as the consequences of the decisions unfold. Loosen your grip. You do not have to control everything or everyone to be an effective leader.

Stay Creative

Creativity has been identified as a key domain of leadership. Leaders need opportunities to practice and develop the skills and behaviors that give rise to creativity. Leaders constantly need to expand on their own experiences while fostering an environment in which others can be creative as well. Leaders need to bring their own character to the team and integrate themselves effectively, all while allowing others to bring their authentic voices and maintaining the integrity of the overall team throughout the process. A critical component of creativity in the workplace is the ability to effectively shape an interaction while being considerate of the style, interests, and focus of others in an exchange. Individuals with improvisational leadership skills are able to integrate ideas quickly while balancing reactions to a situation in a thoughtful manner. Improvisation creates a safe environment to practice these skills. "Yes, and . . . ," a foundational rule of improvisation, guides participants to listen and react thoughtfully, collaboratively, quickly, and creatively.[10]

Through the use of improvisation, leaders and their teams can enter into the unknown, create their environment, and adapt and respond to challenges in the moment and at the top of their intelligence. True improvisation is not composed of a "bag of stock tricks." It is instead a skill set that allows for meeting the challenges of the unknown in the most creative ways possible.

Supporting Lead

Corporate workplaces are dynamic hierarchies in which many are looking to increase both their rank and their status within an organization. It's important for leaders not only to get the best out of people focused on an immediate task, but also to foster talent that might serve as their own replacement when they move on to the next level. Find and support people who are working hard to help you succeed so that you can get the better parking space, move to the bigger office, or even pack up the Speedo and head off on a sexy European vacation (or exec ed improv program). In other words support the people who are there to support you. You don't have to be a looming, micromanaging presence to lead a great team that will step up and make sure the job is done with the quality you expect.

Of course just being there, just distributing leadership, or just stepping away does not necessarily make the team great. The groundwork has to be laid down and the architecture for success has to be put in place. Improvisational communication habits have to be understood, embraced, practiced, and repeated as part of the team's culture. Special forces units, NBA champions teams, and concert jazz quartets all display a dazzling, in-the-moment improvisational flow, and that flow is the direct result of hours and hours of training and practicing and communicating. A leader must commit that kind of effort to create an elite improvisational team in business. Understand that such training isn't done for the moments when things are easy for the team—it's for when all hell breaks loose. If through your leadership you have established best improvisational practices through their repeated and consistent use, then in the moments when you most need a team to rise to greatness, they will deliver.

Leading Roles

How exactly does the improvisational leader get a team to rise to greatness and achieve the best results in the end? Good question. I would break it down by following this path:

Keep the end in sight. Don't let the idea of being "improvisational" throw you. The improvisational leader still begins any team-leading task with an absolute focus on results and a strategy how to achieve the mission.

Communicate. The leader must clearly and specifically communicate expectations and targets to the people in the team. Be explicit.

Be mindful. A leader must be just as clear and specific in determining what he or she needs to do personally to achieve the desired results. Be aware of your actions and your language. Make sure you are actually doing your job at the same level you think you are.

Self-audit. Once you are mindful of your attitude and behavior, be aware of your physical presence and then make minor (or major) adjustments in real time to make sure you are affecting the people around you in the way you intend to.

Know your team. A leader should know every team member's specific capabilities and utilize those core competencies to the fullest extent. Not everybody is good at every job. Know a team member's strengths and weaknesses and lead the person accordingly. Do not put people in a position where they can only fail. On the other hand, audit your own thoughts and behaviors so that you do not create a bias and limit a worker to assumed strengths; provide everyone with appropriate developmental opportunities ("appropriate" means that your strategic mission is never put at risk by granting such opportunities). Understand that as leader you give meaning to each member's position in the team. Make it clear that you respect what members have to say, and value their input. You create the atmosphere in which all members can flourish. In the end they will support you just as you have supported them, and in turn you strengthen your network and team. If you're not clear about your team members' strengths and weaknesses, ask questions. Know the goals and ambitions of your workers beyond the specifics of the team task. Look for opportunities for them, even if those opportunities fall outside of the team's parameters. The driving principle here is that if you facilitate the success of the people you are leading, they will work harder to facilitate your success as a leader.

Constantly take action. Make initiations and declarations. Too many corporate tasks begin with a PowerPoint presentation or a series of memos and then are left to drift without proper follow-up. A leader needs to keep the energy of a team focused and on task. If nobody takes action, a job doesn't get done. However, taking action doesn't mean just doing things to look or sound busy. Take action that not only maintains an energy sweet spot but also drives toward results.

Action might take the form of reaction—once you put a plan in place you must be able to react, adapt, and adjust to make it happen.

Push. Push your group in a way that motivates and inspires (rather than frustrates or intimidates). Ask yourself, "Will people spend their weekend working for me to get a job done without my asking them to?" "Motivation" and "inspiration" are attractive words that get proper lip service from a lot of corporate consultants, and most corporate leaders agree that motivation is relevant to the workplace.[11] Let's create a working definition of both to make sure we are on the same page. For our purposes *motivation* is a drive caused by an external incentive—something outside of oneself that compels a person to succeed; *inspiration* is a drive caused by an internal incentive, that which stirs the heart and pushes a person to succeed. In the leader/team dynamic motivation and inspiration are a leader's call to action that resonates to the core of every team member. The real question though is, "How can I create *intrinsic motivation?*" Such motivation is effectively created and reinforced through improvisational leadership. In order to motivate, the improvisational leader creates and communicates a clear vision, develops a welcoming environment to work in, removes obstacles to success, constantly searches for process improvement opportunities, maintains team energy, trusts a team to do its job, and always maintains open, honest, candid channels for two-way communication. The outcome of this effort results in team members who are inspired, intrinsically motivated, and driven from the heart to work hard.

Set the ego aside. Make sure that your subordinates and colleagues perceive your own motivations as a leader to be the achievement of positive team results, not personal gain. If you have created a strong, improvisational team and a "Yes, and" environment wherein everyone is working to help each other succeed, then team success is personal success and personal success is team success. A good team will make a leader look good, which is of course a personal gain for that leader. However, few things kill teamwork and motivation faster than a leader who appears to be making decisions only on the basis of personal aggrandizement.

Be vulnerable and take risks. An improvisational leader should strategically experiment and innovate wherever possible and constantly seek out new ways to improve performance. Improv is by nature about change and evolution and failure. Create periods of time in which it is okay to take chances and fail. Moreover don't settle into a routine just because it has worked in the past. These blocks of time in which it is okay to fail are prime moments to challenge the status quo. Create new workplace routines that will work in the present and in the future. If you develop great methods and effective protocols, you can certainly hold on to them. At the same time always be prepared to move forward and to adapt. Understand that the mind has infinite potential. There are excellent ideas you haven't thought of yet. Be ready to embrace them when they come your way.

Own the failure. The effective leader makes it very clear to the team that the leader is responsible for negative results. This is a simple matter of integrity and accountability. The buck does indeed stop with you. Way too often business leaders take credit for a team's success and blame the team (or individuals within the team) if there is a failure. I've seen much better results achieved with just the opposite approach: a leader credits the team when there is a success and shoulders the responsibility when there is a failure. Obviously if one or more members of a team are truly incompetent or don't follow a leader's instructions, that is a strategic matter and perhaps even an HR issue. Yes, if you've done your job as a leader and somebody on your team did not do theirs, heads should roll. Generally, though, a team's chances of achieving desired results rise when a leader allows members to be invested in success and to be free of a fear of failure, and then shows appreciation and respect when success is achieved.

Know where you end up. Honestly evaluate and reevaluate results, process, and team performance to look for ways to improve. An improvisational leader should use the results achieved by the team as a litmus test for continuing, discontinuing, and adapting the leadership practices that led to those results. The leader should always be willing to assess results to help dial in best practices. This in fact is the idea behind the concept of best practices. If a tweak or an adaptation in your leadership style will increase the chances of achieving a better result, then make that tweak, pronto. Engage in development activities and opportunities that will help you produce better results next time you lead a team. Be willing to seek feedback from others in the organization about how you and your teams can improve outcomes. Determine what you need to do to personally improve as a leader.

Lousy Leaders

All of the above will create a road map that guides you toward excellent improvisational leadership. However, I'm sure it comes as no shock when I tell you that there are some less-than-inspiring leaders out there working off of very different maps. This begs the question, what makes a bad boss? What leadership traits are guaranteed to demotivate, demoralize, deflate, and drive a potentially great team into disastrous decline? Perhaps it is best to walk you through ten lousy leadership attributes by way of a narrative.

A lifelong resident of Anytown, USA, Johnny C. wants to play a part in the town's upcoming bicentennial celebration. To divide and conquer this monumental event, the town's mayor has formed a bunch of subcommittees. In the past Johnny has served on other town committees that were dysfunctional and ineffective. One was led by a "Buddy," who tried so hard to befriend everyone on his team that he was unable to serve the needs of the project. Johnny has also had experience working for a Grinch—a leader who was heartless and only interested in self-gain. Johnny knows his committee experience this time will largely be determined by the quality of the committee leader he works under. So he shops around.

First John thinks about joining the parade committee. However, the man he'll have to directly report to is a "Yes, but-er." It is hard for John to tell if this guy is unaware of his actions or if he knows and just doesn't care. Regardless this man has not embraced the notion that mindfulness and the self-audit matter. He says "Yes, but . . . " without understanding that the framing of his language makes a difference in collaboration, ideation, engagement, relationship building, and influence. In fact this man says "Yes, but" even when he means "Yes, and" and simply does not recognize the effect his language has on others. Believing he would not have the opportunity to bring value to this team, Johnny looks to join another committee.

So John takes a look at the decorations committee, where he'd have to work with a leader who is perpetually negative and low energy and who chooses to shine a light only on flaws. If something turns out right, ol' Aunty Poopie Panties feels compelled to point out that it could have been done better. Believing his internal flame would be extinguished by her, Johnny C. looks to join another committee.

John thinks about the food and beverage committee; however, the man running this group is a true Dr. Know-It-All, an individual who has never heard a good idea that couldn't be dismissed in favor of his "better" idea. Often you can hear this man profess that it is his job to say no, claiming a role of high status and judging the decisions of others without collaborating or contributing to the team in any meaningful way. He has no problem highlighting his own achievements, accolades, and rank. He is driven by ego, pride, and arrogance. Left unchecked he becomes a tyrant, and nobody wants to work for a tyrant. On to the next committee!

The entertainment committee is right up Johnny's alley, except that team is run by a passive-aggressive leader. She never actually says no; instead she plays the role of the victim or the martyr and looks to manipulate other people by using the emotions, goals, or actions of others to get what she wants. She's been known to bait people on to her team with the promise of helping or giving a gift, only to refocus her energy—once you come in—with what she really wants (from you) all along. Johnny has seen this approach horribly divide a team by quietly sowing discontent.

A little frustrated, John approaches the "kids corner," wherein the leader of this committee questions everything. What she considers to be "ways to get at the heart of an issue" are actually interrogation tactics. The ultimate result of questions delivered relentlessly over time is that everyone coming up with ideas begins to feel the Question Lady is really questioning the value of the person rather than the value of the idea itself. This too is not the right team for Johnny.

Growing more discontented, he tries to set a quick meeting with the booths and vendors committee head, who puts him off. On sniffing around a bit, John realizes this leader is a Stone-Waller who just waits. And waits. And waits—which is followed by excuses for not making decisions. This "leader" simply doesn't understand that not making a decision is the decision to not make a decision.

Now disgruntled, Johnny aims to join the last committee, the one in charge of the after-hours party! It's easy to connect with this leader, as she quickly makes herself accessible. However, she talks a mile a minute and doesn't take time to consider what Johnny, or anyone else, is saying. Perhaps this is due to too much caffeine or unchecked ADHD, but she is a Freight Train and the concept of "Thinking Slow to Move Fast" is lost on her—and so is Johnny.

Depressed and discouraged but not completely deterred, John aims to talk to the big boss, the mayor, for some inspirational leadership; however, the mayor is a LINO—a Leader in Name Only. To date he has provided absolutely no guidance or support. Perhaps due to his schedule this leader has a "dead bolt" policy, in which he insists he has an open door but keeps that door shut at all times. He claims to prize creativity and innovation but when he actually is available to connect, he just continues to demand that the same old things be done in the same way they've always been done. His words say one thing and his actions scream something else. No doubt he will take all the credit for success at this event and absolutely no responsibility or accountability for the current struggles and challenges. This approach to leadership can be so pulseless, mindless, and lacking in energy that one deadly bite spreads apathy, a zombie-like apocalypse, throughout the workplace.

Now completely dejected, Johnny C. packs up his bags and moves to a competing town (Anyville, USA) where the people value his contributions. He is now the head of the party committee there and has avoided all the traits of the horrible leaders he has known. As a result Anyville is thriving, and is known far and wide for its great parties.

Leading Questions

I would like to assume that nobody sets out to deliberately be any of the kinds of poor leaders described above. However, I know that effective leadership isn't easy. It takes work. If you're making a commitment to adopt an improvisational approach to leadership, you're taking a huge step toward open, honest, heartfelt communication with the people working for you. With leadership traits that range from love to passion to self-awareness to trust, an improvisational leader is a heart-led leader.[12] That kind of communication can't help but produce better results, no matter what goal you're leading your team toward. However, to achieve those results the initial commitment to an improvisational style has to be maintained. One of my favorite gut checks for testing if you're on path to leading with authority is a series of four simple questions, introduced to me by my colleague Kate Duffy. For my dollar, to lead effectively, not only should you be able to answer these four questions for yourself; you should also be able to answer them from the perspective of those you are leading:

Why this?

Why now?

What do I have to do?

What's in it for me?

By answering these questions as a leader, you put yourself in the position to lead anything, and this approach is particularly useful when you are leading change in the workplace. Let's suppose for a moment that by virtue of my endowed (or implied) status as author I am in a leadership position and you, the readers, are my team. My goal is to challenge you to change your own leadership style from whatever you're currently doing to a style based in improvisation. Here's how I would handle the four questions if it were my goal to bring the tenets of improvisation into my firm.

Why this?

Because, as mentioned, improv thrives at the critical point where strategy and planning meet execution. Because improv provides a communications-based set of tools and techniques that forces you to be present and in the moment, listen intensively, respond candidly, consider the thoughts and needs of others, and adapt to unexpected challenges and opportunities. Improvisational communication develops that clarity of thought by forcing the brain to slow down and pick up details, nuances, and subtext that might otherwise be missed. The tenets of improvisation are techniques to develop mindfulness and self-auditing. Improvisation is about reacting and adapting and having a level of awareness that allows a leader to accurately assess any group of people, any situation, and any environment. Improv also strengthens the skill sets necessary for teamwork, creativity and innovation, collaboration and ideation, situation assessment, crisis management, adaptive problem solving, conflict management, engagement, and influence. In fact improvisation strengthens all of a leader's soft skills, which often turn out to be hard skills after all.

Why now?

Because change is happening all the time. Technology is continually forcing us to change, and global competitors are evolving. An ever-increasing number of unknown and uncontrollable variables as well as an overwhelming amount of new information are readily available to us. There's an immediate need for adaptability, creativity, innovation, and risk taking, and improv can help a leader achieve each one of these difficult-to-reach end goals. We live in a world in which VUCA (volatility, uncertainty, complexity, and ambiguity) is a regular challenge. Based in nimbleness, flexibility, adaptability, and communication, improvisation techniques provide you with a way to lead teams that can function well through times of crisis. Moreover training and learning as a whole are changing. The traditional learning methodology of sitting in a classroom session for hours at a stretch has been challenged and has lost to experiential learning. Improvisation offers a new methodology for corporate learning and development—a cross-fit for the brain. And as for change, change is a constant. You can either lead change, follow change, or get dragged along behind it. Which do you prefer?

What do I have to do?

Learn to live in the moment. Connect and engage with people. Build relationships. Strengthen focus and concentrations skills. Develop the ability to postpone judgment. Create trust. Become a better communicator and a better listener. Be more adaptable and open. Influence people by choice and create great workplace habits. Embrace the art of improvisation, and valuable leadership skill sets will be strengthened simultaneously. And (here's a great thing) when you do it, most of the people you are leading won't even know you are practicing it. They will simply respond positively. This is a great, risk-free, fail-safe investment (that doesn't cost a thing).

What's in it for me?

Positive results. You will turn hard-to-reach buzzwords like creativity, ideation, collaboration, risk taking, innovation, and adaptability into a workplace reality. You will create teams that know how to achieve excellent outcomes, and you will create a culture in which excellent teams thrive. You will learn to cut redundancy and streamline meetings. You will develop the ability to influence people in the manner you desire, both in person and on the phone. You will develop the ability to hone great ideas through the blend of divergent and convergent thinking, and in doing so you will develop a positive attitude that focuses on possibilities and potential in addition to more critical, judgmental thinking. You will reduce turnover by creating a workplace that retains excellent employees, because they know they are valuable and valued.

•

Great leaders are not created through an equation or formula and they are not mass-produced out of an assembly line. Leadership traits (good and bad) are developed and fine-tuned over time, and the most enlightened leaders make their personal leadership development part of their overall strategy for success.

Now that we've explored what leadership could look like, let's dive into the "how" around applying improv techniques to create a positive corporate culture on a personal level, an interpersonal level, and then on a team level. In the next chapter we'll look at how the tenets of improv can be used to influence, inspire, and create intrinsic motivation in others, and we'll then look at how practices including accountability can be put into place to maintain the rules, principles, philosophy, and shared language of the improvisational corporate workplace.

Chapter 9

HOW TO EAT AN ELEPHANT

CHANGING A CORPORATE CULTURE is a big task. Adopting an improvisa-tional "Yes, and . . . " attitude and introducing it to a workplace that hasn't been running in accordance with that philosophy can certainly seem daunting. Again, the purpose of this book is not to provide a pleasant, improv-oriented escape from the average workday. A pre-scriptive book—or an experiential-learning program—is only as good as the ways you can actually put it to use. I want to be sure that after you read this book and, I hope, experience the benefits of improv, you will know exactly how to take what you've learned directly to work. To that end the concepts of transferability, applicability, and sustain-ability are extremely important. This chapter will focus exclusively on these concepts and address ways to apply improv techniques on a per-sonal level, interpersonal level, and team level. Then we'll shift to the arena of putting improv practices in place to hold others accountable for following the rules, principles, philosophy, and shared language of the improvisational corporate culture.

If you've been intrigued enough by the promise of improvisation to read this far, then it's time to consider how improvisation will actu-ally work for you when you put the book down and head to your office tomorrow. It's time to think about how you can, step by small step, ini-tiate positive change in your energy, your communication, your peers, and your workplace. Perhaps that sounds like a lot to take on. Fair enough. Then again, how do you eat an elephant?

One bite at a time.

Talk to Me

We started this book by focusing on personal development because any change that you're going to initiate has to start with your own behavior. Pay attention to the person staring back at you in the mirror. And talk to yourself.

At the end of my programs I use an accountability exercise that requires participants to team up and vocalize exactly what they've learned in the program and how they are going to use that. I do this to address a primary concern, which is the almost unavoidable gap between mind and mouth—an inherent disconnect that often takes place between our thinking and our speaking. Actors experience this all the time when trying to memorize and perform monologues, just as most business professionals might when trying to present off of a slide deck. As humans we can hear or read something and understand it fully; however, when we try to express those thoughts to someone else, there can be a great deal of stumbling and fumbling over our words to the point that what we're trying to express fails to convey our thoughts with significant weight or clarity. This is especially true the first time we try to explain an experience we haven't put into words before. Those stumbles can become major detriments if we are trying to lead or teach in any capacity.

Some of this stumbling comes from a very natural performer's anxiety that most of us experience at some point. In the theater an actor may have a complete and thorough understanding of a monologue as he reads it on the page. As soon as those words must be spoken without the support of the page—performed that is—that monologue becomes an entirely different beast requiring a full range of vocal nuances and emotional choices in order to be properly presented. If the actor makes the mistake of listening to his voice speaking the words rather than allowing the monologue (message) to flow from his lips organically, that performance is going to be, as we say in show business, an epic fail. That kind of awkwardness doesn't just happen on a stage of course. All of us who have ever been midspeech, midpresentation, or mid-conference call and have found ourselves focusing on the sound of our own voice—rather than the expression of our thoughts—know the awful feeling of having our thoughts derailed and the effectiveness of our communication diminished, if not totally squandered.

Happily the solution to the mind–mouth gap is simple: practice. Practice saying what you want to say, alone and aloud. Talking to yourself might seem a little silly at first. However, this is exactly how actors practice vocally expressing the written word. Once you get used to actually saying what you want to say, you set yourself up for success when it's time to express your ideas to other people. Further, by speaking your objectives for, say, a collaborative meeting aloud, you also start putting into play some subtle accountability practices for yourself. You are much more likely to hold yourself to words you have spoken out loud rather than something that could be considered a passing, unspoken thought. And when you speak your goals aloud you're asking listeners, without actually having to ask, to hold you to a new level of accountability. Others are more likely to hold you accountable to what you've actually avowed out loud as opposed to something conveyed as part of a larger group e-mail. One of the goals here is for you to figure out how to express to others, directly and specifically, that you have a plan for better communication and that your strategy for accomplishing that mission is to embrace improvisational techniques. Once you've practiced what you want to preach enough to be comfortable and confident, you've taken a great (very easy) first step toward having a positive impact on the culture around you.

It may take a few chewy bites of the elephant to get to that point, though. Most conscientious workers don't just assume that the right words will come to them when it's time to make an important presentation; they practice and practice until the precise ideas they wish to communicate flow as effortlessly as possible. If you're going to introduce what may be seen as a significant change in your workplace culture, you want to be just as well practiced. So don't doubt the power of specific, purposeful vocalization. Saying out loud, "I know what I want to say" is not at all the same thing as actually practicing the exact words you want to say.

Start by practicing in the comfort of your own home—maybe your own shower. Tell your shampoo bottle exactly how you are about to lead an improvisational meeting. Explain divergent and convergent thinking to the hair conditioner. If you stumble, self-audit for a moment, regroup, and reapproach. Think about what you want to communicate, then give it another go until the words flow like water. Have a "Yes, and" conversation with a significant other (if this can take place in the shower as well, more power to you).

Logically enough if you *get* comfortable saying something out loud, then you're going to *be* comfortable saying it out loud. The bonus is that even if you think you fully comprehend something, when you take the step of successfully putting it into your own words—and speaking those words out loud to communicate meaning to other people—you develop another level of comprehension. Once you're in a position to articulate your thoughts to others, your understanding of those thoughts deepens.

The hidden benefit of vocalizing goals to a partner is that it creates an accountability practice. By telling someone specifically what you want to do and when, where, why, and how you want to do it, you put yourself in the line of fire, and by declaring it you will more likely practice what you preach. This creates the level of ownership often needed for leadership. If you desire to make an impact back in your workplace, at some point you are going to have to articulate to someone else what you have learned, and that's exactly what we are practicing. If you are going to initiate change one of the questions almost guaranteed to come your way is, "Why are we doing this?" Before you answer that to a coworker or team in a real-world setting, it helps to know that you as an individual have a solid, well-rehearsed answer ready to go.

Makes Perfect

Let's practice. Answer this typical improv question out loud for your-self, right now: "What is the purpose of warming up before a meeting or presentation?"

There are of course many ways to hit this piñata, and the "right" answer might incorporate some of the following: "The purpose of the warm-up is energy manipulation and getting into a better, more focused mental and physical space. We are going to treat our brains as muscles, and we are going to use a warm-up to get that muscle ready to function at peak capability by oxygenating it. The outcome will be raised levels of focus and concentration and increased speed of thought and adaptability so that we are all present in this moment. We are doing a warm-up so that when we move ahead to the task at hand we will be operating at high levels of awareness and engagement."

Now take a shot at answering some meatier questions out loud:

1. "What is 'Yes, and . . . '?" What is the purpose of it? Why are we using it? For how long will we use it? What is the desired effect (the end goal)?

2. "What, if anything, is the difference between 'Yes, and' and 'Yes, but'?"

(For the record, asking and answering these basic questions is a great way to set up a divergent thinking or brainstorming session.)

Once again, please speak your answers to these questions aloud, right now, even at the risk of drawing dirty looks from family members, fellow rail commuters, or other passengers on the airplane. I implore you, please commit to this.

Some of the many appropriate responses might sound something like this:

1. "Yes, and . . . " is a technique for slowing the brain down, to be present and in the moment. "Yes, and" is a way to dramatically strengthen the skill set related to listening, focus and concentration, and engagement. It is a tool for postponing judgment and increasing adaptability. "Yes" indicates that

you have heard what somebody else has said and have taken time to understand it. The "and . . . " is the bridge to your own perspective and authentic voice in articulating how you understand what was said. "Yes, and" implies and creates inclusivity, flow, and momentum. It is an invitation. "Yes, and" is a connector for inclusivity that feels like it is pulling people into a conversation and an exchange of ideas. It is a statement that reflects a positive approach to relationship building.

2. Conversely "Yes, but . . . " feels like it is pushing people away. The "but . . . " eliminates everything said before it. A "Yes, but" communication comes across as a restriction, a denial, a contradiction, or a deflection. Even when "Yes, but" is meant to express a positive attitude, it is rarely heard or understood that way. It feels like a negation, especially when it is delivered consistently, over time, or with volume and energy. "Yes, but . . . " shuts people down and makes them feel defensive. "Yes, but" is essentially a condescending way of saying no.

If you like the sound of your own voice, keep going. Try vocalizing how you would lead a brainstorming session or a team collaboration. Push yourself to think about what you would actually say to coworkers to set up the proper framework for ideation or idea sharing. Be specific and explicit, as in this following swing at the piñata:

"We're going to do a warm-up, to loosen our inhibitions and get us energized for this meeting. Then we are going to split the meeting into two 20-minute sections. In the first section we will emphasize divergent thinking: how far can we get away from Point A (that is, your issue)? We are going to use 'Yes, and' to explore and explode as many ideas as possible. This is about the number of ideas we can come up with, not the number of good ideas. So no one is allowed to say 'No,' and no one is allowed to question, judge, or analyze for these first 20 minutes. The key here is to drive potential and endless possibilities. Fail early and fail often, for 20 minutes. We must all embrace this fully and be diligent with this task.

"Critical perspective will come in the second 20-minute section, when we will emphasize convergent thinking. At that time we will take the ideas we have produced in the first section and pick them apart, prioritize them, analyze them, question them, deconstruct them, and otherwise use our great critical thinking skills to come up with best ideas or viable solutions."

Smaller Bites, Bigger Bites

One of the greatest things about improvisation techniques is that you can practice them by yourself without anyone around you knowing what you're doing. You can develop a "Yes, and" philosophy wherein you frame your thoughts to look for the positive and the potential, rather than the negative and the dead ends. Further, you can "Yes, and" yourself to unleash personal creativity and establish and maintain momentum on projects, conversations, and meetings. Once you've put a foundation in place for personal growth, build it out to use improv techniques on and with strangers.

If you're nervous about practicing these techniques in the workplace, first practice in no-risk situations with strangers like flight attendants, TSA workers, bank tellers, and bartenders before you move on to the coworkers you have to see every day. Though the likelihood of getting caught is small, it is highly likely that you will begin to have a big impact on others. (The first time a bartender buys you a round, you know your "Yes, and" skills are in great shape.) When you get comfortable naturally speaking the language of "Yes, and," take it to work. Continue with small bites, moving from the personal to interpersonal in the workplace. Practice with allies—one or two friends who have your back. Be completely transparent with allies and explain what you are doing. Practice using the "Yes, and" technique in small, interpersonal interactions around the office. Make the effort to really simulate important conversations or meetings in a controlled, safe place with safe people. Keep the stakes as low as you like—you are just practicing techniques at this point and shouldn't necessarily be thinking about real-world results.

Be strategic in the workplace. Start using "Yes, and" for one-on-one conversations in a single meeting, or on one phone call one afternoon. Put a "Yes, and" Post-it note on your office desk or landline phone to remind you to do this—hold yourself accountable. Practice a range of improv strategies: use eye contact as well as some of the intensive listening exercises I've described in Chapter 3, such as focusing on keys words you hear someone else speaking and then repeating those words in your responses.

Decide that you will be using a particular technique only for the next 20 minutes of your workday. Have a five-minute conversation in which you use "Yes, and . . . " and a five-minute conversation in which you use "Yes, but . . . " Then evaluate and see if that shift in communication techniques made a difference. Remember that you're not trying to change an entire culture right away and you're not obligated to take an improvisational approach in every conversation across the board. What you're trying to do is create mental muscle memory: once you practice enough and have started to get positive results, you'll catch yourself beginning to slip into improvisational form naturally without having made the explicit decision to do so.

Think back to the example of riding a bicycle. The very first time you got on that Schwinn the only thing you were thinking about was not falling off the bike. You gripped the handlebars way too tightly, oversteered, had trouble staying balanced, and had no natural feel for the pedals. You were deeply focused on what your body was doing, and in your hyperawareness of yourself you likely had very little consciousness of the environment around you and the possibilities it presented. Wobbling without falling was a triumph. Once you practiced just a bit, though, it quickly became possible to forget what your body was doing and to put all your bike-riding skills on automatic as you truly engaged with your environment. You weren't riding just to stay upright—you were riding to actually get somewhere. You stopped thinking about technique and started enjoying the journey, the wind, the surroundings—the ride. That's what we want to do here.

As "Yes, and" techniques begin to feel more natural, encourage co-workers to offer some pushback. Ask someone to intentionally ask you difficult questions or resist in some capacity. Start light (give yourself practice coming up against "Yes, but") then move toward bigger resistance (dealing with "No," the flat-out denial "I don't want to do this," and oppressive personalities). Practice: train yourself well enough so that resistance doesn't throw you.

I generally loathe the concept of "devil's advocate." To me most people use it as a coward's cloak to hide behind as they pretend to agree with you rather than just having the courage to say that they disagree with you. However, for the purpose of turning "Yes, and" into a leadership tool, getting your allies to take the role of devil's advocate to actually help you is important because you'll have to be able to handle yourself when you get into more uncontrollable, real-world situations with people who consider it their job to say no, and people who consider it their job not to listen to anyone else. Give yourself plenty of time to practice. This is not a competition to see how much of the elephant you can devour in one day. Change can be a very slow, deliberate transition that takes patience, tenacity, and diligence. Focus on your growth the same way and develop a degree of personal comfort and expertise using these tools and techniques, even if you start applying them your next meeting. It is all about the development that comes with continued and consistent practice. When you practice enough, you'll have an arsenal full of ways to deal with this kind of resistance. Practicing "Yes, and" allows you to create your own tools for open communication and gives you the experience of using those tools successfully. When you get to that point, that big roasted elephant is a few, considerable bites smaller.

All You Can Eat

Once you feel like you've talked enough to yourself, strangers, and individual coworkers and have properly practiced what you want to preach on a personal and interpersonal level, then you have steeled yourself for a role in leading change on a greater scale—across teams, departments, and the workplace as a whole. (Depending on who you are, your comfort level, and your actual need to enact these techniques in your workplace, this could take a day, a week, or much longer.) So grab the knife and spork and put your bib on: it's time to really dig into that elephant. You want to bring improvisation deeper into the corporate culture. How do you do it? What exactly should your initiation of this change look like, sound like, and feel like?

It's much easier to initiate change when the people who are going to be affected by the change feel they have a say in the process (remember the build-in strategy from Chapter 5?). With that in mind change can be very effectively initiated when agents of change allow themselves to be vulnerable rather than issue dictatorial commands. Find a place and situation at work in which it's okay to be vulnerable. It should be perfectly acceptable to say to a small team of coworkers: "I really want to try out this new approach I've read about. I'm not an expert in this. I just believe it will help us." Improv can get positive results even without perfect mastery of it, and while there is always talk about how fast-paced and high stakes the business world has become, honesty and vulnerability can make a great impression—especially toward relationship building in a controlled environment.

Not too long ago I did an intense, three-day strategy session with one of the world's premier global providers of warranty solutions, The Warranty Group. The executive vice president of Latin America was addressing the presidents of each of the company's territories, looking for ways to shift the business model to open up and facilitate communication between the regions (he was looking to do some major silo busting). His message to these head honchos was—I'll paraphrase here—"I don't know exactly how to chart through the unknowns that are facing us; we're going to have to chart through them together, because we absolutely must in order to succeed in the future. And we will succeed." That's a level of honesty and vulnerability and confidence that I find inspiring (so did the presidents, as the EVP's remarks created a sense of urgency and purpose), and this example points to the fact that great leaders don't always have to have all the answers in order to lead, especially if there is tremendous change being contemplated. When leaders allow themselves to open up, the possibility of increasing employee buy-in increases because they are "building in" to help the change take place. As a leader you want and need that buy-in from the people you are leading through change.

On the other hand, if you're trying to lead change you can't just be vulnerable. There has to be direction and toughness too—a laying down and protecting of the law of the land. If you're going to bring an improvisational approach to a workplace environment, be clear about your objectives, specific about your intentions, and explicit about your goals. Set parameters and be up-front about them. You don't have to be dictatorial but you have to mean what you say and then back it up. Start to take controlled risks. If you think improvisational thinking would be dangerous or scary in a particular environment (a presentation to top executives perhaps), then direct it to situations that are not so high stakes. You don't ever want a desire for improvisational communication to get in the way of actual strategic goals. However, if you eventually want to be able to use that kind of communication when the stakes really are high, you've got to practice.

Lead the Way

In asking you to take what I hope you've learned about improvisation and apply it within the overall culture of your workplace, I am in effect asking you to become a very powerful agent of change. In transitioning from someone who is aware of improvisational techniques to someone who is actually going to apply those techniques to have an impact on others, it's important to know where you stand in leadership qualities. To get you ready for the challenge, here's a quick gut check on improvisational traits for leadership:

1. *Vision*. Remind yourself that improvisation is not a magic cure-all for every workplace, and not a silver bullet for every problem. It is a tool that has to be used properly. Think hard about how and when the tool of improvisation can be used to help you execute strategy.

2. *Commitment.* One "Yes, and" conversation with the FedEx guy is good practice. That said, if you're going to embrace the use of improvisation, make the commitment to apply it thoughtfully and consistently in the situations where it can make a difference.

3. *Courage.* It takes guts to initiate change. Be courageous. Be daring. Let the people around you know: "We're going to use these techniques, for this (specific) period of time to reach these (specific) desired outcomes, and I will lead us through it." And keep things in perspective: we're not talking about slaying a dragon here; we're talking about making a meeting run better, and impacting people in a profound way.

4. *Time.* Give yourself time to struggle as well as time to figure out what your authentic voice is. Finding your voice may require knocking yourself out of your comfort zone or trying out some voices that don't feel natural at first. Find the one that fits and then practice with it over and over again. The purpose of improv is better, more authentic communication, so if you're leading from your heart your voice must be authentic.

5. *Integrity.* Be cognizant of your core values and who you are as a person. That's a big part of what you bring to your work role and your leadership position.

6. *Awareness.* Be mindful of your emotions, actions, and language. Practice the skill of a self-audit daily to be certain you are impacting others the way you want to impact them. Additionally, be mindful of your team, the individuals in the team, your environment, and yourself. The variables in the equation that makes up a team, leading a team, and leadership are dynamic and can shift from day to day. Mindfulness and self-auditing should be part of your daily work routine.

7. *Objectivity.* Be mindful at the end of the day to assess what worked for you and what didn't work. Why did something not go the way you thought it would? Or why did something start to succeed and then fall apart? What can you do differently to

avoid these pitfalls in the future? Conversely why did something succeed? Or why did something feel like a train wreck at first and then work out after all? What can you replicate for future success? Things don't just work because they work, or fail because they fail. Be as thoughtful about your process after the results are achieved as you were before the process started.

8. *Adaptability.* Just like there is no single, universal equation to create a great leader, there is no formula to stick to when applying these techniques. This is improvisation, for Pete's sake. Adapt and tweak as necessary to get things to work the way you want them to work. Take the foundation that we have been building in this book and make the process your own.

Talk to Your Team

Improvisation is about collaboration, so even if you are in a leadership role initiating change be careful not to micromanage. Once again, early in my Business Improv career, as I was just beginning to learn my voice as a leader, I fell into the very deep trap of micromanaging. The tight grip of micromanaging suppressed my team's initiative, suffocated their voice, and almost snuffed out my own vision. If it were not for my great team, relying on the tenets of improvisation to talk openly with me, not only would I not have gotten out of that anxiety-ridden place; I seriously doubt I would have a company at all.

The people in your team want a voice and they want to be trusted. Give them things to do and then send them off to learn and grow and produce without your assistance. Trust that they will succeed for you (not in spite of you). If you want people to be able to manage the unexpected, you have to allow them to confront and deal with the unexpected on their own. Break up teams and create new ones to foster a collaborative spirit. In teams small and large, level status and cultivate an environment where any one member can learn from any other. Jack Welch has spoken of "reverse mentorship," in which older employees learn from younger ones.[1] In a high-functioning improv team, mentorship can take place from top to bottom, bottom to top, and side to side. Lead with loose enough reins so that this kind of connection, bonding, and learning is allowed to happen.

Shared language and shared rituals are significant elements of establishing culture. Make sure the language of improvisation is clear to everyone and push coworkers to become comfortable using this language. Make sure that if you speak about the difference between "perspective" and "agenda" this does not simply register as jargon or corporate-speak but truly communicates an idea that everyone understands. At the very least make sure that everyone knows precisely what "Yes, and" means and how it works compared to "Yes, but." A great way to make this distinction come alive for people is to use a warm-up I call "Party Planner." This is wonderfully simple:

> Ask a small group, from 5 to 15 people, to plan a party—an office holiday bash, someone's birthday, the anniversary of a new department, the introduction of a new pencil sharpener; anything will do. One by one, each group member has to contribute a single idea to the party and each person must begin their idea sentences with "Yes, but." Let 'em rip. After a round or two ask the group, "How many ideas did you fully agree on?" The answer is usually along the lines of "Not many" (if any at all). If "but" does its usual nasty job, it will have succeeded in negating, dismissing, or contradicting every idea that it follows.

> Now give the same group another opportunity to take on the same task, except this time everyone has to begin every idea sentence with "Yes, and." After a round or two ask the group, "How many ideas did you fully agree on?" The answer is usually along the lines of "All of them." That little switch in conjunctions will do its magic, and invariably the group will find it gets a lot more done when their communication and collaboration are framed by "Yes, and." Mission accomplished.

If it's possible to have shared experiences outside the workplace, take advantage of that opportunity. Putting people together outside of their comfort zones creates bonding that is hard to duplicate in any other way. When you put a group of people in a situation in which as individuals they at least initially feel uncomfortable and vulnerable, they will often galvanize and collectively become stronger as a team. Simply inviting everyone to a happy hour doesn't always do the trick. Social outings without deliberate focus can pull people together; however, they do not always pull people together. You can easily get through a corporate outing at Applebee's without ever talking to someone you've never talked to before, or bonding with anyone you haven't already bonded with. Instead I would recommend something like a team adventure challenge, a group cooking class, or a Business Improv workshop (I may be showing a little bias with that last one, though).

Talk up and promote improv successes that have taken place outside of your own workplace. Make it easy for people to understand that by bringing improvisation into your particular workplace you are not asking everyone to get weird. You are not asking them to eat homemade granola while group hugging. That's not what SEAL Team 6 does or what a team of emergency medical technicians do, and those are teams of exceptional, successful improvisers who have made the improvisational flow of "Yes, and" an indispensable dynamic of their respective workplace interactions.

One of my favorite improv successes to trumpet is the story of Apollo 13, the 1970 moon-landing mission that had to be aborted when an oxygen tank exploded and led to such unplanned complications as limited power, loss of cabin heat, and shortages of fuel and water. There was no contingency plan for this kind of accident, and the NASA support team had to work through all kinds of potential fixes they had never considered before. NASA flight director Gene Kranz, memorably played by Ed Harris in the film *Apollo 13*, confronts the unexpected circumstances with the great line, "Failure is not an option." Of course failure is not an *ultimate* option, though to get to "success" Kranz and his team had to work tirelessly and improvisationally through a lot of failure, including literally making a round filter fit into a square hole.[2] That they were able to react and adapt to a previously unconsidered catastrophe and find their way to literally life-saving solutions shows just how powerful improvisational thinking can be in moments of crisis.

Be diligent. Once you've started to eat the elephant, keep going. Leading change takes tenacity, focus, and fortitude, so stay dedicated to what you're doing. That doesn't mean you can't be flexible or that you might not have to apologize if something doesn't turn out the way you intended. I remind you again: showing vulnerability is not a sign of weakness. In fact it takes great strength to acknowledge your own weaknesses. And in learning a new skill, this type of honesty is imperative to achieve greatness—or at least to achieve unconscious competence. So be strong. Along those lines once you've started to initiate change and have established the beginnings of an improvisational environment, protect the heck out of it. I guarantee that when you attempt to initiate any kind of significant change there will be people who do not buy in, as well as people who will intentionally or unintentionally undermine the process you are trying to establish. Don't be afraid to stand strong and put up a fight when needed.

Culture Club

In this book's Introduction I discussed an interview I had with Navy SEAL captain Jamie Sands. In the interview Captain Sands stressed how training and repetition are techniques to develop muscle memory and avoid brain freeze. He also had some incredibly interesting things to say about the culture of his workplace. Specifically, he said: "An adaptive culture is part of the SEALs' identity, and we take tremendous pride in this. Our mind-set is that we are problem solvers and we can handle anything. There is a pressure from the group to perform. No one wants to let the other members of the team down. *We all do better when we are part of a team.*" The SEALs are an excellent example of how training, a shared philosophy, accountability practices, and even conformity pressure create an adaptive, improvisational culture.

As talented and motivated individuals we often believe we can step into any group and initiate changes we think are necessary. In actuality the vast majority of people don't ever get around to changing the company or the team they become part of. Instead *they* adapt to fit inside the team or inside a particular culture.[3] This is understandable enough when viewed as a kind of risk reduction and survival instinct—nobody wants to be the nail in the board that is going to get hammered down. Even if we accept the fact that an overarching culture tends to dominate and assimilate individuality, we as individuals *can* be agents for change within the culture. We just need to be fully prepared for the challenge we're taking on.

That challenge hinges on a particular psychological aspect of a dominant culture: does the culture create "groupthink" or "group mind"? *Groupthink*, a term created by social psychologist Irving Janis, takes place when a group's desire to get along and conform overtakes their desire to consider dissenting opinions and alternative viewpoints. As a result debate and critical evaluations are suppressed and irrational decision making takes place.[4] In groupthink individuals give up their own perspectives and accept the dictates of the group unquestioningly: "This is what the group wants and there's nothing I can do about it, so I might as well just give up and go along with it." Or, "I *thought* this is what everyone else in the group wanted, so I just said I want it too." In a *group mind* setting, individuals retain their unique perspectives and use them for the betterment of the bigger picture. In fact each individual perspective is valued and celebrated; at the same time, the group never loses focus on what is most important: the process, the product, the group itself.

In either case there is pressure for individuals to conform to the existing culture. It is just a matter of being thoughtful and creating the culture to which you want others to conform. So, before attempting to change a culture, then, one needs to be very aware of how the existing culture functions and in what direction it should be nudged. Ideally all teams should get away from groupthink and facilitate group mind. We want to create a culture in which individual perspectives are maintained within a unified agenda. Further, we want a culture where for certain periods of time and in certain situations people are not afraid to take risks, not afraid to experiment, not afraid to dissent, and not afraid to fail.

If a fear of failure becomes deeply ingrained in a corporate culture, eventually the fear itself fades back to be replaced by something even worse: learned helplessness. When a workplace is permeated by learned helplessness, work is nothing but a grind. When a boss continually shoots down any and all ideas, that boss is training employees to accept that nothing will ever change whether their ideas are fantastic or terrible. After a while employees have no fear of coming up with a bad idea because they just stop coming up with ideas altogether. Whatever improvements or innovations might come from the employee talent pool are essentially buried in cement. Newer employees accept this as part of the culture and never consider going up against it.

Learned helplessness was perhaps best illustrated by extensive laboratory research conducted by psychologist Martin Seligman.[5] For our purposes let's look at an example of a Seligman-like experiment on primates. Several monkeys are in a pen that features a flight of stairs, at the top of which is a bunch of bananas. Stepping on the steps at the top of the flight triggers a powerful jet of water, which strikes the monkey going for the bananas and knocks him back to the bottom of the steps. After several attempts to get the bananas, and several powerful blows of cold water, the monkeys all experience the hopelessness of ever attaining a banana snack and give up climbing the stairs. They learn not to try. When new monkeys are introduced into the pen, they naturally want to go for the bananas. Now however, instead of being repelled by the jet stream, the new monkeys are aggressively held back by the other monkeys until they too give up trying. The new monkeys are trained by the original monkeys not to try. Finally, one by one the original monkeys are removed from the pen, and with each original monkey's departure a new monkey is introduced. However, the behavior does not change: when each of the newest monkeys tries to head up the stairs, it is oppressively held back by the veterans; this holds even after "generations" of monkeys have been rotated in and out. The takeaway from this experiment: you end up with monkey after monkey who have no idea why they should not go up the steps. Most of them have never been hit by the water. They just know—they are taught—that they are not allowed to try.

Created as a model for environmental and circumstantial depression, Seligman's research presents a cautionary tale in creating culture. You can create a culture in which it is not okay to *try*—to succeed, to take risks, to obtain whatever "bananas" your team might desire. You can teach people it is not okay to try. You can also create a culture in which, at least for specific periods, it is okay to try, to just simply *try*. It is up to us as leaders to understand that creating a culture is a choice, and once a culture is in place the individual group members will help uphold the laws of the land.

When the routines and attitudes of culture seem deeply ingrained, the challenge of changing a culture is greater. Yet change is possible. I can demonstrate how a bit of improvisational thinking might steer culture with an example drawn from my experiences working with some of the top business schools in the United States. At one in particular the faculty had a subsidized meal plan that gave them a great discount on a beautiful buffet laid out each day in the business school's very comfortable executive education hotel on campus. The school then built a brand-new university center, a spectacular sun-filled space, a covered atrium with a great, welcoming, wide-open feel to it. The university's intention was that this would be a great common place for students and professors to commingle—all the facilities were tailored with that as a goal. As beautiful as the new place was, though, the professors wouldn't eat there; they were still hidden away at the exec ed hotel enjoying the buffet. The university's solution was to shift the subsidized faculty discount from the hotel to the atrium. No professor was going to be forced to eat with students if they really didn't want to, but there was no longer a financial incentive to stay away from the students. The university wanted a particular change to take place in its culture and it created a framework in which that change could take place, which in turn influenced the behaviors (routines) of the professors. The university wanted interaction and it made a simple change that drove people to interact. I'm sure there was some pushback from the most ardent buffet-lovers, but from the university's perspective the upside of greater student–faculty interaction outweighed the benefits of unlimited mac and cheese for a few of the hungrier profs.

Of course for most individuals in a workplace it's not possible to initiate grand policy actions that will bring about the change you desire. Once you're comfortable enough with "Yes, and" to begin to apply it in the workplace, it's worth thinking about where and when its application could best benefit you and how to use it in a simple step-by-step action plan. Again, this is about "Yes, and-ing" yourself and framing your thought. Instead of focusing on elements of the workplace that are truly out of your control, tweak your thoughts to focus on the workplace changes that you can make. Remind yourself that you are not helpless. Change can be daunting, though, so if this elephant seems too big and it is difficult to take a bite, look at the distinction between the possible and the unchangeable in terms of "controllable pluses and minuses."

Need help? Try this exercise:

Take a piece of paper and write down a list of things you don't like about your workplace (diverge). On a second piece of paper make a list of all the things that you would want to be part of your dream workplace; think limitlessly as if the whole world is yours (diverge, again). Push yourself to think hard about the things you don't like and do want in your environment. Once these lists are created, sort each one by the following categories: (1) what is 100 percent, completely out of my control; and (2) what I have at least some control over.

Now look at the things you really could not do anything about compared to the things you could do something to change. Most will find that they actually have more control over more things than they initially give themselves credit for.

I've been having people put together these lists since 2001, and I have lost count of the number of times that something as simple as "chocolate" shows up on dream job lists. If you're pining to make chocolate a part of your workday, could you have a bowl of your favorite candy on your desk—or at least have some tucked away in your desk drawer? Unless you work in a food allergist's office, I can't imagine any company enforcing a strict no-chocolate policy. So if the sight of M&Ms is going to brighten your day a little bit, make them a part of your day.

The point is, we often have more control than we believe we do. Sure there will be things on each list that are not controllable, and if in examining each list you decide there are only 5 out of 15 things that you can affect even slightly, then you have just boosted your ability to influence the culture around you by 33 percent—not a bad return for less than 30 minutes of divergent and convergent thinking. And in deciding that something is truly out of your control, you can minimize the weight that element of the culture may have on you. You don't have to waste time worrying about things you really can't change. Focus on the things you can change even slightly.

The point here is not just to get the AC turned down or to eat more Hershey's Kisses. The point is to understand that a corporate culture is a dynamic force, always capable of change, and you have the ability to effect change yourself. When you focus on what you can control and you start to frame your interactions with your workplace culture in terms of "What can I do to make this a better place?" (or "What can I do to make myself better in this place?"), you are approaching the workplace with an active perspective rather than a helpless one. That's another big bite of the elephant.

Pushing Back against Pushback

If improvisation will make a workplace run better and allow everyone to do their jobs at the top of their abilities, why would anyone resist it? You could create resistance in others with an improperly executed delivery plan, as well as a lack of awareness of the culture itself. Other individuals may push back through several of the blocks to creativity that we discussed in Chapter 1: fear, insecurity, and any number of biases. Let's acknowledge that changing a corporate culture and establishing new workplace routines isn't easy and that pushback can take many shapes and forms. You have to be extremely strategic and thoughtful about when you will introduce this new way of thinking. In so much of life (including comedy) timing is everything. If you attempt to introduce people to the beauty of "Yes, and" at a rushed, stressful meeting, you're probably not going to have much support or much success. The timing is off and you will get pushback. If a company crisis erupts on Monday afternoon and you need a Tuesday morning meeting to deal with it, that's probably not the best time to introduce a new communications dynamic for the first time. If just too much is going on during a given week and people are understandably distracted, don't make that the week to initiate change. Improvisation techniques are not as effective if they're used only to shake people up for the sake of shaking people up. Structure and purpose must be behind your proposition. Be patient, thoughtful, and deliberate. If you want to lay a foundation that will eventually pay off in times of crisis, then lay it during a time of calm or—if your company culture operates at 150 mph in crisis mode all the time—a moment of relative calm.

The company or team culture itself can also create a climate of pushback. Randomly changing things with no awareness or thoughtfulness of environment (or circumstance) will not further the improv cause. Just as mindfulness and a proper self-audit will help you create a greater awareness of who you are, you have to be very aware of the workplace culture you're in before you attempt to change it. I've come up with an acronym for cultural traits to look out for that will kill an improvisational mind-set: SAD JR. It stands for

Status. If a culture relies heavily on status, most people will not feel they have the freedom to experiment, explore, discover, and improvise without being told to do so. Remember, status is something given to you by other people, and your job is your rank and responsibility in your organization.

Apathy. If people are in a culture or team that has given up, intrinsic motivation will likely be suffocated.

Denial. A culture in which people focus on being negative, shooting ideas down and finding reasons not to try, will likely teach others to focus their energy in the same way.

Judgment. This culture may also be ego based, having a lot of intelligent people who are much more interested in showing how smart they are by sitting back and judging ideas than in generating ideas.

Restrictions. Like the "Yes, but" person, this culture's focus is always on the limitations of something rather than its potential and possibilities.

If any of these are part of the psyche of a corporate culture, the task of initiating change is going to be tougher. Don't surrender to SAD JR though—just be aware of what you're up against, take smaller bites of the elephant, and protect whatever advances you make. And don't make the mistake of assuming all pushback is bad. Some pushback comes from a place of insecurity, and there are times in our lives when each of us feels a bit insecure. If people are simply asking tough questions to try to understand what your goals and objectives are, that's okay. That's the learning process in action, even when the questions are a bit aggressive. Remember I suggested that when you first practice "Yes, and" you find an ally to give you some pushback to help you sharpen your skills. The intent here is to give you comfort handling this type of communication as you become a change agent for improvisation. In real-world applications of improvisation, well-intentioned pushback born of curiosity should do the same thing: make you a better improviser. Use "Yes, and" to help facilitate this process.

I hope as you read this that my voice has resonated clearly: improvisation does not require the abandonment of critical thinking skills. It follows that the implementation of improvisational change has to be a matter of thoughtfulness and strategy: What's going on inside the company? What's the larger picture? What's a good time to try this?

Do not give up the idea of change just because there are times when it would be more difficult to execute—you don't want to be the monkey who never tried for the banana. Empathetically understand that there can be legitimate reasons for pushback against change, and be strategic in counteracting the pushback. As you encounter resistance, consider answering those "leader" questions from the previous chapter from the perspective of those pushing back on you: Why this? Why now? What do I have to do? What's in it for me?

We may see our fellow workers as a collection of distinct individuals, but don't forget that everyone within a workplace is affected by the culture of that workplace. Individual actions always need to be assessed in the context of the culture. We might conclude that the professors lining up for that business school buffet were elitists with an antipathy toward the student body—our biggest piece of evidence being that the professors didn't casually eat with the students. Once we know about the faculty discount, however, the assessment changes. The faculty members were not likely acting out of any negative motivation; they were making a choice that seemed like the best one given the culture that had been created around them. I'd be careful assuming that a person who is putting up resistance or employing a "Yes, but" style is doing so because of personal animus toward you. Look at the culture that person is operating within first. Then again, sometimes the people around you really are the problem. Skeptics. Naysayers. Droopy Dogs. Know-It-Alls. Just plain jerks. Unfortunately these types of people do actually exist in the business world. If you're thinking about implementing change in the workplace, you need to think strategically about how and when pushback might come from these problematic persons. I've already recommended a strategic approach to the general use of improvisation: "I'm going to use 'Yes, and' in this meeting at this time with these people for this period of time for this desired outcome." You also need to be strategic about who those people in the meeting actually are and consider whether any of them are apt to create pitfalls for you.

Before a meeting visualize who is going to be sitting around you. Think about who your pushback people are and what kind of resistance they are likely to put up that would interfere with the improvisational communication you're trying to establish. Given the nature of my business, I'm often walking into situations where I know I'm going to get significant pushback from an alliance of "Yes, but-ers." Before those meetings I make a point of playing out specific possible points of resistance that might be raised and how they might be raised, and then I think of what might happen that would make me stumble. I want to make sure I have mastered enough material to counter that resistance. However, I want to be careful not to go so far as to walk into the room in a state of prejudgment or with a particular bias against someone for "Yes, but" crimes that haven't actually occurred yet. Postponement of judgment is still a major part of my approach.

Yet as I've stressed, postponement of judgment is not an abandonment of intelligence or a denial of reality. Consequently the postponement of judgment has to be implemented in a slightly different way because I have an awareness, built over many prior experiences, of what *might* come at me from particular persons of interest. (I say what *might* come at me, because I always want to give those who have been "No" people in the past the chance to surprise me by becoming a "Yes, and" person.) I try to give skeptics and naysayers the opportunity not to be obstacles while at the same time making sure that I am completely prepared to handle any challenges that may come my way. As the saying goes, hope for the best and plan for the worst.

Here are some tips on planning for a group interaction that will include the worst possible, completely resistant, insufferably skeptical, "Yes, but-ing," naysaying coworker—a fellow I'll call Hugh Jazhol:

- Try to spot Hugh early. Stand next to him when you are doing your intro and explanation of activities. Engage Hugh early. Be explicit and tell Hugh that he is an important member of the team and needs to be involved, starting with the meeting about to take place.

- "Yes, and" Hugh, right from the start. A tendency most of us have when trying to promote something in which we believe is to fall into an emotional trap of being defensive and arguing with someone about "right and wrong." Do not argue with Hugh. In fact, *speak no negatives at all.* Hugh never gives a wrong answer. "Yes, and" him! "Yes, Hugh has this opinion and that may be right for now, or right to him. *And* here's another way to look at it. . . . "

- Postpone judgment. Take time to truly understand what Hugh is saying. Do not assume; ask questions to get to the core of what he is saying. Try to understand why Hugh is saying what he is saying and behaving as he is. Is it ego? Is he uncomfortable? Is he scared? Defensive? Or simply a proud member of the Jazhol family?

- Kneel or become lower, physically, to Hugh. You may have seen Amy Cuddy's TED talk, "Your Body Language Shapes Who You Are," in which researchers show that by posing in a given posture you will begin to adapt that attitude and emotion.[6] Why not give the gift of a physical position to Hugh? By placing yourself in a lower position to another person, you actually raise that person's status.[7] This gives Hugh the feeling of power, which most people will not overuse or abuse—at least not in front of a group. Also you can deliver "pushback" of your own, while being in a physically low-status position. Then if it becomes necessary for you to rise, you actually take back power—slightly, anyway.

- If it feels like Hugh is undermining you, ask the group, "Do others agree with Hugh? Does anyone have a different perspective?" By framing with the word "perspective" you are opening up the discussion to different opinions and dissenting views rather than putting Hugh on the spot as the center of a discussion about whether he is right or wrong. In the end if the group clearly does not agree with Mr. Jazhol, you can let the group argue with him (so you don't have to).

- Implore Hugh just to try. Remind him of postponing judgment for a period, for himself and the other people in the room. Thank him for committing to this challenge.

- In a one-on-one meeting (or two-on-one if you need a witness) tell Hugh what is going on, why you are using these techniques, and so on. Be explicit and tell Hugh that he is an important member of the team and needs to be involved—starting with the meeting about to take place.

- If there is a high likelihood that he will resist the whole process and you are confident that subtle guidance will be missed on the thick-headed Mr. Jazhol, here is a somewhat devious and yet very effective method: partner with Hugh, the toughest nut to crack, to jointly develop a strategy to get Jess, one of the easiest people to work with on the team, involved in using the tenets of improv. Frame your challenge to Hugh along the lines of "We are going to use these improv techniques, and we have to get Jess on board. What would you do to make this a success? How would you approach this?" In framing it this way—with the "what" and "how" as opposed to the "should we" question— you are taking away Hugh's power to judge whether these techniques should or should not be employed. By approaching Hugh in this manner, you have essentially created a "build-in" strategy to get Hugh involved by refocusing his energy on helping someone (who is already great to work with!).

If stronger measures are needed:

- Call out Hugh's behavior:
  - Ask the group if they appreciate Hugh's behavior. Ask the group what that behavior looks like. How is it affecting the group? (Again, call out the behavior and not the person.)
  - Identify Hugh's behavior and ask him if he knows he's being a ... Jazhol. Does he know the effect he is having on the group? Is this a conscious decision, a choice? Ask him to define the message that he is trying to send to the group.

- Sidebar! Take a break and pull Hugh to the side. Alone, quietly call out Hugh's behavior, how it is affecting the group. Ask Hugh if this is his desire. If not, ask him to reengage, support other folks in the class, postpone judgment, and so on. If it is his intention to disrupt the group and completely undermine the success of the meeting, then . . .

• Confront Hugh with a decision: "You have a choice. I will respect your decision to leave this meeting. If you want to leave, then go do something you want to do. I will respect your decision to stay. I want you to stay. You are a great asset to the group. However, if you choose to stay, these are the rules of engagement that you must follow." Give Hugh the choice to leave. If he really doesn't want to be part of what you're trying to do, he shouldn't be there. But in leaving—and here is the big caveat—he will forfeit any claim to success the group may achieve or any right to say "I told you so" if the group fails. He will have absolutely no ownership of the group's success or failure.

Good Eats

How's that elephant looking now? I hope I've given you enough tips and guidance to get you excited and confident about bringing improvisation into your workplace. In focusing quite a bit on practice, pitfalls, and pushback, I don't mean to give the impression that improvisation is always a heavy lift. One of the great recent trends in corporate culture—a trend that has made improvisation more relevant than ever—is that it's now okay to have fun in the workplace. And here is a bombshell insight into human nature for you: most people like to have fun.

As I mentioned back in Chapter 5, for years there seems to have been an ingrained corporate bias against fun. Even today in some workplaces, if people seem to be enjoying themselves this can trigger deep concern in management over issues of productivity, quality, and efficiency. I would contend that there's nothing wrong with having a little bit of fun at work, and that people can still be incredibly productive when they're enjoying what they're doing. Bosses don't always seem to get that people know how to be happy and serious at the same time (one of the finer advancements of the human brain).

After years of dealing with people who come from some of the most productive workplaces in the world, I have witnessed the evolution of fun in the workplace firsthand, and I can guarantee you that you do not have to be frowning or panicking to take your job seriously. When I began bringing improvisation into the corporate environment, fun was absolutely taboo. It was not part of the business world psychology. Now more and more companies are looking for ways to inspire intrinsic motivation.[8] Very successful businesses (Google, Twitter, SAS, IDEO) have taken a "Yes, and" approach to building their culture—an approach that's evident in things like flex hours, horizontal hierarchies, free lunches, and free babysitting. All these wonderful benefits have an immediate cost, yet more and more today companies are asking themselves, "What's the cost of replacing a great employee if that employee becomes unhappy working here?" It has become very clear, even to the starchiest accounting departments, that when you treat people positively you get positive results.

Allowing for open communication and fostering creativity, risk taking, innovation, adaptability, and improvisation just happens to be a highly effective way of turning this great bunch of nouns from buzzwords into reality. With that in mind, I leave you with the following:

> Some of our deepest human desires are to be understood.
>> Improvisation can fulfill those desires.
> Business is really the business of relationships.
>> Improvisation is all about relationship building.
> You want to work smarter rather than harder.
>> Improvisation gets the job done.

So go ahead. Take improvisation to work. And have fun.

Chapter 10

AND WAIT . . . THERE'S MORE!

I HAVE GREATLY APPRECIATED the opportunity you've given me to present my perspective on the power and potential of an improvisational approach to the workplace. As someone with a long-held passion for both improvisation and business, I've found the marriage of the two to be effective and inspiring. Improvisation at its core is about communication. It is my deepest hope that in these pages I have communicated some of that passion to you and effectively conveyed what improvisation is, why it can work in a business setting, and how exactly you can start making use of it in your own workplace and life.

In that spirit it seems appropriate to include the following "bonus" materials extending the lessons of this book to cover a few specific, practical, business-oriented areas.

Ten More Ways to Create an Improvisational Workplace

First, let's consider a few basic steps to help any company get started on the path toward a more improvisational corporate culture. By consistently implementing these simple and powerful steps, you will find yourself among employees who are communicating better, managers who are proving to be fine leaders, and an office culture with dramatically improved levels of creativity and teamwork.

1. *Make the time.* It's within your power to make the time to learn (try, fail, succeed), make changes, take risks, and provide wiggle room for errors and unexpected developments as well as organic discoveries.

2. *Be explicit with your intent.* Tell your team what you want, why you want it, and how you are going to get there.

3. *Create a common language.* The phrase "Yes, and" is one of the foundational techniques of all improvisation. It means acknowledging an idea and adding to it. Talk with team members to ensure everyone understands the power of using this phrase when sharing opinions and suggestions, then use it to hold each other accountable.

4. *Get buy-in.* Find one or two close allies or create a small group who can help you develop an improvisational culture, give you honest feedback along the way, and help you stay consistent with your behavior. Get their support not only through feedback but also through participation, and in doing so you will get their build-in for the success of this endeavor.

5. *Provide a mutually shared experience.* This can include an experiential learning workshop, off-site bonding opportunity, or other structured or less-structured experiences. The key is not only to have everyone in the same place; it is to have them share a memorable experience in the place that will connect them further in the future.

6. *Routinely seek out exercises, techniques, and challenges*, for yourself and your team. (*Practice!*)

7. *Lead by example.* Walk the talk; be consistent; be passionate; be unwavering in your beliefs! Be accountable for your actions, for the success of the mission, for the actions of the group, and for the protection of the culture.

8. *Empower your team.* Ownership is essential in creating an inclusive environment. Empower your team to help you create and protect this culture.

9. *Weed out.* Remove from the team those who refuse or undermine the process—otherwise, they may undermine you as well.

10. *Be diligent!* There are always speed bumps on the road of change. Stay focused on the final destination and you will get there sooner than later. Be tenacious to make change happen. Your team needs you!

Five More Ways for Dealing with Pushback

My team and I prepare for pushback before every program. Conveying the true importance of improv to our intelligent audiences is paramount to us, and sometimes we need to crack some hard nuts to break through to an entire group. Here are a few additional tips for dealing with doubters, skeptics, naysayers, and negative know-it-alls:

1. *Find an ally.* I'm not talking about teaming within a team or creating dissension within a group. Rather, what I am suggesting is finding one or two people whom you trust and who trust you, with whom you can talk and work through the improvisational techniques to gain needed practice, insight, and comfort. Once you have this elite group you will have support. Then it will not be you alone attempting to implement these techniques—it will be you and your team.

2. *Frame thoughts.* Instead of asking, "Can I do this?" which asks for permission and ultimately puts the power of the decision in the hands of the person you are asking, frame the question so that the answer must address the challenge of *how* to succeed (e.g., "This is what we need to do. How would you suggest we implement these techniques?"). That way if your boss or colleague tries to say "but" or even "no," it will be at a sharp right angle

from the direction you are currently heading, and the negation
will be painfully obvious.

3. *Take personal accountability.* The only thing you can truly control is
how you react (for some, that may be an incredibly difficult task
as well). Take one minute before a meeting to think about how
you want to, and can, control your energy and your attitude.
Take time to put yourself in the right mental place—the game
state—to be your best in the meeting.

4. *Be thoughtful.* Take a few minutes before a meeting or a call to
think about whom you are working (dealing) with in this meeting
and how you will "Yes, and" them. Don't let the "Yes, but-ers"
or the "It's my job to say no" folks train you to be helpless and
undermine you before a meeting even begins.

5. *Cling to "Yes, and . . ."* The more you practice using the literal
words "Yes, and," the more they will seep into your brain. You
will embody "Yes, and" as a life philosophy, a positive approach
to how you react, and a core decision-making tool.

What's Your Point? Storytelling Matters

The Duke Fuqua School of Business leaders have consistently challenged me to develop original programs for new challenges their students face. (I'm speaking to you, Col. Joe Leboeuf, Dean Morgan, and
Dean Boulding.) Here is how we took on the students' challenge of
creating a 90-second elevator pitch to respond to the request to "tell
me about yourself" that so many of us face in networking events.

An easy first step is to develop a personal "logline"—a one-sentence summary used in Hollywood to describe the basic premise of
a TV series or movie (e.g., *Star Wars: The Force Awakens*: "An orphaned
scavenger and a cowardly defector become the unlikely guardians of
the location of Luke Skywalker, the last Jedi alive and the last hope
for the Republic to defeat the sinister First Order who have risen
from the ashes of the Empire"). Another way to frame the need for

a one-sentence summary of yourself is, "What is your Twitter bio?" Who are you, in 160 characters or less. To get there, try the following:

- Give yourself two minutes to describe who you are without listing what is on your resume or anything a person could find online.
- Reduce that story to one minute.
- Don't forget the passion!
- Bulk it back up to 90 seconds. This is your elevator speech.
- Don't forget the passion!
- Now create a Twitter bio (or logline) out of it.
- Passion!

Improv Tips for MBAs Transitioning to Career

The transition from MBA life to a full-time career can be tricky if not overwhelming. I have often been approached by business students to address a number of outgoing challenges those students continually face. Here are a few hard-earned and hard-learned tips:

1. You are your brand. Know your brand! What are your behavior patterns? Are your behaviors in line with your goals? Have you aligned your personal(ity) goals with your career goals and with what you want to achieve in life? Take a moment to create a strong self-audit. Recognize your strengths and weaknesses. Be able to succinctly answer the directive "Tell me about yourself" in 90 seconds or less. (See above exercise.)

2. Create the brand you want. If you have a good idea of who you are and what you stand for, then you can adapt to become the person you want to be in your new job. After all, most people do not know who you are at your new job. You have the unique opportunity to create the person you want to be and train your new peers how to react to you. Warning: be consistent!

3. Do not be shy. Just be polite.

4. "Yes, and" yourself in your new role. Your impact on your team and organization will happen over time. There are bound to be mistakes and places where you stumble. Give yourself permission to make mistakes, adapt to those mistakes, and learn from them. In baseball, hitters are not judged by a single turn at the plate; they are evaluated by their batting averages over the course of the entire year. Do your best each time you're at bat and be consistent with your improvement over the course of your entire career.

Improv for Presentation

Delivering a presentation in the workplace really is a bit of theater—your own one-person or small-group show. If you're looking to take your "performance" to the next level, improvisational techniques can make all the difference.

1. *Warm up!* It's not enough to review your notecards and double-check your PowerPoint. Speaking before a group is a physical act as well as a mental undertaking, so make sure you give yourself time to get your body and mind ready for peak performance.

2. *Relax, and "Yes, and" yourself.* You've done all the prep work and you know what you're talking about, so give yourself permission to adapt to changes in your presentation as they occur. All you have to do is share the points that you have worked hard to become an expert in. You don't ever have to memorize every word in a speech (no one will remember every word anyway). Loosen up, and hit the big points hard!

3. *"Yes, and" unexpected opportunities.* You cannot plan for every question and no matter how much you prepare there will always be uncontrollable surprises (such as technology malfunctions) that pop up and potentially undermine your presentation. Don't try

to control them. Try to adapt to them. And remember, you can always seize the unexpected challenge as an opportunity for a group discussion.

4. *Focus on engaging.* Put your energy into making sure that you are communicating your points cleanly and effectively. You are not talking to a group; you are talking to individuals within the group. Keep your eyes on individuals. They will signal what they want to see more of, or less of, and what they do or do not understand. Look at them as your team and look to support that team.

5. *Be yourself.* You are not bound by slides. Your slides are there to support you, not vice versa. Don't worry about being a "Proper Presenter." Let your natural energy come out and let your personality shine. Being a dynamic speaker is about bringing out the best of yourself, connecting with your audience, and communicating a simple message memorably.

Improv Tips for Entering and Exiting Small Groups (Networking)

Networking turns out to be one of the biggest challenges for people just getting into the business world. Specifically people are challenged because they don't know how to enter a conversation already going on; they don't know what they will talk about with strangers; and they don't know how to (gracefully) leave a conversation that they are in. The trick here, like everything else in life, is practice. The more you practice, the more comfortable you get with these transitions. Here are a few ideas to help you in those pesky (mandatory and occasionally awkward) networking events.

1. Smile a lot. Cognitive psychologists have proven that moods are contagious. The small act of smiling shows warmth, confidence, and a good attitude. Further, a positive mood will help you find positive colleagues. So relax and just smile.

2. Listen a lot. My mentor (Martin de Maat, who created The Second City training center) used to say, "To be interested is to be

interesting," meaning that people are drawn to those who care about what they have to say. Listen for offers, gifts, and clues in the moment that reveal opportunities to make connections to the people talking and build on what they have just said. In other words, "Yes, and" them.

3. When entering an already formed group, simply ask if you can join the conversation. If it is private they'll say no and you can move on instead of standing awkwardly next to the conversation. If it is not private they'll say yes and then boom, you're in!

4. When entering and exiting groups, use the phrase "Yes, and . . . " a lot. Assume a default position of acceptance. Your "Yes" demonstrates a level of understanding of what others in the group are offering; "and" shows how you understand (or don't understand) what others are saying. This shows that you are engaged in the conversation. If the conversation is going well when you need to exit it, ask for a card or some other means of continuing the conversation at a later time.

5. When exiting a continuing conversation, I "Yes, and" myself into any one of a number of great outros (excuses). I start with "It has been great talking with you" and then transition to

   - "I'm going to refill my drink."
   - "I'm going to the restroom."
   - "I'm gonna bounce around the room and mix it up a bit." (This is my go-to. It's a networking event after all!)
   - "Oh my goodness, I have to go. I just remembered I left my cat in the oven!"

Again, if the conversation is a good one, I ask for their card and whether we can continue the conversation off-line when it is not so chaotic.

Whenever you need a quick refresher on improvisational keywords, techniques, or principles, I hope you will use this book as a reference to support you in all your personal, team, and workplace successes.

ACKNOWLEDGMENTS

Thank you, Bonnie Solow, for finding me as I charted the sea of business books, giving me direction and challenging me every step of the way.

Thank you, Margo Fleming, for believing in me. You and Stanford University Press took a chance on me when others would not. Your guidance and support has been a true motivation.

A huge thank-you to Chuck Crisafulli. You are a prime example of commitment, diving so fully into Business Improv and becoming a truly curious student of this life in improv. I am so privileged to have had the opportunity to work with you on this book and can't wait to watch you jam out with the Doublewide Kings.

Thank you, Gary Rudoren and Samantha Dulther. Without you I'm not sure where I'd be. I still don't know where I am . . . that's neither here nor there. I just know that without your support, this book would likely not be a reality.

For your unconditional friendship and support, thank you, Tom Tillisch, Ken Schainman, Kip Kelly, and Ray Smith. And Ray, thank you for your mentorship and thoughtfulness. You are always a welcome voice of wisdom.

Thank you, Bruce Craven, the master storyteller, for being a freakin' rock star! I look forward to our next bourbon together.

Thank you, Captain Jamie Sands, Alex Gallafent, Craig Robinson, John Perez, Lindsay Caplan, Jeff Golde, Thom Little, and Gregg Hilker for all of your friendship, help, and support.

Thank you, Andy Cutright, Kendall Case, and all my great Effingham, IL, friends.

Thank you, Alex Burke, Ryan McPheeters, Bill Connolly, and Mark Stetson: work hard, stay focused, do great work, impact people in a positive way, and have fun!

Thank you, Alan Barinholtz. You have always been there for me and so many other improvisers, and you are an important part of the improv family.

Thanks to Maureen Brooks, Tommy Spaulding, Rick Barrera, and everyone at The Center For Heart Led Leadership. You are truly inspirational (to say the very least). Thank you for adding me into your family. I love working with you!

Thank you, all of the brilliant professors with whom I've had the extreme good fortune of working and collaborating at Duke Fuqua School of Business, Columbia Business School, and UCLA Anderson School of Management. I have learned so much from all of you as we've created great programs together.

Thanks to everyone at the University of Florida Warrington College of Business Administration, especially Jason Rife and Kara Cupoli, who embody joy and happiness.

Thank you, all the folks at UCLA Executive Education, especially Kelly Bean, who continues to believe in me and to demand excellence in everything.

Thank you, Michael Morris and all the folks at Columbia Business School and Columbia Executive Education, and a huge thank-you to Paul Ingram, a truly intelligent, thoughtful, and caring professor.

To the Duke Fuqua School of Business: thank you! In 2000, I was (as I still am today) just an improviser with a tremendous drive to link improv to business. You were so incredibly ahead of the curve, and you still are in this field! You continue to challenge me to develop new exercises, new programs, and new courses and to bring immense depth to the material I create and teach. Without all the great folks throughout Fuqua, the Career Management Center, and Duke Executive Education, I do not know that any of this would have ever taken place.

I would be remiss if I did not spotlight Rick Staelin, Sim Sitkin, Douglas Breeden, James Smith, and Jack Soll, each of whom has influenced me greatly. Thank you, Dean Russ Morgan and Dean Bill Boulding. You have shown me enormous guidance, motivation, and unconditional support, at times when it was needed most.

And a very special thank-you to Colonel Joe Leboeuf. You are the personification of leadership. You push incredibly hard; you are brutally honest; you demand nothing shy of the absolute best from those with whom you work; and you care immensely for those you command. You lead by example, and I have learned so much from you. I consider you a mentor and a friend and it has been an honor and privilege to have been led by you and to have worked alongside you.

Thanks to everyone who has ever taught a Business Improv program. You are truly a who's who of elite improvisers. Thank you for your hard work, great intelligence, tireless energy, and tremendous passion for this amazing thing of ours.

Kate Duffy, Jess Eason, Cesar Jaime, Deanna Moffitt, Sean Monahan, Marion Oberle, Chris Roberti, Scot Robinson, and Pat Shay: you are rock stars! Thank you for being such caring, thoughtful, and passionate leaders at Business Improv, and thank you for being centurions of this wonderful art form. You inspire everyone who has ever taught for BI. An extra shout goes out to Mr. Monahan: thank you for being my consigliere over, lo, these many years. Westside Corporate Creativity is being led by a genius. (That genius is you, by the way, just in case you don't know.)

Josh Pryor you are a fellow workhorse and a stud at that. Thanks for grinding it out in BI with me every day.

Thanks to all my friends and family from the world of improv: more than twenty-one years in the muck with you . . . where do I start to say thank you and where do I end? There are just so many great folks I have worked, lived, loved, and laughed with—I am so incredibly fortunate in that way. You are among the most talented people on the planet, and the world is finally catching up to this fact. Performing in improv is one of the most magnificent things anyone will ever know—and we know. Thanks for a great life.

Thank you, Mick Napier, Jack McBrayer, T. J. Jagodowski, Jordan Klepper, and Susan Messing for being ridiculously smart dummies and brilliant improvisers and for getting my back.

Thanks to Baby Wants Candy, Weaseliscious, To: Idiots, Guilty Party, Monster Island, The Armando Diaz Experience, and The Windy Pendejos? and all of the other kick-butt improv and sketch comedy groups with whom I've had the extreme fortune of playing. Thanks to Charna Halpern and iO, Jennifer Estlin and The Annoyance Theatre, The Second City, Chicago ComedySportz, ImprovAcadia, UCB, Magnet and PIT, and all the other great improv houses around the globe. Big shout out to the Mission Improvable folks and M.i.'s Westside Comedy Theater in Santa Monica!

Thank you, Martin de Maat. I miss you every day.

To those great, passionate, caring teachers, directors, and coaches who dedicate so much time to those they lead and the art of improv, Thank You So Very Much. Without you, this world would not exist. The art is better because of you.

Thank you Sheldon Patinkin for everything that you did.

Thanks to my "family" family for their love and support. To my parents, Bob and Kathy Kulhan—without you I would not be here. (Dad, I learned so much about leadership from you!) To my sisters Michelle (Muki International) and Tracy and their families, and to all the Caswell, Wussow, Legge, Molnar, and Kulhan peeps in Chicago, Nashville, London, the East Coast, and around the world.

And thanks to my beautiful, understanding, caring wife, Denise, and our magnificent son—and any children that we might be so lucky to eventually have one day (including our baby girl, who will be premiering around the same time as this book).

NOTES

Introduction: More than One Way to Hit a Piñata

1. O'Leonard, Karen, *The Corporate Learning Factbook 2014: Benchmarks, Trends, and Analysis of the U.S. Training Market*, January 2014, www.bersin.com

2. Owen, Mark, and Kevin Maurer, *No Easy Day: The Firsthand Account of the Navy Seal Mission That Killed Osama bin Laden*, Dutton Adult, Printing Edition, 2012.

3. "What a Downed Black Hawk in Somalia Taught America," *All Things Considered* (NPR), October 5, 2013, www.npr.org/player/v2/mediaPlayer.html

4. Owen and Maurer, *No Easy Day.*

5. "Six Soft Skills to Hire For in 2015," January 2015, http://blog.adeccousa .com/hire-candidates-soft-skills-2015/ (accessed January 4, 2016).

Chapter 1: Thinking Outside of Thinking Outside of the Box

1. Shankland, Stephen, "Moore's Law: The Rule That Really Matters in Tech," *CNET*, October 15, 2012, www.cnet.com/news/moores-law-the-rule-that -really-matters-in-tech/

2. Hummel, Denise Pirrotti, "Understanding the Importance of Culture in Global Business," *Profit Magazine*, May 2012; Kante, R. M., "Strategy as Improvisational Theatre," *MIT Sloan Management Review*, Winter 2002, 76–81.

3. Spaulding, Tommy, *The Heart-Led Leader*, Crown, 2015.

4. Shaughnessy, Haydn, "15 Ways to Make Much Better Decisions," *Forbes*, December 9, 2013, www.forbes.com/sites/haydnshaughnessy/2013/12/09/15-ways -to-make-much-better-decisions/2/#1d07f3494337

5. Modarresi, S. Jamileh, Asiyeh S. Modarresi, S. Mahmoud Modaressi, and Mohammad Ali Dehestani, "Individual and Organizational Barriers to Creativity Advance in Environmental Biology," *American-Eurasian Network for Scientific Information*, September 2013, 24–32.

6. Allan, Leslie, "Employee Resistance to Change—Why?" *Business Performance*, 2008, www.businessperform.com/change-management/resistance_to_change.html

7. Chicago Improv Festival, CIF 8 Awards, "Del Close" Ensemble of the Year Award, April 21, 2005, www.chicagoimprovfestival.org/2005/awards.php

8. Small, Deborah A., George Loewenstein, and Paul Slovic, "Sympathy and Callousness: The Impact of Deliberative Thought on Donations to Identifiable and Statistical Victims," *Organizational Behavior and Human Decision Processes* 102, no. 2, March 2007, 143.

9. Guilford, J. P., *The Nature of Human Intelligence*, McGraw-Hill, 1967.

10. Atchity, Kenneth, and Chi-Li Wong, *Writing Treatments That Sell: How to Create and Market Your Story Ideas to the Motion Picture and TV Industry*," 2nd ed., Holt Paperbacks, 2003.

Chapter 2: Just Say "Yes, and . . . "

1. Bellanger, Caroline, "Learn to Say 'Yes': Mindfulness in the Workplace," *Right Hand HR*, Straight Forward People Management, September 8, 2015, www.rhhr.com/learn-to-say-yes-mindfulness-in-the-workplace/

2. Cherry, Kendra, "What Is the Difference between Extrinsic and Intrinsic Motivation?" *Verywell*, January 15, 2016, http://psychology.about.com/od/motivation/f/difference-between-extrinsic-and-intrinsic-motivation.htm

3. Elfenbein, H. A., "Team Emotional Intelligence: What It Can Mean and How It Can Affect Performance," in *Linking Emotional Intelligence and Performance at Work: Current Research Evidence with Individuals and Groups*, Lawrence Erlbaum Associates, 2006, ch. 8, 165–84.

4. Schwartz, Tony, "Why Appreciation Matters So Much," *Harvard Business Review*, Managing People, January 23, 2012, https://hbr.org/2012/01/why-appreciation-matters-so-mu.html

5. Moore, Karl, "Millennials Work for Purpose, Not Paycheck," *Forbes*, October 2, 2014, www.forbes.com/sites/karlmoore/2014/10/02/millennials-work-for-purpose-not-paycheck/#ed75a3d5a225

6. Goleman, Daniel, "What Makes a Leader," *Harvard Business Review*, Emotional Intelligence, January 2004, https://hbr.org/2004/01/what-makes-a-leader

7. Mosley, Richard, "CEOs Need to Pay Attention to Employer Branding," *Harvard Business Review*, Talent Management, May 11, 2015, https://hbr.org/2015/05/ceos-need-to-pay-attention-to-employer-branding

8. Manjoo, Farhad, "Dick Costolo Thinks It's O.K. to Never Tweet," *New York Times*, February 25, 2015, www.nytimes.com/2015/03/01/magazine/dick-costolo-thinks-its-ok-to-never-tweet.html?smid=tw-nytmag&_r=2

9. Chatzisarantis, N., and M. Hagger, "Mindfulness and the Intention-Behavior Relationship within the Theory of Planned Behavior," *Personality and Social Psychology Bulletin* 33, 2007, 663–76.

10. Haririar, Tessitore A., V. S. Mattay, F. Fera, and D. R. Weinberger, "The Amygdala Response to Emotional Stimuli: A Comparison of Faces and Scenes," *Neuroimage* 17, no. 1, September 2002, 317–23.

11. Glaser, Judith E., and Richard D. Glaser, "The Chemistry of Positive Conversations," *HBR Blog Network*, June 12, 2014.

12. Langer, Ellen, "The Mindlessness of Ostensibly Thoughtful Action: The Role of 'Placebic' Information in Interpersonal Interaction," *Journal of Personality and Social Psychology* 36, no. 6, 1978, 635–42.

13. Pavlov, I. P., "The Scientific Investigation of the Psychical Faculties or Processes in the Higher Animals," *Science* 24, 1906, 613–19.

14. Fang, Janet, "Your Brain Is 'Hard-Wired' to React without Thinking," *IFL Science*, March 14, 2014, www.iflscience.com/brain/your-brain-hard-wired-react -without-thinking

15. Keep, Deborah, "Influence and Empowerment through Consciously Chosen Language," *Training and Development* 40, no. 1, February 2013, 18–19.

16. Bolton, Robert, *People Skills: How to Assert Yourself, Listen to Others, and Resolve Conflicts*, Simon & Schuster, 1979, 72.

17. Business Dictionary, www.businessdictionary.com/definition/active-listening .html

Chapter 3: I'm with the Brand

1. Napier, Nancy K., "The Myth of Multitasking: Think You Can Multitask Well? Think Again," *Psychology Today*, May 12, 2014, www.psychologytoday.com/ blog/creativity-without-borders/201405/the-myth-multitasking

2. www.psychologytoday.com/basics/mindfulness

3. Mehrabian, Albert, *"Silent Messages": A Wealth of Information about Nonverbal Communication (Body Language)*, Personality and Emotion Tests & Software: Psychological Books & Articles of Popular Interest; self-published, 2009.

4. Hatfield, Elaine, John T. Cacioppo, Richard L. Rapson, and Margaret S. Clark, eds., "Primitive Emotional Contagion," in *Emotion and Social Behavior: Review of Personality* and Social Psychology, Sage, 1992, 151–77.

5. Arno, Christian, "Create Content That Effectively Crosses Cultural and Linguistic Borders," Localization/Understanding Your Audience, September 24, 2012, http://contentmarketinginstitute.com/2012/09/create-content-that-effectively -crosses-cultural-and-linguistic-borders/

6. Feinstein, Ashley, "Why You Should Be Writing Down Your Goals," *Forbes*, April 8, 2014, www.forbes.com/sites/85broads/2014/04/08/why-you-should-be -writing-down-your-goals/

Chapter 4: Energy Independence

1. Paris, Mary Jane, "Attitude: The Power of Positive in the Workplace," *Self-growth*, www.selfgrowth.com/articles/Attitude_The_Power_of_Positive_in_the_ Workplace.html

2. Barsade, Sigal G., and Donald E. Gibson, "Why Does Affect Matter in Organizations," *Academy of Management Perspectives*, February 2007, 36–59.

3. Loehr, Jim, and Tony Schwartz, *The Power of Full Engagement: Managing Energy, Not Time, Is the Key to High Performance and Personal Renewal*, Free Press, 2003, 65.

4. Bench, Shari, "Why Is Positive Energy Important in the Workplace?" www .airbestpractices.com/energy-manager/personal-productivity/why-positive-energy -important-workplace

5. Divine, Mark, *Unbeatable Mind: Forge Resiliency and Mental Toughness to Succeed at an Elite Level*, 3rd ed., CreateSpace Independent Publishing Platform, 2015.

6. Chan, Amanda L., "Digestion Foods: The Best and Worst Foods for Your Digestive System," *HuffingtonPost*, Healthy Living, November 29, 2012, www .huffingtonpost.com/2012/11/29/digestion-foods-best-worst-digestive-system -gut_n_2206641.html

7. Franke, A., H. Harder, A. K. Orth, S. Zitzmann, and M. V. Singer, "Postprandial Walking but Not Consumption of Alcoholic Digestifs or Espresso Accelerates Gastric Emptying in Healthy Volunteers," *Journal of Gastrointestinal and Liver Diseases* 17, no. 1, March 2008, 27–31.

8. Tourish, Dennis, David Collinson, and James R. Barker, "Manufacturing Conformity: Leadership through Coercive Persuasion in Business Organizations," *M@n@gement* 12, no. 5, 2009, 360–83.

9. Cameron, Judy, W. David Pierce, Katherine M. Banko, and Amber Gear, "Achievement-Based Rewards and Intrinsic Motivation: A Test of Cognitive Mediators," *Journal of Educational Psychology* 97, no. 4, 2005, 641–55.

10. Arnold, Carrie, "Following the Crowd: Changing Your Mind to Fit In May Not Be a Conscious Choice," *Scientific American*, August 25, 2011, www.scientific american.com/article/following-the-crowd/

11. "What Are the Rules of the Conch?" www.answers.com/Q/What_are_ the_rules_of_the_conch

12. Barsade, S. G., "The Ripple Effect: Emotional Contagion and Its Influence on Group Behavior," *Administrative Science Quarterly* 47, no. 4, 2002, 644–75.

13. Ramanujam, Nanda, "Fostering Productivity, Organizational Effectiveness via Employee Engagement," *Wired*, April 14, 2014, http://insights.wired.com/ profiles/blogs/fostering-productivity-organizational-effectiveness-via-employee ?xg_source=msg_appr_blogpost#axzz3zpy83ebC

14. Jeffcoat, Kellmeny, and Jane Whitney Gibson, "Fun as Serious Business: Creating a Fun Work Environment as an Effective Business Strategy," *Journal of Business and Economics Research* 4, no. 2, 2006, www.cluteinstitute.com/ojs/index.php/ JBER/article/view/2634

15. Chartrand, T. L., and J. A. Bargh, "The Chameleon Effect: The Perception-Behavior Link and Social Interaction," *Journal of Personality and Social Psychology* 76, 1999, 893–910.

16. Émond, Caroline, "Les corrélats prosodiques et segmentaux de la parole souriante en français québécois" [Prosodic and segmental correlates of smiling speech in Quebec French], master's thesis, Université du Québec à Montréal, 2008.

17. Liraz, Meir, "Nonverbal Communications," *Bizmove*, Management Skills, www.bizmove.com/skills/m8g.htm

18. Émond, "Les corrélats prosodiques et segmentaux de la parole souriante en français québécois."

19. Kraemer, Harry M. Jansen, Jr., "The Mantra for Successful Startups Is 'Team First, Ego Last,'" *Entrepreneur*, May 22, 2015, www.entrepreneur.com/article/246537

20. National Aeronautics and Space Administration (NASA), www.grc.nasa.gov/www/k-12/WindTunnel/Activities/first2nd_lawsf_motion.html

21. O'Doherty, J., J. Winston, H. Critchley, D. Perrett, D. M. Burt, and R. J. Dolan, "Beauty in a Smile: The Role of Medial Orbitofrontal Cortex in Facial Attractiveness," *Neuropsychologia* 41, 2003, 147–55.

Chapter 5: Teaming Up

1. Anderson, Erika, "21 Quotes from Henry Ford on Business, Leadership and Life," *Forbes*, May 31, 2013, www.forbes.com/sites/erikaandersen/2013/05/31/21-quotes-from-henry-ford-on-business-leadership-and-life/#247c22bd3700

2. Brooks, Frederick P., *The Mythical Man-Month*, Addison-Wesley Professional, 1996, www.amazon.com/Mythical-Man-Month-Software-Engineering-Anniversary/dp/B005GM4EBS/ref=asap_bc?ie=UTF8

3. Brounstein, Marty, "Ten Qualities of an Effective Team Player," Dummies.com, www.dummies.com/how-to/content/ten-qualities-of-an-effective-team-player.html

4. Heathfield, Susan, "Ten Tips for Better Teamwork," About.com, Money–Human Resources, December 16, 2014, http://humanresources.about.com/od/teambuilding/f/team_work.htm

5. Parker, Glenn M., *Cross-Functional Teams: Working with Allies, Enemies and Other Strangers*, Jossey-Bass, 2015, www.wiley.com/WileyCDA/WileyTitle/productCd-111912462X.html

6. Six, Janet M., "Teamwork and Collaboration across Departments," UX-matters, May 23, 2011, www.uxmatters.com/mt/archives/2011/05/teamwork-and-collaboration-across-departments.php

7. Erb, Marcus, "Seven Ways to Boost Employee Morale," *Entrepeneur.com*, July 19, 2011, www.entrepreneur.com/article/220000

8. Spreen, Vanora, "The Right Attitude, Your Secret Weapon for Team Performance," *The Art of Teamwork*, July 29, 2012, https://theartofteamwork.wordpress.com/tag/positive-attitude/

9. Haden, Jeff, "How to Build a Great Team with Imperfect People," *Inc. Magazine*, March 22, 2012, www.inc.com/jeff-haden/how-to-build-a-great-team-with-imperfect-people.html

10. Bastian, Brock, Jolanda Jetten, and Laura J. Ferris, "Pain as Social Glue: Shared Pain Increases Cooperation," *Psychological Science* (online), Sage, September 5, 2014.

11. Cross, Rob, Andrew Hargadon, Salvatore Parise, and Robert J. Thomas, "Together We Innovate," *Wall Street Journal*, September 15, 2007, www.wsj.com/news/articles

12. Moran, Gwen, "Why Your Job Title Means a Lot More than You Think," *Fast Company*, September 9, 2014, www.fastcompany.com/3035359/hit-the-ground-running/why-your-job-title-means-a-lot-more-than-you-think

13. Heathfield, Susan M., "How to Build a Teamwork Culture," About.com, Money–Human Resources, December 16, 2014, http://humanresources.about.com/od/involvementteams/a/team_culture.htm

14. Blue Angels Team (video), www.youtube.com/watch?v=L51wzOF9KT0

15. Webb, Caroline, "How Small Shifts in Leadership Can Transform Your Team Dynamic," *McKinsey Quarterly*, February 2016, www.mckinsey.com/business-functions/organization/our-insights/how-small-shifts-in-leadership-can-transform-your-team-dynamic

16. Zwilling, Martin, "How to Delegate More Effectively in Your Business," *Forbes*, October 2, 2013, www.forbes.com/sites/martinzwilling/2013/10/02/how-to-delegate-more-effectively-in-your-business/#29efedac2891

17. Bywater, Liz, "The Flexible Leader: An Adaptable Approach to Managing Your Team," WJM Associates, April 2012, www.wjmassoc.com/insight/the-flexible-leader/

18. Firstenberg, Iris, and Moshe F. Rubinstein, *Extraordinary Outcomes: Shaping an Otherwise Unpredictable Future*, Wiley, 2014, 107–8.

19. Singleton, Singer, "Create a Culture of Teamwork with Mutual Trust and Respect," *TechRepublic*, April 22, 2002, www.techrepublic.com/article/create-a-culture-of-teamwork-with-mutual-trust-and-respect/

20. "13 Ways to Prepare Your Team in a Crisis," *Upstart Business Journal*, September 11, 2013, http://upstart.bizjournals.com/resources/advice/2013/09/11/ways-to-prepare-for-a-business-crisis.html?page=all

21. Stern, Tom, "Ten Ways to Inject Fun into the Workplace," *Fast Company*, My Work-Life Balance Sheet, February 16, 2007, www.fastcompany.com/659698/ ten-ways-inject-fun-workplace

Chapter 6: Must Be Something Ideate

1. Osborn, Alex, *Applied Imagination: Principles and Procedures of Creative Problem Solving*, 3rd ed., Creative Education Foundation Press, 1963.

2. Catmull, Ed, "How Pixar Fosters Collective Creativity," *Harvard Business Review*, September 2008, http://hbr.org/2008/09/how-pixar-fosters-collective -creativity/ar/1

3. Rubinson, Joel, "Innovating Innovation: The Best Ideas Can Come from Any-where," *Fast Company*, June 16, 2009, www.fastcompany.com/1296086/innovating -innovation-best-ideas-can-come-anywhere

4. Mankins, Michael, Chris Brahm, and Gregory Caimi, "Your Scarcest Re-source," *Harvard Business Review*, May 2014, http://hbr.org/2014/05/your-scarcest -resource/ar/1 (accessed September 20, 2014).

5. Dib, Farah, "How Workplace Fear Rots the Brain," Chartered Manage-ment Institute, February 20, 2015, www.managers.org.uk/insights/news/2015/ february/how-workplace-fear-rots-the-brain

6. Sinek, Simon, *Leaders Eat Last*, Penguin Group, 2014, ch. 17, 127–47.

7. Tiedens, Larissa, and Alison Fragale, "Power Moves: Complementarity in Dominant and Submissive Nonverbal Behavior," *Journal of Personality and Social Psychology* 84, no. 3, 2003, 558–68.

8. "Frequent Multitaskers Are Bad at It," University of Utah, January 23, 2013, http://archive.unews.utah.edu/news_releases/frequent-mulitaskers-are-bad-at-it/

9. Rhodes, Justin, "Mind and Brain: Ask the Brain," *Scientific American* 24, no. 3, 2013, www.scientificamerican.com/article/why-do-you-think-better-after-walk -exercise/ (accessed August 9, 2014).

10. Nadler, Ruby, "The Influence of Mood and Motivation on Cognitive Flex-ibility," doctoral diss., University of Western Ontario, 2013.

11. Govindarajan, Vijay, and Jay Terwilliger, "Yes, You Can Brainstorm with-out Groupthink," *HBR Blog Network*, July 25, 2012.

12. Page, Scott E., "Making the Difference: Applying a Logic of Diversity," *Academy of Management Perspectives* 21, no. 4, November 2007, 6–20.

13. www.businessballs.com/consciouscompetencelearningmodel.htm

Chapter 7: Busted

1. Stone, Florence, "Deconstructing Silos and Supporting Collaboration," *Employment Relations Today* 31, no. 1, April 8, 2004, 11–18, 200.

2. Dorrell, Kathryn, "Silo-busting," *Benefits Canada* 26, no. 6, June 2002, 49.

3. www.dhs.gov/publication/proposal-create-department-homeland-security

4. Dwyer, Jim, Kevin Flynn, and Ford Fessenden, "Fatal Confusion: A Troubled Emergency Response; 9/11 Exposed Deadly Flaws in Rescue Plan," *New York Times*, July 7, 2002, www.nytimes.com/2002/07/07/nyregion/fatal-confusion-troubled-emergency-response-9-11-exposed-deadly-flaws-rescue.html

5. Pink, Daniel, *To Sell Is Human: The Surprising Truth about Moving Others*, Riverhead Books, 2012, 43.

6. Abrashoff, D. Michael, *It's Your Ship: Management Techniques from the Best Damn Ship in the Navy*, Grand Central Publishing, 2012, www.amazon.com/Its-Your-Ship-Management-Anniversary/dp/145552302X

7. Michaels, Adrian, "Dubai's Rise as a Family Destination," *The Telegraph*, Travel Section, October 3, 2003.

8. Schwab, Lars, and Oliver T. Wolf, "Stress Prompts Habit Behavior in Humans," *Journal of Neuroscience* 29, no. 22, June 3, 2009, 7191–98, www.psy.unihamburg .de/arbeitsbereiche/kognitionspsychologie/publications/schwabe2009c-jneurosci .pdf

9. Kahneman, Daniel, Jack L. Knetsch, and Richard H. Thaler, "Anomalies: The Endowment Effect, Loss Aversion, and Status Quo Bias," *Journal of Economic Perspectives* 5, no. 1, Winter 1991, 193–206.

10. Lionnet, Annie, *Brilliant Relationships: Your Ultimate Guide to Attracting and Keeping the Perfect Partner*, 2nd ed., Pearson Business, 2013.

11. U.S. Naval Academy, "Change from Below: Creativity, Dissent and Reshaping," 2014 Leadership Conference, www.youtube.com/watch?v=8ranv-Pct8 Q&index=4&list=PLY2Foc7RFdI0s-Su_P22xCmABJX3dIiGm

Chapter 8: Take Me to Your Leadership

1. Spolin, Viola, *Improvisation for the Theater*, Northwestern University Press, 1983, 61.

2. Goleman, Daniel, *Emotional Intelligence: Why It Can Matter More than IQ*, Bantam Books, 2005.

3. Lind, E. A., and S. B. Sitkin, "Six Domains Leadership Survey," Delta Leadership, Inc. (Chapel Hill, NC), 2007.

4. Goleman, *Emotional Intelligence*.

5. Bennis, Warren, *On Becoming a Leader*, 4th ed., Basic Books, 2009.

6. U.S. Naval Academy 2014 Leadership Conference, "Change from Below: Creativity, Dissent and Reshaping," 2014, www.youtube.com/watch?v=8ranv-Pct 8Q&index=4&list=PLY2Foc7RFdI0s-Su_P22xCmABJX3dIiGm

7. Sy, Thomas, Stephane Cote, and Richard Saavedra, "The Contagious Leader: Impact of the Leader's Mood on the Mood of Group Members, Group

Affective Tone, and Group Processes," *Journal of Applied Psychology* 90, no. 2, March 2005, 295–305.

8. Voirin, Rick, "Rick Voirin Covers the 10 Leadership Skills That Are Essential for Leading in a VUCA World," online lecture, Duke Fuqua Executive Education, October 16, 2011, www.fuqua.duke.edu/programs/other_programs/executive_education/advanced_management/vuca_video

9. Mack, Oliver, Anshuman Khare, Andreas Kramer, and Thomas Burgartz, *Managing in a VUCA World*, Springer, 2016.

10. ILE 2—Improv Detailed Design Sheet, Duke Corporate Education, v9, Business Improvisations, LLC, 2004.

11. Witt, Chris, "How to Motivate and Inspire Your People in Difficult Times," reliableplant, June 29, 2009, www.reliableplant.com/Read/18525/how-to-motivate-inspire-your-people-in-difficult-times

12. Spaulding, Tommy, *The Heart-Led Leader: How Living and Leading from the Heart Will Change Your Organization and Your Life*, Crown Business: 2015.

Chapter 9: How to Eat an Elephant

1. Kwoh, Leslie, "Reverse Mentoring Cracks Workplace," *Wall Street Journal*, November 28, 2011.

2. Kranz, Gene, "Failure Is Not an Option: Mission Control from Mercury to Apollo 13 and Beyond," Simon & Schuster, 2000, chs. 18 and 19, 306–33.

3. Arnold, Carrie, "Following the Crowd: Changing Your Mind to Fit In May Not Be a Conscious Choice," *Scientific American*, August 2011, www.scientificamerican.com/article/following-the-crowd/

4. Janis, I. L., *Victims of Groupthink: A Psychological Study of Foreign-Policy Decisions and Fiascos*, Houghton Mifflin, 1972.

5. Maier, S. F., and M. Seligman, "Learned Helplessness: Theory and Evidence," *Journal of Experimental Psychology: General* 105, 1976, 3–46.

6. www.youtube.com/watch?v=Ks-_Mh1QhMc

7. Carney, Dana R., Amy J.C. Cuddy, and Andy J. Yap, "Power Posing: Brief Nonverbal Displays Affect Neuroendocrine Levels and Risk Tolerance," *Psychological Science* 21, no. 10, October 2010, 1363–68.

8. Ford, R. C., J. W. Newstrom, and F. S. McLaughlin, "Making Workplace Fun More Functional," *Industrial and Commercial Training* 36, no. 2/3, 2004, 117–20, www.emeraldinsight.com/doi/abs/10.1108/00197850410532131

INDEX